Hawaii Under the Rising Sun

Japan's Plans for Conquest After Pearl Harbor

John J. Stephan

UNIVERSITY OF HAWAII PRESS · HONOLULU

Library of Congress Cataloging in Publication Data

Stephan, John J.
  Hawaii under the rising sun.

  Bibliography: p.
  1. World War, 1939–1945—Hawaii.   2.   World War, 1939–
1945—Japan.   3.   Japan—Military policy.   4.   Hawaii—
History—1900–1959.   I.   Title.
D767.92.S835   1984   940.54'0952   83–9101
ISBN 0–8248–0872–X

In memory of

WILLIAM L. MAGISTRETTI
(1914–1982)

GEORGE RICHARD STORRY
(1913–1982)

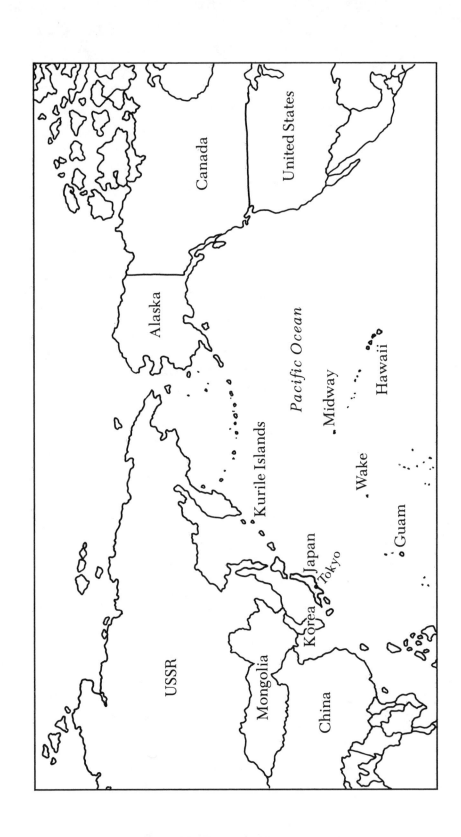

Contents

PREFACE   vii

INTRODUCTION   1

   I. A MID-PACIFIC FRONTIER   10

  II. THE PREWAR JAPANESE COMMUNITY   23

 III. HAWAII JAPANESE IN JAPAN   41

 IV. INVASION SCENARIOS, 1909–1941   55

  V. HAWAII IN IMPERIAL NAVAL STRATEGY   69

 VI. THE BIRTH PANGS OF "EASTERN OPERATION"   89

 VII. STILLBORN INVASION   109

VIII. VICTORY DISEASE   122

 IX. HAWAII IN GREATER EAST ASIA   135

  X. HAWAII UNDER JAPANESE RULE   148

CONCLUSION: THE PERSISTENCE OF ILLUSION   167

NOTES   179

SELECT BIBLIOGRAPHY   207

INDEX   221

MAPS   iv, 178

A NOTE ON JAPANESE NAMES

All Japanese surnames will be placed after the given name. While this sequence does not follow Japanese practice, it avoids the confusion that would arise if different word orders were used for Japanese and Japanese-American names.

For the sake of consistency, all Japanese transliterations of the word "Hawaii" will be rendered as "Hawaii."

Preface

A number of historical topics have attracted attention only years after the events themselves took place. Delayed recognition can occur when hitherto silent witnesses give testimony, when new documentation comes to light, or when someone asks new questions and probes into areas that others have overlooked. Japanese planning for the invasion and occupation of the Hawaiian Islands during the Second World War is such a topic.

Many historians of World War II may assume that this topic does not exist. In a sense, they are right. There are no books, no articles, no dissertations on Japanese plans for Hawaii. It is conventional wisdom that Japan sought to destroy the U.S. Pacific Fleet at Pearl Harbor but did not intend to invade Hawaii. Why? The Japanese leaders supposedly felt that Hawaii was too difficult to capture and retain. Military strategists in the Imperial Army and Navy supposedly regarded Hawaii as outside of the Pacific perimeter deemed essential to secure basic war objectives. Tokyo did not, it is often assumed, intend to include Hawaii within the Greater East Asia Co-Prosperity Sphere.

In fact, the conquest and occupation of Hawaii constituted an important part of the Japanese Empire's war strategy. Seizure of the entire archipelago was a major objective in the Combined Fleet's long-term plans from the day after Pearl Harbor until the Battle of Midway on 5 June 1942. Well into 1943 civilians prepared scenarios of Hawaii's political administration, economic reconstruction, and social transformation under Japanese occupation.

Why have over forty years elapsed before these plans have come to light? Upon what sources is our knowledge of these plans based? Three conditions suggest why Japanese planning for Hawaii has hitherto eluded historical investigation.

First, aside from the useful work by Robert Butow, Akira Iriye, and Joyce Lebra, there has been relatively little detailed research on Japan's war aims after 7 December 1941. The subject did come under scrutiny at the International Military Tribunal for the Far East (1946–1948), but the prosecution's emphasis on proving certain charges against accused Class A war criminals obscured rather than illuminated many of Tokyo's motivations in 1941 through 1943. Consequently, the transcripts of the Tokyo trials cast only faint light on Hawaii.

Interrogations of Japanese officers immediately after the war, notably those conducted by the United States Navy, focused on what had occurred on the battlefields (in this case on the high seas) rather than what had gestated in the minds of those planning long-term strategy. Planning attracted attention largely where operations ensued. Such an approach to information gathering served a practical purpose at the time, but one suspects that in the long run it contributed to a tendency of military historians to dwell upon the tactical rather than the strategic dimension of Japan's war effort. This predilection is readily evident in the American popular consciousness of the Pacific War. The Battle of Midway is still almost a household word. History buffs can even guess roughly how many carriers Admiral Yamamoto lost. But how many have grasped Midway's intended role in Japan's overall war objectives? How many know that Midway was the first step toward an invasion of Hawaii?*

A second factor that has discouraged research on planning for Hawaii is that sources are scattered and difficult of access. During the two-week interim between the emperor's decision to accept the Allies' Potsdam Declaration on 14 August 1945 and the arrival of American forces on Japanese soil (28 August), vast quantities of government and private documents were destroyed. The Imperial Navy carried out this procedure with efficient dispatch, for the most sensitive naval documents had been filed separately for just such a contingency. Nor were only military entities turning their

---

*Midway is in fact part of the Hawaiian archipelago.

records into ashes. A specialist on Hawaiian affairs at Kyoto Imperial University recalled in 1979 how shortly after the surrender he and his colleaques had burned notes, reports, and books in order to keep them from falling into the hands of Occupation authorities. Materials that have by chance or design survived are dispersed throughout repositories in Japan and the United States.

Third, wartime planners and commentators are not readily available for interviews. Time has taken a heavy toll. The survivors are generally not listed in reference works and are hence difficult to locate. Some of those who have been traced are reluctant to discuss wartime activities that they feel might constitute a source of embarrassment.

The sources upon which this study is based are of three varieties: one, documents, diaries, and depositions in the archives of the War History Office at the National Defense College in Tokyo; two, wartime publications of professional societies and research institutes in Japan; and three, interviews with individuals directly or indirectly engaged in wartime research on Hawaii. Additional material (translations of wartime Japanese broadcasts, United States Army intelligence reports from Hawaii) was located in the Naval Historical Center of the Washington Naval Yard and in the National Archives at Suitland, Maryland.

The War History Office of the Natiional Defense College has assiduously collected documents that escaped destruction in 1945. Some of this material had been confiscated by the United States Army and held for several years near Washington before being returned to Japan. Other documents never fell into American hands. For example, records of the Army General Staff's Second Section (Operations) were saved from both the incinerator and the Americans by being surreptitiously removed from Imperial Headquarters to a hiding place somewhere in Tokyo on 14 August 1945 by a staff officer to whom historians owe a debt of gratitude. In 1946 these records came into the possession of another staff officer, Colonel Takushirō Hattori, who kept them for the duration of the Occupation. After Colonel Hattori's death in 1960, his heirs donated the records to the War History Office. From among such materials surfaced operational orders for three divisions to commence training for an invasion of Hawaii.

For civilian perceptions of Hawaii and civilian scenarios of Hawaii under Japanese occupation, in-house reports of research institutes such as the Kokusaku kenkyūkai (National Policy Research Society) and the Nan'yō keizai kenkyūjo (South Seas Economic Research Center) have been invaluable. The Library of Congress and the National Diet Library have many of these reports. Additional wartime publications (books, pamphlets, journals) have been examined at the Hoover Institution on War, Revolution and Peace (Stanford) and in the East Asian collections at Harvard University, Columbia University, and the Universities of Maryland, California at Berkeley, Chicago, and Hawaii.

Finally, surviving military and civilian personnel who engaged in Hawaii-related research during the Pacific War have been traced and interviewed.

The above sources—published and archival, written and oral—could not have been accessible without the assistance of many individuals on both sides of the Pacific.

I owe a particular debt to those whose lives were touched by the subject of this book. Former officers of the Imperial Japanese Navy shared memories of what is found in no written record. The unstinting cooperation of Admiral Suguru Suzuki, Admiral Michise Matsuki, Admiral Akira Yamaki, Captain Takaji Terasaki, Captain Minoru Nomura, and Commander Eijirō Suzuki is gratefully acknowledged. Invaluable insights were gained through conversations with Captain W. J. Holmes, Drew W. Kohler, Professor Saneshige Komaki, the late William L. Magistretti, Dr. Klaus Mehnert, Professor Tsugio Murakami, Captain Roger Pineau, and Hanama Tasaki.

Without the guidance of archivists and librarians in Japan and the United States, this project would have been stillborn. It is a pleasure to express special appreciation to Professor Hisao Iwashima, chief of the First Research Section of the War History Office, and to Junko Kinoshita of the War History Office Archives. I am also deeply grateful to Shōichi Izumi, Atsumi Kumata, and Ken-'ichi Hoshi of the National Diet Library; Ken Kurihara, Yukie Togawa, Shōichi Saitō, and Masahiro Tanaka of the Foreign Ministry Archives; Yukio Fujino, former librarian of the International House of Japan; Key Kobayashi of the Library of Congress; T. Lane Moore, Gibson Smith, and John Taylor of the National Archives; Frank J. Shulman of the University of Maryland's East Asian Collection; Miwa Kai and Philip Yampolsky of Columbia University's East Asian Library; John J. Slonaker of the United

States Army Military History Institute and Colonel William F. Strobridge of the Center of Military History (both agencies are within the Department of the Army); D. C. Allard of the Naval History Center, Department of the Navy; Kenneth Tanaka of the University of Chicago's East Asian Collection; Emiko M. Moffitt of the Hoover Institution's East Asian Collection; and Eiji Yutani of the East Asian Collection of the University of California at Berkeley.

Scholars from Japan, the United States, Great Britain, and Australia have assisted this study with helpful comments and suggestions. Thanks are due Gordon M. Berger, Hilary Conroy, Alvin D. Coox, James B. Crowley, John W. Dower, Ikuhiko Hata, Russell N. Horiuchi, Akira Iriye, Hiroshi Kimura, Joyce C. Lebra, Gail Nomura, Mark R. Peattie, the late Gordon W. Prange, Robert S. Schwantes, and the late G. R. Storry.

Hawaii residents have played a special role in this study through their guidance and support. The Library of the University of Hawaii has provided outstanding services. My profound thanks to Dr. Masato Matsui, Tom Tomoyoshi Kurokawa, and Minako Song of the East Asia Collection. Also very helpful were Genevieve Correa, Renée Heyum, David Kittelson, Ellen Chapman, Takumi Tashima, Misao Shibayama, and Pat Polansky. Colleagues have given thoughtful advice. I am particularly grateful to George Akita, Gavan Daws, Akira Iriye, Marius B. Jansen, Andrew W. Lind, Judge Masaji Marumoto, Earl K. Nishimura, Franklin S. Odo, Jeffrey S. Portnoy, Minoru Shinoda, and George Yamamoto who read all or portions of the manuscript and made many valuable comments and suggestions. Yukiko Kimura, Mitsugu Sakihara, Yukuo Uyehara, and John A. White generously shared their time and experience to discuss bibliographical and interpretive issues. Cynthia Timberlake graciously made available microfilm copies of *Hawaii hōchi* deposited in the Bishop Museum Library. Agnes Conrad located issues of *Jitsugyō no Hawaii* in the Hawaii State Archives. Useful information was kindly provided by Gwenfread E. Allen, George Chaplin, Mary Fujii, Ritsuka Fujioka, the late Kengi Hamada, Michiko Kodama, Laura Kurokawa, Satoko Lincoln, Tsuruko Ohye, and A. A. Smyser. The author is very grateful to Iris Wiley for her editorial expertise and thoughtful suggestions during the manuscript's preparation for publication.

My wife Barbara supported this project with cheerful encouragement and constructive criticism throughout several years of research and writing.

As much as others have contributed, the author assumes full responsibility for factual errors, debatable inferences, and lapses in style.

Introduction

On 9 December 1941, less than forty-eight hours after the attack on Pearl Harbor that launched the Pacific War, Admiral Isoroku Yamamoto, commander in chief of the Combined Fleet and at that moment the most celebrated officer in the Imperial Japanese Navy, ordered his staff to prepare plans for an invasion of Hawaii. This order set in motion what was to be the most ambitious and far-reaching Japanese operation of the Second World War. A Japanese conquest of Hawaii would have changed not only the course of the war but the nature of the eventual peace. This book will describe the genesis of the idea of a Hawaii invasion, show why the Army and Navy general staffs at first opposed and then supported it, and reveal how civilian planners envisioned Hawaii under Japanese rule.

Located 2,300 miles from San Francisco and 3,900 miles from Tokyo, Hawaii in the spring of 1942 was a pivotal mid-Pacific American base for which there was no substitute. Following the fall of Guam, Wake, and the Philippines, Hawaii became the only remaining bastion between Japan's victorious forces and the West Coast of the United States. As headquarters of the damaged Pacific Fleet, Hawaii was a crucial repair facility, a vital intelligence center, and an ideal springboard for any counteroffensive against Japan. Hawaii was also the anchor for air and maritime communications between the United States and the southwestern Pacific. If Yamamoto could seize Hawaii, American forces would be obliged to fall back on Washington, Oregon, and California, leaving Australia and New Zealand, not to mention Alaska and the Panama Canal, exposed and vulnerable.

Although there were voices which advocated an assault on Hawaii as the first step toward an invasion of California, Admiral Yamamoto had a more realistic grasp of Japan's capabilities. He saw Hawaii in Japanese hands as a safeguard against American carrier strikes aimed at Japan's home islands. He saw Hawaii in Japanese hands as a hostage that could be used to convince the Americans to negotiate a quick peace. The admiral knew that Japan could not win a war of attrition against America's superior resources and industrial might. But he was willing to gamble that Japan had the edge in short-term operational initiatives and in political willpower. He calculated that once the American people beheld the spectacle of 400,000 fellow citizens living under Japanese rule, President Franklin D. Roosevelt would be forced to the peace table by public opinion. Tokyo could thereby terminate the war on favorable terms before America's superior power could be mobilized.

Unlike Yamamoto and his staff, wartime civilian commentators saw Hawaii's occupation as an end in itself. The outbreak of hostilities between Japan and the United States unleashed a torrent of emotions, emotions which for decades had gestated beneath the surface of public discourse but which suddenly found expression in the euphoric sense of release that removed customary constraints in the aftermath of Pearl Harbor. Hawaii suddenly came to signify more than palm trees and hula dances. It emerged as the symbol of a monumental Japanese victory over the United States, a victory of Yamato spirit over American materialism, of heroic determination over complacent arrogance, of a Greater East Asian revival over "Anglo-Saxon" colonialism.

Speculation accompanied rejoicing. To a number of journalists and academics, Pearl Harbor was but an overture to invasion. The prospect of Hawaii under Japanese rule animated the public imagination. Newspapers, magazines, and books on Hawaii poured forth in unprecedented quantities. The islands were portrayed as legitimate objects of Japanese overseas expansion, linked by geography and by history to Dai Nippon and inhabited by 160,000 *dōhō** allegedly yearning for reunification with their ancestral

---

*Dōhō (compatriots), sometimes pronounced *dōbō*, in prewar and wartime Japan, was applied to all ethnic Japanese at home and abroad, regardless of their citizenship.

land. Hawaii, in this view, had been temporarily detached from Asia by "Anglo-Saxon" interlopers. Restored by the Imperial Army and Navy to its roots, Hawaii would soon regain its true identity within the benevolent embrace of the Greater East Asia Co-Prosperity Sphere.

Most of the intellectual energy generated by this wave of excitement and expectation was consumed in rhetoric, but a significant portion remained to fuel serious research. Bureaucrats, academics, and journalists composed scenarios of postwar Hawaii. Conceptualizing social and economic policies for a multiracial community at the crossroads of the Pacific tapped idealistic as well as whimsical impulses. On the tentative agenda were restructuring of agriculture, disbandment of the Big Five,* land redistribution, revival of the Hawaiian monarchy, and re-education of *nisei*. Some of the researchers had no firsthand knowledge of Hawaii. Others were by birth or residence intimately familiar with the islands.

Although fictional accounts of Japanese invasions of Hawaii can be found in both Japanese and American literature, historians have been unaware of the real military and civilian preparations for the seizure and occupation of the Islands between 1941 and 1943. Within the corpus of writings on the Pacific War there is not a single study of this topic in any language. In this case, the language barrier may have been a factor for Western writers. Yet Japanese scholars who have access to the relevant documentation are as silent on the subject as their American counterparts. Curiously, postwar Japanese works on the Greater East Asia Co-Prosperity Sphere do not, insofar as I am aware, make any reference to the fact that Hawaii was explicitly included within the Sphere in both public and classified wartime documents.

This historiographical lacuna has reinforced a widely held assumption that Japan had no definite intention of invading Hawaii after the Pearl Harbor attack. In an authoritative account of Hawaii's war years published in 1950, Gwenfread E. Allen stated this view unequivocally: "Actually, Japanese documents now available show that Japanese concentration on the war in Asia and the South Pacific, coupled with the logistic difficulties of taking

*Five corporations that dominated the economy of the Islands before the Second World War: Alexander & Baldwin, Castle & Cooke, C. Brewer, Theo. H. Davies, and American Factors.

and holding Hawaii, eliminated an attempt to capture the Islands from any definite enemy plans."

The late Stanley D. Porteus, a University of Hawaii psychologist, went one step further in a 1947 book about wartime Hawaii. "As we now know, the Japanese did not include in their plans any invasion. . . . Invasion, the threat of blockade, were convenient bogeys [of the U.S. Army] with which to scare civilians."

The assumption that no real threat of invasion existed except as a "bogey" wielded by American military authorities to frighten the civilian population is a seductive one. There is a certain specious legitimacy in the notion that what was not attempted was not planned, or that what is not known did not exist. Moreover, martial law in Hawaii was unpopular and by a general consensus continued longer than any military necessities warranted.

Yet a Japanese invasion of Hawaii was no "bogey." True, the American military did not possess definite information about it, at least insofar as I know. But the military's instincts about the danger during the first half of 1942 were correct.

We might ask at this point what purpose is served by probing into plans that however momentous in their implications were never put into practice. Should not the historian confine himself or herself to what happened and leave what might have happened to the novelist? Of course. And it is precisely what *did* occur that endows this subject with significance and interest.

For one thing, the Hawaii plans throw new light on Japan's general war aims. Through the prism of Hawaii, one can get a sense of broader strategic questions that historians have yet to explore. What did Japan's military and civilian leaders hope to achieve in the Pacific Basin if operations against the United States proved successful? Was the United States to be driven permanently from Hawaii and Alaska? Was the North American West Coast to be invaded? Were Central and South American republics to be turned into Japanese protectorates or left independent? Were Australia and New Zealand to be seized and incorporated into the Greater East Asia Co-Prosperity Sphere? How were Japan's aims in the Pacific to be achieved in view of the crushing superiority of America's industrial might and formidable war potential?

Second, the planning for Hawaii casts Japan's wartime internal divisions into sharp relief. It does so in ways that will come as a surprise to many. The early breathtaking triumphs (Pearl Harbor,

Hong Kong, Singapore, Manila) emboldened some strategists but also created uncertainty and disagreement about how to capitalize upon such unexpectedly easy successes. Interservice negotiations over Hawaii in early 1942 reveal a complex interplay of conflicting strategic priorities between the Army General Staff, the Navy General Staff, and the Combined Fleet. In addition, the extravagant recommendations of a number of journalists and academics challenge common stereotypes about military aggressiveness and civilian passivity in Japan.

Third, in preparing occupation policies, research produced revealing analyses of social and economic conditions in Hawaii. Containing a paradoxical blend of realism and illusion, these wartime appraisals afford a rare glimpse of Japanese perceptions of the United States at a time when writers could and did dispense with the constraints normally observed in peacetime discourse.

Fourth, preparations for the occupation of Hawaii involved prognoses of how the local population would be treated. These prognoses raised the question: how would Hawaii's 400,000 residents react to Japanese rule? Would there be extensive collaboration? How would the Islands' Japanese community, which in 1941 numbered about 160,000 or just under 40 percent of the Territory's civilian population, respond?

The last question merits discussion, for it touches upon a raw nerve in modern American history. In 1942 about 120,000 Japanese-American residents of the West Coast (a majority of whom were American citizens) were forcibly relocated to camps in inland states. The rationale for mass relocation was that common ancestry with the enemy rendered this ethnic group vulnerable to penetration by spies and saboteurs. The fact that relocation was racially determined raised legal and moral questions, which have reverberated more insistently in recent years in connection with discussions about reparations for victims of internment. The fact that thousands of California and Hawaii *nisei* volunteered for service in the United States Army and fought with magnificent courage against German forces in Europe compounds the difficulty of treating the subject of potential collaboration in Hawaii.

Japanese-Americans have been subject to two genres of stereotypes. The first, traceable to anti-Japanese sentiment in California at the turn of the century, assumed a virulent form in the early days of World War II when Japanese victories in the Pacific and

Southeast Asia generated an invasion hysteria in some West Coast communities. This stereotype depicted Japanese-Americans as a cohesive, unassimilated minority with questionable loyalty to the United States. The other stereotype, which superceded but did not entirely replace the former between 1943 and 1945, stressed the "100 percent American" character of Japanese-Americans. This view was given a strong impetus by the combat achievements of *nisei* units in Europe and has been fostered by leaders of the Japanese-American community since the war.

Both stereotypes commit serious oversimplifications. They treat Japanese-Americans as a monolithic unit. During the 1930s, Hawaii's Japanese community was divided by generations, by educational experiences, by politics, and by personalities. Attitudes toward Japan varied widely. Some *nisei* joined the University of Hawaii ROTC program, others went to Japan and volunteered or were drafted into the Imperial Japanese Army or Navy. A vast majority embraced the American ideas of freedom and democracy, but there were others who felt disillusioned and alienated by the racial discrimination in Hawaii. Some of the latter responded to the call of their ancestral land which in the 1930s was embarking upon a crusade to build a new order in East Asia (after 1940 in Greater East Asia).

Another weakness of both stereotypes is that they treat Japanese-American loyalty as a black-and-white issue when in reality the situation in Hawaii was very complex. It is hard to believe that any Japanese-American in Hawaii felt 100 percent loyalty to Japan or to the United States in the 1930s if such loyalty meant the exclusion of emotional feelings and respect toward one or the other country. Available evidence and common sense suggest that a majority felt an attachment to both countries. The proportions of this attachment, of course, varied from individual to individual. There were important differences between *issei* (first generation immigrants from Japan) and *nisei*. The *issei* quite naturally loved the land of their birth and were proud of Japan's emergence as a world power. At the same time, they felt a deep attachment toward the land where they had spent in many cases most of their lives, the land where they had built their careers and raised their families. The *nisei* could hardly be expected to reject their ancestral land, the birthplace of their parents, and the home of their grandparents, uncles, aunts, and cousins. At the same time, almost all *nisei* considered themselves Americans and were in terms of dress, language, and tastes largely Americanized.

In short, an intricate web of human ties bound Hawaii to both sides of the Pacific. The eastern and western strands of this web could be severed only at the cost of considerable pain and disorientation. The situation of many Hawaii Japanese in 1941 was not unlike that of a child of divorced parents, where each parent castigates the other and demands the child's undivided love.

An examination of Japanese planning for Hawaii reveals that a number of Japanese-Americans went beyond sympathy and collaborated with the Japanese authorities. Yet in retrospect their actions need to be understood within the turbulent and complex conditions prevailing during the war years. Some Hawaii *issei* spent the war in Japan acclaiming the anticipated "restoration" of Hawaii to Asia by the Imperial Japanese Army. One even prepared a report for a research institute subsidized by the Navy Ministry, and he recommended how Hawaii might be politically restructured. Strictly speaking, these *issei* were more "loyal" than their compatriots in the United States who bought Uncle Sam's war bonds and hung Franklin Roosevelt's portrait in their homes. After all, as Japanese citizens, *issei* had no business collaborating with the American enemy.

Nor can *nisei* who called for Hawaii's "liberation" by Japan be labelled disloyal. They had Japanese as well as American citizenship. Moreover, they acted from understandable if at times misguided motives: bitter memories of racial discrimination in Hawaii, opposition to what they perceived as militarization of the Islands, and an idealistic belief in Japan's self-proclaimed mission to build an Asia for Asians, an Asia free of European and American intruders be they capitalists or communists.

Hawaii *nisei* who fought in Japan's armed forces, whose experiences have been portrayed apologetically or passed over in silence, need to be understood in the context of their times. Their sacrifices, unlike those Hawaii *nisei* who served in the United States Army, have not been recognized. Today, the memory of those who fell in battle is preserved neither at the Yasukuni Shrine in Tokyo nor at the National Memorial Cemetery of the Pacific in Honolulu's Punchbowl Crater. The survivors have not enjoyed the prestige and perquisites of veterans of the highly publicized *nisei* combat units in the American Army: the 100th Infantry Battalion and the

442nd Regimental Combat Team. Yet the hardships of *nisei* veterans of the Imperial Japanese Army and Navy have been if anything more severe; they have in many cases persisted long after the war, and they have for the most part been borne in silence.

Collaboration is a pejorative word. Often misused, it is inappropriate for those Japanese-Americans whose circumstances and inclinations led them to serve Japan during World War II. On the other hand in Hawaii, potential collaboration was by no means confined to Japanese-Americans. Any resident of the Islands in 1942, regardless of ethnicity, probably speculated on what life would be like in the event of a successful Japanese invasion. Any rational mind considering that contingency would most likely conclude that a degree of collaboration would be hard to avoid. Unlike the Philippines, Hawaii was physically too small for anyone to avoid contact with occupation authorities. A guerrilla movement would have been virtually suicidal. There is little evidence that either the military or civilians were prepared to fight to the last man should Hawaii have been assaulted. On the contrary, many probably shared the views of a State Department special agent who in a report written several weeks before 7 December 1941 acknowledged: "If the Japanese fleet arrived, doubtless great numbers of them [Hawaii Japanese] would then forget their American loyalties and shout a 'Banzai' from the shore. Under those circumstances, if this reporter were there he is not sure that he might not do it also to save his own skin, if not his face."

These words were not written by a coward. Dying to the last man, woman, and child (*gyokusai* as the Japanese called it in those desperate defenses of Saipan, Iwo Jima, and Okinawa) was neither a tenet of American military doctrine nor consonant with American historical experience, the Alamo notwithstanding. Moreover, Hawaii in 1942 was still a territory, not a state. It is doubtful that an assault on what were then considered distant islands inhabited largely by Polynesians and Orientals would have precipitated the national upsurge of determination that would have occurred if, say, several Imperial Army divisions had landed at Long Beach or Monterey.

Consequently, if the choice were to collaborate or face suicidal odds, there is little doubt but that Hawaii's residents would have opted, in the British phrase, to "carry on" with as much dignity as possible. The scale and degree of collaboration would probably have depended upon many obvious and subtle factors, among them individual character, the content and style of occupation policies, the conduct of occupation authorities and garrison troops, and the local assessment of Japan's prospects for winning the war or at least for repelling an American counterattack.

The Japanese literary critic Jun Etō remarked that his countrymen can at last look at World War II with a sense of psychological distance, contemplating it as a historical event. Americans too should be able to view that war with more detachment, if only because most of them have no personal memory of it. Topics that a generation ago were too emotionally charged to be approached can now be discussed in a calmer atmosphere. Time has healed wounds, cooled passions, and witnessed a growth of mutual trust between Japanese and Americans, creating an atmosphere in which it is possible to recognize wartime planning for Hawaii as an interesting and significant historical phenomenon worthy of serious scholarly attention.

CHAPTER I

A Mid-Pacific Frontier

About 1,400 miles north of the equator and roughly midway between Asia and America stretches a long, slender archipelago called the Hawaiian Islands. Unlike the insular galaxies that spray the South Pacific, this archipelago stands alone, forming an oasis in a vast watery expanse.

On a map of the entire Pacific Basin, the Hawaiian Islands look like wayward specks, dwarfed by the oceanic and continental masses that surround them. Closer inspection shows these specks to be more numerous than they first appeared. Some even have a respectable size, by island standards. The Hawaiian archipelago extends for 1,523 miles along a northwest-southeast axis. It consists of 132 islands that have a total area of 6,425 square miles or slightly larger than Connecticut and Rhode Island combined and a bit smaller than the Japanese island of Shikoku.

Ninety-nine percent of Hawaii's area is accounted for by eight islands which cluster in the southeastern quarter of the chain. In descending order of size these are Hawaii (the Big Island), Maui (the Valley Isle), Oahu (on which is located the city of Honolulu and the naval base at Pearl Harbor), Kauai (the Garden Isle), Molokai (the Friendly Isle), Lanai, Niihau, and Kahoolawe. The remaining 1 percent of land consists of islets and atolls strung out over 1,200 miles of ocean from Nihoa in the central part of the arc to Kure in the extreme northwest.

Hawaii, because of its location, is called "the crossroads of the Pacific." Indeed, the archipelago has a spatial relationship to continental masses around the Pacific Basin much like that of a hub to the rim of a wheel. East-west and north-south trans-Pacific routes converge in Hawaii like spokes. From a Hawaii perspective, conventional geographic nomenclature has an anomalous ring. Asia's Far East is not very far and it lies to the west. The American Far West is also not far and it lies to the east. Moreover, relative distances look different from a Hawaii vantage point. Panama is about the same distance from Honolulu as are the Philippines. Alaska is no farther away than is Samoa, nor are the Pacific shores of Siberia more remote than the beaches of southern California.

There is one spatial relationship, however, of which even many Hawaii residents are unaware. The archipelago's western end is closer to Japan than the eastern end is to the American mainland.

Geography and history have brought various Pacific, Asian, and European peoples to Hawaii. The aboriginal Hawaiians were descended from maritime Polynesian migrants from Tahiti and the Marquesas who reached the arc more than a thousand years ago. When Captain James Cook "discovered" the Sandwich Islands (as he called them) in 1778, the Hawaiian population was estimated to be about 300,000. During the next two hundred years, pure Hawaiians declined in numbers largely as the result of diseases. Meanwhile, as a result of mixed marriages, the part Hawaiian population grew until by 1980 it had reached 173,000 or about 19 percent of those who make the state of Hawaii their home. The bulk of today's Hawaii residents are immigrants or descendents of immigrants from the mainland United States, Japan, the Philippines, Portugal and its territories, China, Korea, Samoa, and —most recently—Vietnam. Direct immigration from European countries other than Portugal has been limited, although at various intervals in Hawaii's history there have been modest influxes from England and Scotland, Germany, Scandinavia, Spain, and Russia.

From the 1890s until the 1960s, the Japanese constituted the largest single ethnic group in Hawaii. This plurality put the Hawaii Japanese community in a different environment than that of its scattered and less numerous counterparts on the American mainland. In Hawaii, as the late *nisei* journalist/historian Tamotsu Murayama observed, social and cultural traditions were more faithfully preserved through the years. It is probably also fair to say that before the Second World War Hawaii community ties with Japan were on the whole closer than were those of West Coast communities.

The first Japanese to reach Hawaii were probably fishermen,

swept across the North Pacific by storms and currents. There are a number of well documented cases of Japanese castaways reaching Hawaii in the first half of the nineteenth century, and one cannot rule out the possibility of earlier contacts. But like the Chinese, Portuguese, and Filipinos, most Japanese came to Hawaii as laborers to fill manpower demands on local sugar plantations.

Until the 1870s native Hawaiians worked the cane fields, but economic, cultural, and demographic considerations led plantation owners and their agents to supplement and eventually replace Hawaiians with imported labor. Chinese were brought to the Islands in 1852. By the 1860s, agents recognized Japan as a potential source of labor. In 1868, 148 Japanese were transported to Honolulu and assigned to plantations on Oahu, Maui, Kauai, and Lanai. This inaugural group had no immediate successors, because disagreements over working conditions led the newly established imperial government* in Tokyo to prohibit further shipments.

The bulk of Japanese laborers reached Hawaii between 1885 and 1907. In 1885 the authorities in Tokyo permitted two boatloads to embark for Hawaii. In the following year Japan concluded a Convention with the Kingdom of Hawaii, according to which laborers were engaged under a three-year contract and brought in under official supervision. From 1886 until 1894 some thirty thousand Japanese came to Hawaii under the convention-contract arrangement. The convention was terminated in 1894, after the overthrow of the Hawaiian monarchy (1893) and the creation of the Republic of Hawaii. Thereafter, private entrepreneurs imported Japanese workers and supplied the manpower-hungry plantations, despite rising opposition to Japanese immigration from elements of the politically dominant, white, propertied class. This opposition temporarily abated after Hawaii's annexation by the United States in 1898, and the influx from Japan increased dramatically. There were 24,407 Japanese in Hawaii in 1896. By 1900 this figure had risen to 61,111, which was more than double that of any other ethnic group.

The tide of Japanese immigration to Hawaii ebbed in 1908

---

*The Tokugawa shogunate was overthrown in 1868 by a group of warriors from southwestern Japan who established an Imperial government in Tokyo under the nominal leadership of the young Emperor Meiji.

when, responding to anti-Japanese agitation in California, the United States and Japan concluded a Gentlemen's Agreement wherein Tokyo quietly undertook to restrict the trans-Pacific flow of laborers. Only relatives of immigrants and prospective wives (including the so-called picture brides) continued to come to Hawaii until the 1924 Exclusion Act virtually closed the door.

Japanese immigrants to Hawaii had much in common with each other. Geographically they came overwhelmingly from southwestern Japan—from Hiroshima and Yamaguchi prefectures of Honshū and from Fukuoka and Kumamoto prefectures of Kyū-shū. Socially they were from those elements of the peasant class that were hardest hit by the economic dislocations that rocked rural Japan in the 1880s and 1890s: small farmers, tenant farmers, and agricultural laborers. Physically hardy, they were more willing than most of their compatriots to take risks, to venture into an alien and unknown environment in order to improve their economic situation and social status. They came to Hawaii intending to accumulate some capital and then to return home upon the expiration of their contracts.

Of the approximately 180,000 Japanese who reached Hawaii between 1885 and 1930, the majority returned to Japan. Some did so as soon as their contracts had expired. Others lingered on for various lengths of time ranging from a few months to four decades. Hundreds hurriedly sought repatriation in 1941 as war clouds gathered over the Pacific.

Those immigrants who did not return to Japan followed several courses. A few continued to work in the cane fields. Most removed themselves at the earliest opportunity from the drudgery of plantation life with its low pay, cramped bunkhouses, and narrow horizons. Japanese made up over 70 percent of sugar plantation labor in 1900 but less than 20 percent in 1932. Some found employment in the pineapple industry. Some became independent farmers and grew vegetables near one of the towns, harvested rice on Kauai, or raised coffee crops along the Big Island's Kona Coast. Others took to the sea as fishermen. A few entered domestic service in one of the more affluent white households or became gardeners. Many, moving to Honolulu or Hilo, opened stores with savings accumulated through hard work and frugal living. Finally, there were those who moved on to the West Coast in search of better opportunities.

A Japanese community started to develop in Hawaii before the turn of the century. It took shape as the unmarried transient contract laborer gradually gave way to the married resident, who more often than not had moved off the plantation. In fostering the social, religious, and educational institutions that would sustain and enrich their lives in an alien land, the first generation of Hawaii Japanese turned to their homeland for models and guidance. Buddhist temples and Shinto shrines were built. Japanese language schools were founded to impart the mother country's speech and moral values to the next, Hawaii-born, generation. Japanese-language newspapers appeared, informing the community of local, national, and international events. Eventually, a Japanese Chamber of Commerce, prefectural societies (which brought together those from the same prefecture back home), professional associations, and philanthropic organizations proliferated, strengthening the community's cohesiveness and sharpening its identity.

Several factors reinforced the *issei's* ties to Japan and simultaneously insulated the *issei* from Americanization. First, there was a language barrier, far more formidable than that encountered by most European immigrants. Second, Japanese men usually did not marry Chinese, Hawaiian, or Caucasian women. Instead, they brought brides from Japan. Third, Japanese were excluded from the white community's social circles and corridors of power. Fourth, after Hawaii became an American territory in 1898, Japanese immigrants who were already in the Islands and who subsequently arrived were barred from acquiring United States citizenship. Finally, strong feelings of patriotism and ethnic pride gave *issei* an inner strength that reduced the lure of assimilation with white American culture.

Patriotism among Hawaii Japanese took sustenance from their homeland's brilliant achievements during the reign of Emperor Meiji (1868–1912). Divided, vulnerable, and patronized by the West when the Tokugawa shogunate fell in 1868, Japan by 1912 had won international recognition as a world power. Within four decades Japan had built a modern centralized state, equipped with a Prussian-inspired constitution, managed by a well-trained and highly motivated bureaucracy, and defended by a battle-tested army and navy. A national educational system was eliminating the last vestiges of illiteracy, instituting universal primary education, and administering an impressive array of middle schools, higher schools, vocational schools, and prestigious universities. The economy was advancing briskly if unevenly along the road to industrialization without inflation, serious unemployment, or heavy indebtedness to foreign creditors. An overseas empire had been won, stretching from southern Sakhalin to Taiwan and including Korea and enclaves in Manchuria. In 1914 the Imperial Navy occupied Germany's Micronesian colonies (the Mariana, Caroline, and Marshall islands), bringing the frontiers of the Rising Sun to within twelve hundred miles of the Hawaiian Islands—less than half the distance between Hawaii and the West Coast of the United States.

Japan's successes excited both admiration and misgivings throughout the world. These reactions were pronounced in Hawaii because of the Islands' proximity to Japan, their ethnic composition, and (until 1898) their uncertain political future. Japan's military exploits not only stirred the patriotism of Hawaii Japanese but gave them a heightened sense of their own status and prestige. Victory over China in the Sino-Japanese War (1894–1895) promoted feelings of superiority over local Chinese. The epochal triumph over Russia in 1904 and 1905, a triumph in which a number of Hawaii Japanese participated as volunteers in the Imperial Army and Navy, was felt deeply in the Islands. Russia was perceived as a European country. Russia's defeat therefore constituted a victory of Asians over Caucasians. The implications of this victory were not lost upon Hawaii Japanese, who continued to live under the political domination of white Americans.

The motherland's achievements were brought to the attention of the community by more than local vernacular newspapers and language schools. In 1885, Tokyo opened a consulate in Honolulu and within a few years was appointing consular agents (unpaid volunteers) within the community. Regular visits of Japanese naval vessels began in 1876 and continued until the eve of the Second World War.

Naval visitations were often accompanied by festivities and warm hospitality, particularly so at times when members of the local community felt discriminated against by the Hawaiian authorities. When the monarchy was replaced by a republic in 1893, allowing the white propertied class to consolidate its power, Tokyo reacted by dispatching the warship *Naniwa* to demonstrate Japan's concern. *Banzais* greeted the ship in Honolulu. In 1897, when the Hawaiian Republic levied a heavy tax on *sake* and turned back three boatloads of Japanese immigrants, the *Naniwa* made another appearance. This time it was met by a local "Welcome the *Naniwa* Committee."

The captain of the *Naniwa* on both occasions was Heihachirō Tōgō, who subsequently won fame by leading Japan's battle fleet to its greatest victory: the destruction of the Russian Baltic Squadron in the Tsushima Straits on 27 May 1905. Tōgō's popularity in Hawaii was said to have been so great that some local Japanese families named their children "Tōgō" or "Naniwa." Whether this actually occurred cannot be established with certainty. But it is a fact that until just before World War II a brand of *sake* brewed in Hilo on the Big Island bore the name Tōgō Masamune. A portrait of the admiral adorned the label.

Tokyo was by no means indifferent to its subjects in Hawaii. Concern derived largely from sensitivity to matters of international prestige. During the last three decades of the nineteenth century, the Meiji government strove in general to gain the respect of the major western powers and in particular to convince these powers to revise the "unequal treaties"* which in effect denied Japan full membership in the community of what was then called "civilized" nations. Tokyo regarded its overseas compatriots *(dōhō)* as representatives of the empire, and their status abroad reflected directly upon that of Japan. The government's prohibition of emigration to Hawaii from 1869 to 1885 stemmed in part from anxiety that if Japanese laborers were treated like Chinese coolies, the analogy would place Japan in a lower international category of states.

By the 1890s, however, once a sizeable Japanese community had been established in Hawaii, Tokyo adopted the position that any unreasonable *restriction* of further immigration by Hawaiian authorities impinged upon Japan's national honor. It will be recalled that when the Hawaiian Republic denied three boatloads of immigrants permission to land in 1897, Tokyo dispatched the warship *Naniwa* to Honolulu to back up the foreign minister's protest.

---

*Treaties concluded between the Tokugawa shogunate and major powers during the 1850s which granted extraterritorial privileges to foreigners in Japan and deprived Japan of the right to set its own tariffs on imported goods.

Did Japan hope that Hawaii might someday come under its wing? The evidence is complex and contradictory, for there was a discrepancy between expressed hopes and actual behavior.

The Meiji government behaved with scrupulous discretion toward Hawaii, even when tempting opportunities presented themselves. For example, in the wake of the 1871 Treaty of Commerce and Friendship between Japan and the Kingdom of Hawaii, certain Hawaiian entrepreneurs broached the idea of Japanese "men of means" leasing Hawaiian land and building productive colonies with imported Japanese labor. Tokyo ignored these propositions. While on a visit to Japan in 1881, King Kalakaua offered to renounce Hawaii's extraterritorial rights in Japan. The king also proposed the marriage of his niece to a Japanese prince in order to forge a bond between Japanese and Hawaiian royalty. Finally, Kalakaua urged Japan to organize and lead a federation of Asian nations of which Hawaii would become a member.

Tokyo politely declined all three of Kalakaua's proposals. However welcome Hawaii's renunciation of extraterritorial rights, Japanese statesmen prudently realized that accepting such a gesture might jeopardize Japan's chances for a comprehensive revision of the unequal treaties. Britain's consent would be crucial to achieve that objective. As to the marriage proposal and Asiatic federation, Tokyo regarded them as premature. For the time being, territorial expansion would take second place to treaty revision. Moreover, American interests in Hawaii were extensive, and Japan in the 1880s could not risk alienating the United States. In short, Meiji leaders were acutely aware of Japan's weaknesses and at the same time determined to gain acceptance by the great powers. Guided by these conditions and goals, Tokyo exercised caution and kept bolder impulses under tight control.

While the Meiji government was cautious in practice, certain individuals nurtured acquisitive aspirations with respect to Hawaii. Occasionally these aspirations were openly expressed. During the 1890s, for example, a number of intellectuals, influenced by currently fashionable social Darwinism and impressed by the colonization of the Americas, Australia, and Siberia, wrote that Japan should also expand overseas through emigration. At this time, Hawaii was a household word, signifying the earliest destination for Meiji emigrants. Publicist Setsu Nagasawa in 1893 called the Islands a "springboard" for peaceful expansion.

More forthright in their formulations were activists such as Keishirō Inoue who urged throughout the 1890s that Japan must rule Hawaii in order to protect itself in the Pacific. It was at this time that Hiroharu (Kanji) Katō, later chief of Navy General Staff, felt deep regret that Japan did not use its naval power during the 1893 Hawaiian revolution to expel American influence from the islands and maintain the monarchy's "independence."

There is some evidence that government officials entertained the idea of gaining control over Hawaii. Foreign Secretary Taneomi Soejima is reported to have considered taking over the Islands during the 1870s. Emperor Meiji's answer to King Kalakaua's 1881 proposal for a Japan-led Asiatic federation including Hawaii also contains some revealing hints. After politely declining the Hawaiian monarch's proposal, the emperor (in words probably drafted by Foreign Secretary Kaoru Inoue in consultation with other leaders in the government) went on to say: "However, I ardently hope that such Union [of Asian nations and Hawaii] may be realized at some future day, and keeping it constantly in mind I never fail, wherever time allows me, to discuss the means of bringing about that result. . . . it cannot only be the fortune of Japan and Hawaii, but also of whole Asia." These innocuous words anticipate the rhetoric of the Greater East Asia Co-Prosperity Sphere sixty years later, when publicists loudly called for Hawaii's "reunification" with Asia.

Whatever hopes Japan may have had about acquiring Hawaii through peaceful expansion were dashed in June 1897, when the United States and the Republic of Hawaii concluded a treaty of annexation. As soon as the treaty became known in Japan there was an outcry in nationalist circles. The newspaper *Kokumin* declared that the entire nation disapproved of the treaty and demanded that the Imperial government issue a strong protest. Tokyo did submit an official protest on 19 June, after President McKinley had submitted the treaty to the Senate for ratification.

While informing Secretary of State John Sherman of his government's displeasure, Tōru Hoshi, Japan's minister in Washington, assured him that Japan "did not have and never did have" designs upon the integrity and sovereignty of Hawaii. Yet two days earlier, in a telegram to Foreign Minister Shigenobu Ōkuma, Hoshi had urged the following course of action: "I submit my plan, which I believe to be the only possible means of frustrating scheme of

Hawaiian annexation, that is, our occupation of that Island by dispatching, without any delay some powerful ships under the name of reprisal, taking advantage of present relation between Japan and Hawaii."

Hoshi's advice was not taken by his superiors, but the matter did not end there. One Japanese diplomat, disgusted by his government's weak response to the American action, attempted suicide en route home from Honolulu on the *Naniwa*.

In the longer run, the obstruction of Japan's peaceful expansion into Hawaii through restrictions to immigration, together with the disappointment of vague but deep-rooted expectations for a closer relationship with the Islands, left a residue of frustration. Both the frustration and the expectations were resurrected forty-four years later when Hawaii suddenly emerged as a strategic target and visionary object in the Greater East Asia War.

One of the ironies of history is that yesterday's problem can become today's pride (and vice versa). In the 1890s, Hawaii was the scene of the first serious Japanese-American friction. In the 1980s, Hawaii is a symbol of Japanese-American cooperation. Japan's profile in Hawaii today is more visible than at any time before World War II. Yet with few exceptions, the Japanese presence in the Islands is welcomed both locally and in Washington.

Hawaii has become a favorite meeting ground for American and Japanese officials. Heads of state have conferred there. Ministers and department chiefs regularly consult there. Prime Minister Zenkō Suzuki spoke about "Pacific solidarity" in 1982, having been introduced by State Governor George Ariyoshi, who delivered a welcoming address in accented but appropriately composed Japanese. Units of Japan's armed forces regularly visit Hawaii. In 1980 and 1982, Japanese naval vessels participated in maneuvers with the Hawaii-based U.S. Seventh Fleet. It is not uncommon to see Japanese sailors sightseeing at Pearl Harbor's Arizona Memorial. More recently, Japan's Ground Self-Defense Forces have held joint command post maneuvers with the United States Army at Schofield Barracks. In honor of the first such joint exercises on American soil, a reception was held at the Honolulu Japanese Chamber of Commerce on 23 June 1982 for some three hundred Japanese and American army officers, with a welcoming speech by the state governor.

In the economic sphere, Japanese corporations have invested in

Hawaiian businesses, real estate, and tourism. Any number of high-rise hotels that cluster along Waikiki Beach are Japanese owned. Some 690,400 Japanese tourists came to Hawaii in 1981, more than three times the number of immigrants from Japan between 1885 and 1941. Japanese restaurants, theaters, banks, and retail stores can be spotted throughout Honolulu. A Mitsukoshi Department Store opened in Waikiki in 1979, fulfilling a project that began in 1940 only to be interrupted by the war. To manage and help staff these enterprises, some thirteen thousand Japanese nationals have taken up residence in Hawaii.

Japanese culture, traditional and modern, pervades the islands. In addition to festivals, temples, shrines, theaters, and language schools, there are three Japanese-language newspapers, two Japanese-language radio stations, and—until recently reduced to evening programs only—one full-time Japanese-language television channel. The University of Hawaii has more specialists on Japan than does any other institution of higher education in the United States. The university trains one quarter of those studying the Japanese language in this country. From Japan come well-known writers, artists, movie stars, pop singers, television personalities, and *sumō* wrestlers, assured of appreciative local audiences. Emperor Hirohito received the most effusive welcome of his 1975 American trip when he paid a visit to Honolulu.

To be sure, the Japanese presence in Hawaii has provoked some complaints. Several years ago there were voices that blamed big-spending yen investors for driving up real estate prices. Some criticism attended the purchase of a Honolulu golf course by Japanese interests, after local users discovered that they had to pay steep membership fees. Eyebrows were raised when the local press revealed that Tokyo *yakuza* (gangsters) operated a Waikiki hotel whose services to specially introduced Japanese clients were said to extend into areas normally associated with certain massage parlors. But these incidents have been infrequent and relatively minor. Despite grumblings and jokes from members of all ethnic groups about the Rising Sun completing peacefully what it started to do at Pearl Harbor, Japan's presence in Hawaii is on the whole accepted.

Hawaii's Japanese-Americans in the 1980s, a vast majority of whom are descendants of immigrants who came to the islands from 1885 to 1924, have both fulfilled and belied predictions about them made fifty and sixty years earlier. Contrary to what observers of the 1920s were saying, the Japanese community in Hawaii has not soared to numerical dominance. It has grown from 160,000 in 1941 to 227,000 in 1980, but proportionately it has decreased from a peak of 43 percent of the total Island population in 1920 to only 23.5 percent in 1980. Current immigration from the American mainland and the Philippines will probably further reduce this proportion.

Nor has the prediction that Japanese would not assimilate come true. The past fifty years have witnessed a steady erosion of insularity by intermarriage, education, travel, and generational changes. Today the *issei* have dwindled to a small minority within a shrinking minority. Most surviving *issei* are elderly women who came to Hawaii as brides more than a half-century ago. Meanwhile, the *nisei* generation has passed into middle age and beyond. While many of its members are still in the prime of their careers, the generation as a whole is older than was the *issei* generation on the eve of the Second World War. It is the *sansei* and *yonsei* (third and fourth generations) who predominate numerically. Their ties to Japan are comparatively diffuse, although many of these young Japanese-Americans have a serious and thoughtful intellectual and emotional interest in their ancestral land. This attraction derives in part from a search for "roots" and in part from a reaction against the Americanization embraced by their parents.

One prediction that has come true after a fashion is that the *nisei* have transformed Hawaii's political landscape. The old business and financial elites who enjoyed political dominance from the 1890s until a few years after World War II have been succeeded by a more complex power structure in which organized labor plays a notable role. The once reigning Republican Party has lost its preeminence. The Republicans have been a minority in the state legislature since 1954 and for several years have had no candidate elected to the United States House or Senate. The political fortunes of Hawaii's Japanese-Americans have been closely bound with the rise of the Democratic Party since the Second World War. That Japanese-Americans occupy the governor's office, both United States Senate seats, a number of key legislative positions, and a strong position in the state civil service has been more a product of Democratic Party politics than of ethnic solidarity.

Amid these trends, memories of World War II have grown both

indistinct and selective. Physical vestiges of the war can be found, if they are looked for. In Pearl Harbor the submerged rusting skeleton of the battleship *Arizona* has been made a memorial to the 1,177 officers and men who perished when the ship was wracked by explosions on 7 December 1941. The National Memorial Cemetery of the Pacific in Honolulu's Punchbowl Crater commemorates those who served in and who gave their lives in World War II and other wars. A solitary Japanese tank, almost toylike in comparison with contemporary behemoths, rests incongruously in a recreation area at Fort DeRussy on Waikiki Beach. On the northern slope of Punchbowl Crater, with its embrasures facing Pearl Harbor, stands an abandoned concrete pillbox. It was built shortly after 7 December 1941 in anticipation of a Japanese invasion. Dozens of tour buses pass it daily. Recently, someone covered its grey pockmarked exterior with a coat of bright yellow paint, brushed on representations of flowers in green, and inscribed in bold pink letters the Hawaiian word for (among other things) welcome: *Aloha.*

CHAPTER II

The Prewar Japanese Community

Wartime Japanese writers asserted that Hawaii *dōhō* were waiting for the Imperial Army to liberate them from American rule. It is tempting to dismiss such views as propaganda. But to do so would be to commit an oversimplification fraught with misleading overtones. Japanese perceptions of the *dōhō* community in Hawaii were largely derived from, and shaped by, members of that community. Therefore, it is important to know something about certain aspects of the prewar community that made it not entirely illogical or insincere for observers in Japan to write about Hawaii the way they did.

In 1932, a book appeared in Tokyo describing life in the Hawaiian Islands. The author began by calling Hawaii "a second Japan." Properly understood in the context of the times, the phrase was neither farfetched nor presumptuous. Hawaii, with about 160,000 Japanese in 1941, contained the third greatest concentration of overseas *dōhō* in the world. China and Brazil had more, but in these countries the Japanese were tiny minorities engulfed by masses of other inhabitants. In Hawaii they were the largest ethnic group, comprising about 40 percent of the Territory's population. Roughly three-quarters or 120,000 of Hawaii *dōhō* were *nisei* born in the Islands. The remaining 40,000 were *issei* who, denied United States citizenship whether or not they wanted it, were subjects of the Empire of Japan. The citizenship status of Hawaii *nisei* was complicated. All were American citizens, under the principle of *jus solis*, by virtue of having been born on American territory. But in 1940 a majority of Hawaii *nisei* (73,281 out of 119,361) also carried Japanese citizenship. The circumstances behind this anomalous situation require an explanation.

Until 1924 Tokyo regarded all children born of Japanese fathers in any part of the world as Japanese citizens according to the principle of *jus sanguinis*. Consequently, *nisei* born in Hawaii during most of or before 1924 were Japanese subjects in the eyes of the Imperial government. True they could seek expatriation, that is renounce Japanese citizenship, but only before the age of seventeen. After the age of seventeen, *nisei* were denied the right of expatriation until they reached their thirty-seventh birthday. Between seventeen and thirty-seven, they were liable to serve a term in military uniform, either in the Imperial Army or the Imperial Navy.

On 1 December 1924 the Imperial Diet (Japan's parliament) passed a law which loosened the bond between mother country and overseas *dōhō*. According to this law, *nisei* born before 1 December 1924 could nullify their Japanese citizenship by submitting formal notification accompanied by appropriate documentation to the Home Minister. Those born after that date would lose their Japanese citizenship within two weeks of birth unless their parents registered them at a Japanese consulate. In other words, any Hawaii *nisei* born after 1924 would have only American citizenship unless his or her parents promptly took steps with local Japanese diplomatic representatives to give the infant Japanese citizenship as well.

After 1924 it was considerably easier to sever the legal link binding *nisei* to Japan. Older *nisei* could renounce their Japanese citizenship. The parents of those born after 1924 needed only to do nothing and their children would have no legal ties with Japan.

These ties, however, were not significantly loosened in Hawaii until the eve of the Second World War. Only 8 percent (5,500 out of 66,000) of *nisei* born before 1924 had renounced their Japanese citizenship by 1933. In the same period, about 40 percent (17,800 out of 39,900) of those *nisei* born after 1924 were registered by their parents at the Japanese consulate so that they could acquire Japanese citizenship. In 1938 it was announced that children of dual citizens (*sansei*, or third generation Japanese-Americans) were eligible for registration as Japanese subjects.

While dual citizenship conferred some advantages, it also had drawbacks. All Japanese male citizens were liable for military service. After the Imperial Army moved into Manchuria in 1931, draft levels increased in order to supply manpower for escalating hostilities with China. Hawaii *nisei* males with dual citizenship were advised to submit an application for draft deferment every year at the Japanese consulate. Should they neglect to do so and then go to Japan, they were required to take a physical exam and faced possible induction into the Imperial Army. Hawaii *nisei* were indeed drafted, but the exact number are not known.

The ambiguities of dual citizenship were only one of several circumstances complicating the lives of Hawaii *nisei* during the 1930s. The *nisei* were a generation suspended between Japan and the United States in a decade of increasing tension. The generation gap with their parents, who clung to traditional Japanese values and spoke little English, was considerable in terms of years (*issei* had married late), education, and social behavior. Many *nisei* bridled at the discipline and obligations imposed by the Japanese family system. Nor was there unanimous enthusiasm among the 85 percent (in 1934) of *nisei* students who attended Japanese language school after their regular school hours. At the same time *nisei* were not generally accepted into Hawaii's white *(haole)* community. They were not readily admitted to private schools that educated the local *haole* elite. *Nisei* with excellent academic and employment records were passed over when the Big Five corporations recruited management personnel. While old-time *haole* residents *(kamaaina)* tended to treat the *nisei* paternalistically, recent arrivals from the mainland—including army and navy personnel—often regarded them with distrust. Consequently, *nisei* with technical qualifications were as a practice not hired for well-paid defense jobs.

Between these complex sets of pressures, *nisei* followed various paths in life and work. Some made up their minds to win the respect and acceptance of the *haole* community through hard work and rigorous Americanization. Others, under parental guidance or on their own initiative, sought to improve their local status by acquiring an education in Japan, becoming in the process *kibei*.* But most *nisei* took an intermediate course, blending their

---

*Literally "return to America". *Kibei*, a term coined within the Japanese-American community, refers to *nisei* who returned to the United States after receiving most of their education in Japan.

ancestral heritage with the peculiarities of the Hawaiian social environment. If asked, as many were, if they were "loyal" to the United States or to Japan, few would have been comfortable contemplating a choice that would be mutually exclusive. As one *nisei* testified to a congressional committee in 1937: ". . . as long as you treat American citizens of Japanese ancestry as Japanese, they are going to be Japanese."

These sentiments were echoed by a University of Hawaii freshman shortly thereafter: "If we Japanese in Hawaii are treated like 'Japs', perhaps in time we shall come to feel like 'Japs'; but if our friends continue to treat us like Americans, we will feel and act like Americans."

Unfortunately, officials in Washington all too often did not treat *nisei* as ordinary Americans. On 14 October 1940 Congress passed the Nationality Act (Public Law 853) in which Section 402 of Chapter IV stipulated that as of 13 January 1941 American citizens of foreign parents could lose their United States citizenship should they remain in their parents' homeland for more than six months. This legislation was aimed at, among others, *nisei* pursuing studies, working, and visiting relatives in Japan. The effect of the law was to demonstrate that American-born men and women of Japanese ancestry were not equal to the vast majority of their fellow citizens. One Hawaii *nisei* who was in Japan at this time was so offended by such statutory discrimination that he decided, notwithstanding the gathering clouds of war, not to return to the United States.

The *issei*, too, had ties to both Japan and the United States. Feelings of Japanese patriotism ran deep, and not surprisingly so, for this generation was born in Japan, spoke Japanese as its mother tongue, and were not dual citizens like most of their children but outright subjects of Japan. Moreover many *issei* attributed what they regarded as their superior status vis à vis Chinese, Filipino, and other non-*haole* minorites in Hawaii to the Japanese Empire's power and to Tokyo's solicitude for its overseas *dōhō*.

Issei opinions were both shaped by and reflected in the local Japanese-language press. There were over a dozen vernacular serial publications during the 1930s, but probably none were more influential among *issei* readers than the Honolulu newspapers *Nippu jiji* and *Hawaii hōchi*. Each paper had a circulation of about fifteen thousand. Only slightly less weight was carried by *Jitsugyō no Hawaii*, published by Tetsuo Toyama.

The tone of all three papers with respect to international affairs shared certain characteristics. They were strongly anticommunist and expressed hostility to the Soviet Union. Britain and France were treated coolly, and at times with outright suspicion. Among the European countries, perhaps Germany and Italy received the most complimentary coverage. *Jitsugyō no Hawaii*, for example, portrayed Adolf Hitler in openly flattering colors. After the Anschluss of the Reich and Austria in March 1938, the Führer's "snapping the chains of bondage" between the two German-speaking nations was equated with Takamori Saigō's exploits in the Meiji Restoration.* Six months later during the Sudetenland crisis, *Jitsugyō no Hawaii* assessed the Munich agreements that dismembered Czechoslovakia in the following words: "Adolf Hitler has stark courage, power, and vision. . . . It required supreme courage on the part of Hitler to defy the threat of 25,000,000 armed men. But he had what it takes—and won!"

Japan occupied a special place in the columns of Hawaii's vernacular press. According to Tadao Tamaru, a former reporter for *Nippu jiji*, "all" editorials were favorable to Japan. Any criticism of the Imperial Army was "unthinkable."

Tamaru did not mention one remarkable editorial policy: that news in the English-language sections and Japanese-language sections of the same paper was reported differently. The *Nippu jiji* and *Hawaii hōchi* were mainly vernacular newspapers, but each carried a few pages of news written in English. In fact each issue had two front pages, each with its own masthead, headlines, lead stories, and photographs—one in Japanese and one in English. Treatment of Japan in the English sections was comparatively detached. However, the sections written in Japanese reverberated with patriotic rhetoric. Whereas the English pages referred to "Japanese Army" and "Japanese planes," the vernacular section spoke of "our army" *(waga gun)* and "our angry eagles" *(waga arawashi)*, the latter a poetic term for Japanese military aviators during the 1930s and World War II.

The extent to which English and Japanese versions of the same events diverged in the same paper can be gauged by comparing

*Takamori Saigō commanded the forces of the allied southwestern *han* (fiefs) which routed supporters of the Tokugawa shogunate in 1868, paving the way for the establishment of an Imperial government under the young Emperor Meiji. The political and social events that witnessed the partial demise of feudalism and the birth of an Imperial state have been called the Meiji Restoration.

the headlines of *Hawaii hōchi*'s 24 September 1937 issue. During this period, the Imperial Japanese Army was fighting Chinese Nationalist forces around Shanghai and was beginning to push inland along the Yangtze River toward Han-k'ou. English-language reports on these events were confined to two articles headlined respectively "Chinese Hold Lotien Lines Against Foes" and "Raiders Bomb Hankow." In the Japanese section, there were eight stories about these and other developments not reported in the English-language section. Sample headlines were: "Our Units Advance Everywhere"; "Enemy Defences Blown Up [at Lotien]"; "Army Ministry Announcement of War Situation"; "Mongol Units Cooperate with Imperial Army and Annihilate Enemy"; "Our Senda and Itakura Units Complete Occupation of P'ing Ch'ih Ch'uan"; "Imperial Army Welcomed, Rising Sun Flags Flutter from Every Door!" (the exclamation mark was in the original headline).

A wave of patriotism swept across Hawaii's Japanese community at the outbreak of hostilities between Japan and China on 7 July 1937. *Nisei* as well as *issei* were caught up in an emotional fervor that reinforced ethnic consciousness and in some families narrowed the generation gap. To a certain extent this emotion was rooted in anxiety that Japan's defeat by China would undermine the local status of Hawaii *dōhō*. As *Jitsugyō no Hawaii* editorialized: "Fellow compatriots, let us with our hearts pray for our ancestral land in her trials. Should the war in the end be lost, the Japanese in Hawaii, insulted and ridiculed by Kanakas [Hawaiians and part Hawaiians] and Pake [Chinese], would in the long run be unable to work."

As the war escalated during 1938 into a Japanese crusade to "reform" China and to build a "New Order in East Asia," idealistic impulses in the Hawaii Japanese community came to the fore. Japan was perceived by many as devoting lives and resources to saving China from its own decadence, to constructing a new Asia in which all Asians would ultimately benefit. In the eyes of these *dōhō*, Japan's challenge to the colonial powers and to Soviet communism was a historical turning point of fundamental importance. The demands of this "holy war" *(seisen)* upon the ancestral land were so great that all *dōhō* were thought to bear a responsibility to contribute what they could for victory.

The vernacular press played the leading role in keeping *issei* informed about the war. Without regular Hawaii *dōhō* correspondents in China, the local press relied heavily upon Dōmei, a Japanese news agency that closely reflected official views.

Dōmei reports had greater credibility for many *issei* than those emanating from American news agencies. According to University of Hawaii anthropologist John Embree, who was studying the Japanese community in Kona on the island of Hawaii during the late 1930s: "The first generation regards the Japanese war news in the Japanese section as infallibly accurate; all other news of the war, such as appears in American papers, is 'Chinese propaganda'."

Professor Embree's remark was substantiated by Shirō Sogabe, a missionary in Hilo, who in 1938 advised readers of *Jitsugyō no Hawaii:* "Japanese press reports are the most reliable in the world. Do not be misled by the English language press. It is all right to read the English language press, but you must first read the Japanese press and make a calm judgment."

Hawaii's Japanese-language newspapers on occasion openly criticized the Honolulu *Advertiser* and *Star-Bulletin* for printing negative allegations about Japan's prosecution of the war in China. For example, when the Imperial Army fought its way into Nanking in December 1937, the local vernacular press openly hailed the fall of China's capital as an epochal triumph. But as stories of atrocities by Japanese soldiers started to surface in the local English-language press, the vernacular papers responded sharply.

Feelings ran particularly high over the so-called slapping incident. During the occupation of Nanking, a young American diplomat named John Allison* was slapped by a Japanese soldier for intervening in what appears to have been the imminent abuse of a Chinese woman. The incident stirred up considerable publicity in the United States, not to mention in the Territory of Hawaii. *Jitsugyō no Hawaii* took Allison to task for "slandering" the Imperial Army.

The China war made its presence felt in Hawaii's Japanese community in many ways. One was through rallies and meetings to support the war effort, such as those held by the *Nihon bunka shinkōkai* (Society for the promotion of Japanese culture). Local theaters such as the Honolulu-za showed Japanese war movies and

---

*John Allison subsequently served as ambassador to Japan (1953–1957). After retirement he lived in Honolulu until his death in 1978.

Dōmei newsreels, inviting viewers with posters hailing the "hero-
ism of the Imperial Army" and promising "excitement inspiring
100 million *dōhō.*" Japanese radio broadcasts were readily accessible, and starting in May 1940 the Tokyo station JZK began evening news programs broadcast especially for Hawaii audiences.
An advertisement in a Honolulu store selling Philco radios urged
shoppers to "Hear Japan, 100 Battles, 100 Victories."

Another way in which Japanese views of the China war were
disseminated in Hawaii was through prominent visitors. A number of the well-known Japanese politicians, journalists, and academics who came to or passed through Hawaii in the 1930s gave
interviews for the vernacular press or delivered lectures to local
audiences for the purpose, as Baron Kishichirō Okura put it, of
imparting "a correct understanding of Japan's goals." These visitors included a postwar prime minister (Hitoshi Ashida), the director of Dōmei (Masanori Itō), the editor-in-chief of the *Mainichi*
newspaper (Shingorō Takaishi), and a retired rear admiral and
Diet member from Okinawa (Kenwa Kanna).

A figure who aroused strong local reactions, both positive and
negative, in the community was the ultranationalist Seigō Nakano.
Nakano made a stopover at Honolulu in February 1938 en route
home from a trip to the Third Reich. In an interview with *Nippu
jiji* he stressed the rising power of Germany, Italy, and Japan. Six
months later, in an article written specially for *Jitsugyō no Hawaii*,
Nakano criticized Tokyo's apology to the United States for the
Panay Incident* and applauded a statement by a hawkish Japanese admiral† that the white man must be driven out of Asia.

Among the most powerful stimuli to patriotism among *issei*
were visits by ships of the Imperial Japanese Navy. Such visits
occurred forty-one times between 1876 and 1939. From Tokyo's
perspective, these calls in the Islands served a number of purposes.
At an official level, they constituted a courteous gesture toward the
United States, providing occasions in which American and Japanese naval officers could establish professional contacts. At a second level, they offered opportunities to observe America's mid-

*Japanese planes strafed and sank the American gunboat *Panay* on the Yangtze
River near Nanking on 12 December 1937.

†Nobumasa Suetsugu (1880–1944), commander in chief of the Combined Fleet
(1933–1934), Home Minister (1937–1939).

Pacific base. Finally, by showing the flag, they conveyed a message to Hawaiian (and after 1898 to American) authorities that Japan was a Pacific naval power that took more than a casual interest in its Hawaii *dōhō*.

For their part, many *dōhō* welcomed naval visitations. The vernacular press gave them prominent coverage. Officers and men were accorded warm hospitality in the businesses, civic and religious organizations, and homes of *dōhō* on Oahu, Maui, and the island of Hawaii. Many *issei* saw the Rising Sun flag on an Imperial naval vessel as gratifying reassurance that the mother country still cared about its overseas subjects. Nor were the *nisei* unaffected. One of them recalled: "A naval ship, being an extension of the suzerainty of the homeland, is a tonic of the first magnitude . . . and the reception is therefore both elaborate and sincere. We were brought up in such an atmosphere, and so the sailors and officers of the training ships were welcomed with both affection and respect."

Editorial policies in the vernacular press fostered the idea that Japanese naval officers who had visited Hawaii subsequently retained a special connection with the islands. Promotions and combat exploits of these individuals were periodically published, sometimes in the form of their letters to a Hawaii vernacular newspaper editor. Rear Admiral Denshichi Ōkōchi, who called at Honolulu in 1934, subsequently commanded a flotilla in Shanghai and wrote to *Nippu jiji* editor Yasutarō Sōga how pleased he was that Hawaii *dōhō* correctly understood and supported Japan's war efforts. Another visitor to Hawaii, Lieutenant Commander Matsuhei Kawasaki, wrote Tetsuo Toyama that *Jitsugyō no Hawaii* editorials enjoyed a good reputation within the Navy Ministry. Toyama also befriended Lieutenant Commander Takaji Terasaki who came to Hawaii in 1922 as a cadet and returned for a second visit in 1936. Promoted to captain in 1937, Terasaki commanded a Yangtze River gunboat during the Nanking campaign and wrote an account of the city's capture which Toyama published. The article was accompanied by a photograph of Admiral Ōkōchi and Captain Terasaki on the deck of a warship under the caption "Shining War Deeds of Naval Stars with Hawaii Connections."

Personal ties between Japanese naval officers and the Japanese community were strengthened by geographical and family bonds. John Embree noted that in Kona local hosts looked for Japanese

sailors with the same prefectural origins and tried to get the men
to stay in their homes. It was not unusual for some of the officers
and men among the visiting ships to have relatives in Hawaii. For
example when the training ships *Ondo* and *Erimo* called at Hilo in
June 1937 they received a particularly warm reception. The commander of the *Erimo* had not only friends but relatives on the Big
Island. About the same time the warship *Sunosaki* dropped anchor
at Honolulu. Its commanding officer had an emotional reunion
with his older brother, who had emigrated to Hawaii from Kagoshima thirty years earlier.

Nor were young women unaffected by the proximity of Imperial
Navy cadets. In 1931 a Hawaii *nisei* girl fell in love with a cadet
visiting American waters on a training vessel. For the next ten
years, both waged a quiet struggle with Washington and Tokyo
bureaucracies for the right to marry. Meanwhile the cadet matured into a naval fighter pilot with the rank of captain. At last, in
the spring of 1941, the couple was united. *Nippu jiji* celebrated the
event by noting the "happy end" to a saga where "pure love"
between a Hawaii *nisei* maiden and an "angry eagle" had over-
come barriers separating the two nations. The Imperial Navy,
however, gave its permission for the marriage only after the
Hawaii girl had come to Japan and renounced her American citizenship.

Although Imperial Navy officers visiting Hawaii were expected
to refrain from political activities, the goodwill and receptivity of
issei led some to assume the role of educators. The public lectures
on Japan's aims in China delivered by naval officers in Hawaii
enjoyed considerable success. For example, on 8 December 1938,
Captain Isamu Takeda, commander of the naval tanker *Shiriya*,
gave a lecture on the China war to an appreciative audience of
160 at the Konpira Shrine in Honolulu. Sponsored by the local
Nippon rengō kyōkai [United Japanese society], the lecture dealt
with more than China. Captain Takeda was quoted approvingly in
the *Jitsugyō no Hawaii* as asserting that future generations of *dōhō*
may be American in form but they would not lose their Japanese
spirit. The captain's presentation was so well received that he was
persuaded to postpone the *Shiriya*'s departure in order to make
similar appearances in Oahu's rural districts.

Such was the local enthusiasm generated by naval visits that
Admiral Suguru Suzuki, when interviewed in 1979, recalled how

in 1937 and 1938 as a lieutenant commander attached to the
Third Department (Intelligence) of the Navy General Staff he had
been regularly detailed to pick up sackfuls of mail from Hawaii
dōhō at a Tokyo post office. The bulk of this mail contained expressions of goodwill and occasional monetary contributions. It is
possible, albeit unprovable, that a few letters came from self-
appointed guardians of *dōhō* patriotism. John Embree noted the
existence of such types in the Japanese community at Kona: "Anyone who acts in a way 'disloyal' to Japan is likely to have some
neighbor write to Tokyo about him and then, if and when he
returns to Japan for a visit, he runs into trouble."

The Imperial Navy was not the only beneficiary of Hawaii *dōhō*
patriotism during the 1930s. From 1937 until 1939, encouraged
by the Japanese Consulate and the Japanese Chamber of Commerce, Hawaii *dōhō* purchased three million yen worth of Imperial war bonds and contributed 1.2 million yen to the National
Defense and Soldier's Relief Fund.* These transactions were handled largely by Honolulu branches of the Yokohama Specie Bank
and the Sumitomo Bank, or through consular agents active on
each island. During this interim, Hawaii *dōhō* reportedly donated
more per capita to the National Defense Fund than did the inhabitants of Japan proper.

Monetary contributions made up only part of total donations.
Through the good offices of *Nippu jiji* and other vernacular newspapers, ties, blankets, lead plates from auto batteries, and tinsel
foil from cigarette packages and Kodak film wrappers were sent to
Japan to help the war effort. Local *kumi* (groups) of housewives
took up collections for and prepared *imonbukuro* (comfort bags)
for troops fighting in China. Imperial Army infantrymen who
were accustomed to foraging for food in Chinese villages prized
these *imonbukuro*, which typically contained as assortment of
Camel and Lucky Strike cigarettes, Dole canned pineapple, Sun-
kist oranges, Sun-Maid raisins, and chocolate kisses. A few Hawaii
women sewed one-thousand-stitch belts to be worn as protective
talismans by Imperial soldiers in combat.

Efforts were made in Hawaii and Japan to direct these remittances to those military units from the same Japanese prefectures
and even from the same villages from which donors had emi-

*At that time the exchange rate was 3.4 yen to one U.S. dollar.

grated. This complicated task was tackled by local prefectural societies, the vernacular papers, the Japanese Consulate, Japanese firms with branches in Hawaii, and the Army Ministry. Whether the articles were always delivered to the intended units in the field cannot be said with certainty, but the cooperation of so many groups was impressive.

Demonstrations of support from Hawaii were appreciated in Japan. On 6 September 1937 Navy Minister Mitsumasa Yonai sent a letter to the editor of *Nippu jiji* commending him and the community for contributions to the war effort. A month later, Army Minister Gen Sugiyama conveyed similar expressions of gratitude to the editors of *Hawaii hōchi* and *Jitsugyō no Hawaii*. Writing from a gunboat on the Yangtze near recently occupied Nanking, Lieutenant Commander Terasaki thanked Hawaii *dōhō* for the *imonbukuro* and added:

> Dedicated to serve until death, we are all deeply moved by the warm sympathy and solicitude overflowing from all dearest Hawaii *dōhō*. I shall never forget the encouragement and hospitality shown by geisha, restaurant owners, innkeepers, merchants, doctors, publishers, Chamber of Commerce officials, bankers, and people of all classes during my stay of only four days.

Expressions of gratitude from the Imperial Navy to Hawaii *dōhō* for material and moral suppport in the "holy war" in China appeared in the vernacular press as late as New Years Day 1940. On New Years Day 1941 Foreign Minister Yōsuke Matsuoka sent a message of encouragement to *dōhō* throughout the world which was carried in the Hawaii vernacular papers.

Notwithstanding the extraordinarily high level of per capita contributions from Hawaii, some felt that even more could be done. In early 1938, *Jitsugyō no Hawaii* exhorted readers:

> Japanese of Hawaii! There's absolutely no need to feel any hesitation. What's wrong with serving your ancestral land? Are not those who vacillate about contributing money at this time of national emergency being unpatriotic? Look! Has not our Army Minister sent a respectful letter of thanks even for those who contributed fifty cents? Isn't this the flower, the sincerity, the essence of our Japanese military?

Nine months later, Harutsugu Tahara, a member of the Socialist Mass Party serving as an electcd representative in the Imperial Diet, remarked that with some real effort Japanese-Americans could channel half of their total assets into war bonds. Some Hawaii *dōhō* did go beyond buying war bonds and filling comfort bags to show their support for Japan's crusade in China. Emissaries ranging from an envoy from a Nichiren Buddhist school to a delegation of dressmakers performed "comfort visits" to the Army and Navy ministries in Tokyo. Some also made forays into China in order to encourage troops in the expeditionary forces serving there. In 1938 a Japanese journalist reported that one or two delegations from Hawaii were touring combat zones in China each month.

One *dōhō* who took a particular interest in the war was a Honolulu educator, Kuwaichi Nōnin. Founder and director of the *Senshōbyōsha Hawaii imonkai* (Hawaii consolation society for war casualties), Nōnin made a five-month tour of military installations in Japan, China, Korea, and Manchuria during the spring and summer of 1938. After paying respects at the Army and Navy ministries in Tokyo, he called at and dispensed "comfort money" to military hospitals and divisional headquarters in Yokohama, Sendai, Hirosaki, Kanazawa, Nagoya, Osaka, Himeji, the Kure Naval Base, Hiroshima, Kokura, the Beppu Naval Hospital, and Kumamoto. Nōnin published an account of his travels in which he described how hospitalized Japanese soldiers were deeply moved, sometimes to tears, when they learned that their solicitous visitor came from Hawaii. Such feelings were especially strong among those from the same prefecture in Japan as was Nōnin himself. Nōnin concluded his account by calling for stronger *dōhō* commitments to the war effort, citing the example of his own son, a *nisei* serving in the Imperial Army in China.

Just how many Hawaii *nisei* joined or were drafted into the Japanese Army is not known. The pages of the vernacular press carried several articles between 1937 and 1941 on the deeds of local youth in China. As most of these were young men whose families were prominent in the local community, it is probably safe to assume that many cases went unreported.

One case not reported in the prewar vernacular press that did eventually attract wide attention was that of Hanama Harold

Tasaki. In 1950 Tasaki achieved recognition in both Japan and the
United States for his autobiographical novel, *Long the Imperial
Way*, which one New York critic compared to Remarque's *All
Quiet on the Western Front*. Born on Maui in 1913, Tasaki studied
a year each at the University of Hawaii and at Oberlin College,
worked as an agricultural laborer in California, and in 1936 went
to Japan. From 1936 until 1939, he served as an infantry private
in the Japanese Army, undergoing grueling combat in various
parts of China.

In the publicity surrounding the publication of *Long the Imperial Way*, it was noted that the author had been drafted. This detail
conveyed the impression that Tasaki had been sucked into the Japanese military machine. However, in a 1980 interview at Tasaki's
home in the city of Fukuyama on the Inland Sea, Tasaki told me
that he had enlisted voluntarily, indeed enthusiastically. Why? For
one thing, his admiration for Japan had been aroused by the spiritual strength of *issei* farmers among whom he had worked in California. Moreover, he had been drawn toward the ideals that
seemed to animate Japan's international policies during the early
1930s. Finally, he had carried a residue of resentment, recalling
discrimination against Hawaii's Japanese. One memory remained
vivid: at PTA meetings his mother and father had been snubbed by
haoles. What really stung was that these same *haoles* socialized
with local Chinese.

Was Tasaki an isolated example of a Hawaii *nisei* who sought
identity and involvement by joining Japan's armed forces? Probably not. *Nippu jiji* noted late in 1937 that the Kona community
was providing a steady flow of recruits. About the same time, the
Hawaii hōchi praised a Honolulu family for sending both of its
sons to China with the Imperial Army.

It is possible that many *nisei* who entered the Japanese military
did so because of parental pressure. Those educated in Japan *(kibei)* were probably more likely to join or to be drafted than those
who grew up in the islands. Whatever the particular circumstances, it is clear that a small number of Hawaii's Americans of
Japanese ancestry donned the military uniform of the Imperial
Army.

One can only conjecture how many Hawaii *nisei* lost their lives
in China. An obituary that appeared in the 5 October 1937 issue
of *Nippu jiji* provides a clue to the atmosphere of the time. A man

from the Kalihi district of Honolulu, Sergeant Torao Morishige, age twenty-four, had been killed in action in North China. The paper carried his photograph (showing him in uniform) and conducted an interview with his surviving family members. The mother was quoted as recalling his parting words: "If news of my death should come, please rejoice." One of two younger brothers added: "We're going to be soldiers too, and we're going to get back at our brother's enemy!"

Service in the armed forces was not the only means by which a small number of Hawaii *nisei* supported Japan's New Order in East Asia. Kan Matsumura, born in the islands and graduated from the University of Hawaii, found work in Osaka with the English-language *Mainichi* newspaper, thanks to the good offices of his UH Japanese language instructor, Tasuku Harada. As a reporter in Japan and Manchuria during the 1920s, Matsumura became increasingly involved in his ancestral land's continental ambitions. When the "Manchurian Incident" (18 September 1931) led to the seizure of northeastern China by Japanese forces and to the creation, in 1932, of a puppet state called Manchukuo, Matsumura joined the Manchukuoan Foreign Affairs Ministry in Hsinking (Shenyang) as a propaganda specialist. By 1939 he had risen to the post of Manchukuoan minister plenipotentiary to Franco's government in Madrid. When Matsumura initialed the Spanish-Manchukuoan Treaty of Commerce on 18 September 1941 (the tenth anniversary of the Manchurian Incident), the *Nippu jiji* treated the event as a Hawaii *dōhō* success story.

These efforts, sacrifices, and achievements by a few Hawaii *dōhō* raised expectations in Japan about Hawaii's Japanese community as a whole. Journalists and politicians envisioned ambitious tasks for them. It will be recalled that a Diet member estimated that Japanese-Americans could (and by implication should) contribute half of their assets to defense bonds. One writer proposed that Hawaii *nisei* and *sansei* should emigrate en masse to the forty-eight states, impress Americans with their probity, and persuade them to revise the 1924 Exclusion Act so that Japan's excess population could flow into the United States. Another writer urged that, since *nisei* were uniquely equipped to understand American psychology, they should spearhead a propaganda drive throughout the United States to convince Americans of the justice of Japan's actions in East Asia.

Others saw a mission for Hawaii *dōhō* in Asia. Seikō Ebizaka, chief of the Information Department of the Honganji Temple in Tokyo's Tsukiji district, declared in a 1940 radio broadcast that Hawaii *dōhō* formed the "advance guard" of Japan's "holy war" for a New Order in East Asia. Early in 1941, journalist Zuimei Azumi called Hawaii's Japanese the *"shishi* of a Shōwa Restoration"* who must be prepared to sacrifice themselves "if worse comes to worse" for the construction of the Greater East Asia Co-Prosperity Sphere.

Not all Japanese shared extravagant expectations about Hawaii *dōhō*, but enough did to suggest that the prewar Japanese perception of Hawaii contained some serious misconceptions. First, Japanese commentators tended to assume that the views and actions of some *issei* and a few *nisei* represented the community as a whole. This was definitely not the case. Second, observers tended to exaggerate the potential services that Hawaii *dōhō* could—or would—perform on behalf of the motherland. These misconceptions persisted well into World War II and help account for the confidence felt by so many Japanese writers that their compatriots in Hawaii were anxiously awaiting liberation.

For their part, many Hawaii *dōhō* had their own illusions, if one is to judge from the vernacular press. There was a stubborn reluctance to recognize that Japan's advance into China carried serious consequences for relations with the United States. One editorial in a Honolulu vernacular paper late in 1938 assured readers that the United States would do nothing even if Japan occupied all of China, because Washington basically had little interest in the Far East.

Another illusion was that American business was eager to cooperate with Japan in rebuilding China. Some 1938 headlines in *Jitsugyō no Hawaii* convey this sanguine prognosis: "American Capital Welcome for New China Construction", "Japan Will Exclude France, Britain, USSR and Will Cooperate with Its Friends: Germany, Italy, USA." One editorial went on to say: "The United States has friendly relations with our ancestral land. Since the out-

Shishi (literally "men of courage") were warrior activists who paved the way for the Meiji Restoration. "Showa Restoration" was a slogan popular among some civilian and military nationalists calling for a renewal of Japan's spirit and a purge of "corrupt" political leadership during the 1930s.

break of the China Incident, perhaps with the exception of Germany and Italy, the United States has been the number one friend in showing understanding for Japan."

Those Americans who criticized the behavior of the Imperial Army and Navy in China were said not to understand Japan's true goals there. There seemed to be an unwritten assumption in Hawaii's vernacular press from 1937 through 1941 that if Washington correctly understood Japan's efforts to guide China toward independence and prosperity, the United States would raise no objections to the "holy war." As late as the fall of 1941, a number of Hawaii *dōhō*, perhaps a great number, saw no contradiction between being pro-Japanese and pro-American.

In the spring and summer of 1941, as relations between Washington and Tokyo steadily deteriorated, Hawaii's vernacular press succumbed ever more to wishful thinking. Again and again commentators discounted the likelihood of hostilities and held out the hope of reconciliation. In April, *Nippu jiji* downplayed the possibility of Japanese military action against Singapore and gave prominent coverage to Prime Minister Konoe's statement that relations with the United States would not worsen. In late July, after Roosevelt had frozen Japanese assets in the United States in retaliation for the Imperial Army's occupation of southern Indochina, *Nippu jiji* emphasized that the freeze would have no influence on Hawaii *dōhō*, who could continue sending money to Japan. During September, October, and November, attention was focused on diplomatic negotiations in Washington which seemed to hold out the hope of a compromise. Hopeful to the very end, *Nippu jiji* headlined on 6 December: "Far East Crises Somewhat Eased, No War Will Occur in the Pacific."

Reactions within the Japanese community to the mounting crisis were varied. Some *issei* took the precaution of putting their property in the name of *nisei* relatives. Others hurriedly changed their dollar savings into yen. Hundreds returned to Japan. A vast majority at least outwardly embraced American patriotism, joining those members of the community who for years had been espousing the cause of Americanization.

Signs of Americanization even crept into the vernacular press during 1941. *Nippu jiji* and *Hawaii hōchi*, while continuing to hail the advances of "our army" in China, carried approbatory articles on *nisei* in the United States armed forces. *Jitsugyō no*

Hawaii, which in the 1930s had carried a portrait of Emperor Hirohito (usually in military uniform) at the outset of each issue, in 1941 bedecked its pages with American flags, photographs of United States Army and Navy commanders, and testimonials from local *haole* politicians and businessmen. Sometime between 1938 and 1941, Admiral Heihachirō Tōgō vanished from the labels of Hawaiian *sake* as the Tōgō Masamune brand was renamed Hilo Masamune.

Despite the upsurge of Americanization, many members of Hawaii's Japanese community clung to the hope that somehow war could be avoided, that somehow the painful choice between ancestral and adopted (or native) lands would not have to be made. The events of 7 December left these people in a state of shock and disbelief, followed by anger, anxiety, and a numbing sadness.

After Pearl Harbor, the vast majority of Hawaii *dōhō* concealed or repressed their emotional ties with Japan. In the charged wartime atmosphere, any open expression of pro-Japanese feeling invited internment or even violence (Japan's invasion and occupation of the Philippines exacerbated antagonisms toward local *dōhō* from Hawaii's Filipino community).

With wartime restrictions placed on the movements of Hawaii Japanese, and with military censorship imposed on the vernacular press, it was natural for Tokyo to base its calculations of Hawaii *dōhō* wartime attitudes on prewar evidence. There was, however, an additional source of information that the Japanese government had at its disposal: several thousand Hawaii *dōhō* who were in Japan at the start of the war. It was from this group that emerged some of the prophets and planners of Hawaii's "liberation."

CHAPTER III

Hawaii Japanese
in Japan

Hawaii *dōhō* who by accident or intent were in Japan on 7 December 1941 constituted a potentially valuable source of information about the islands for both military and civilian planners. As some of these people came to play roles as propagandists and visionaries of Hawaii's "new life" within the Greater East Asia Co-Prosperity Sphere, it is essential to know something about their backgrounds.

Hawaii *dōhō* in Japan fell into two categories: *issei*, who had returned to their mother country after anywhere from a few years to several decades in the islands; and Hawaii-born *nisei*, who were in Japan studying, working, or serving in the armed forces. *Nisei* who had come to Japan as children or adolescents and who had received all or part of their primary, secondary, and higher education in Japan were called *kibei* (return to America) in the United States. In Japan, however, they were referred to as *kinichi* (return to Japan) *nisei*. The appellation *nikkeijin* was also used, but it had a broader connotation, embracing any person of Japanese descent.

In 1938 there were about forty-thousand *nikkeijin* in Japan of whom some fourteen thousand were Hawaii-born. Hawaii *nisei* had started going to Japan in 1918, but their numbers remained modest until the 1930s. After the Manchurian Incident (1931) and especially after the outbreak of Sino-Japanese hostilities in 1937, what had been a trickle turned into a stream.

Hawaii *nisei* came to Japan for a variety of reasons. The most important was to get an education. *Nisei* educated in Japan came back to Hawaii with heightened prestige in the local community. Graduates of Waseda, Meiji, and Dōshisha universities (which were favorites among Hawaii Japanese) enjoyed more status than graduates of the University of Hawaii. Some upwardly mobile *issei* parents did send their bright children to the American mainland for college or graduate degrees, but it was not unusual for a first generation Japanese immigrant couple to want at least one member of the next generation to possess the linguistic abilities and cultural outlook that a Japanese education would impart. Girls were sent to Japan to acquire training in household matters and etiquette that would enhance their suitability as brides. One contemporary observer in Hawaii noted that youth who went to Japan for study, whether male or female, came from better educated elements of the community.

Related to education were the prospects for better employment. Hawaii's *haole*-dominated politics and economy offered bright, ambitious *nisei* limited career opportunities. Unwilling to work in dead-end clerical jobs, some energetic and enterprising *nisei* went to Japan with the hope of acquiring technical skills in Japanese schools and then securing good positions in Japanese corporations, perhaps even with firms having branch offices in Honolulu.

Exchange rates of Japanese and American currencies also facilitated the pursuit of an education in Japan. During the 1930s, the yen was relatively cheap in relation to the American dollar. This helped to make housing and food affordable for *nisei* living on modest remittances from Hawaii. Occasionally, *nisei* could count on help from relatives in Japan.

Patriotism undeniably contributed to a growing number of Hawaii *nisei* going to Japan in the 1930s. Japan's deepening international isolation in the wake of the Manchurian Incident, the escalation of fighting on the Asian continent, and the crescendo of inspirational rhetoric ("Total National Mobilization," "A Hundred Million Hearts Beating as One," "New Order in East Asia") caught the imagination of hundreds if not thousands of *nisei*. The attraction of a beleaguered ancestral land was all the greater for those who for various reasons felt alienated from American society and who yearned to be part of a national community, to be accepted as an equal. Fumiye Miho, who left Hawaii in 1939 to teach English in Japan, recalled many years later: ". . . all the while I grew up and went through the University of Hawaii, I saw all that racial inequality around me. The haoles up there and the Orientals down here. I saw all the injustice. I wanted to go to Japan. In my heart, I felt that as a Japanese in Japan, I wouldn't be treated as a second class citizen."

The emotional experiences of some *nisei* in Japan were so intense that they became almost abrasively nationalistic upon returning to Hawaii. In the words of University of Hawaii sociologist Andrew W. Lind, *kibei* could be "more fanatically Japanese in their disposition than their own parents."

Although most *kinichi nisei* intended to return to the United States, some did not. A few dropped their American citizenship. According to a 1939 survey of *nisei* students in the Tokyo area, 21 percent of the males (but only 7 percent of the females) expressed the intention of remaining permanently in Japan. As it turned out, of the Hawaii *nisei* in Japan between the summer of 1940 and the summer of 1941, only 40 percent returned to the United States before the outbreak of the war, although Washington had repeatedly advised American citizens to do so. The 60 percent who remained, numbering several thousand, included a large number of politically uncommitted victims of circumstance. But if one is to believe Japanese sources, the majority made a deliberate choice to stay.

Life was by no means easy for Hawaii *nisei* in Japan during the 1930s. Their imperfect command of the language, particularly the complicated forms of honorific speech, made them hapless standouts in a country where society was sensitive to proper levels of polite (or impolite) discourse. Some *nisei* unwittingly showed Hawaii-style behavioral traits (easygoing manners, wearing of brightly colored clothing) that made a negative impression on people traditionally attentive to strict etiquette and (after 1931) increasingly conditioned to the spartan, sober atmosphere of the "national emergency." Some Japanese looked down on *nisei* as the children of emigrants who had "abandoned" their homeland. There were also unspoken feelings in some quarters that no *nikkei-jin* could really understand traditional aesthetic and moral values. Consequently, *nisei* were all too often treated, in the words of one who had direct experience, "with condescension if not actual disdain." Among the more unflattering appellations for *nisei* heard in Japan at this time were *hikokumin* (stateless people), *ai no ko* (half-breeds), and *ketō* (hairy Chinese). On 28 July 1941, the Tokyo *Hōchi* went so far as to call for the return of American *nisei* to the United States on the grounds that they were "too Americanized" and thus had an undesirable influence on Japanese society.

Acutely aware of the prejudice that their American associations brought upon them, some *kinichi nisei* threw themselves into an intensive study of Japanese history and language in order to compensate for their "deficiency." A few memorized the Imperial Rescript on Education to convince Japanese of their sincerity.

Nisei recruits in the armed services are said to have felt under pressure to prove themselves. In one instance, a Hawaii *nisei* private serving with Japan's expeditionary forces in China happened to be assigned to a squad commanded by a Hawaii *nisei* sergeant. The latter went out of his way to impose a harsh regimen on this particular subordinate, because he felt himself under observation by the other soldiers.

To lend each other support and comfort, Hawaii *dōhō* formed a number of organizations in Japan during the 1920s and 1930s. Some of these were purely social groups, such as the Aloha Society (established in 1925) and the Tokyo Hawaii Society (established in 1932). Others undertook educational programs, such as the Japan-America-Hawaii Society (founded in 1930) which built and managed dormitories for *nisei* students, conducted Japanese language courses, offered guidance on university entrance examinations, and assisted *nisei* seeking employment in Japan and other parts of East Asia.

One of the central figures in the education of Hawaii *nisei* in Japan was Kaju Nakamura, founder and director of *Tōyō bunka kaki daigaku* (Oriental Culture Summer University). Located in Tokyo's Akasaka district, the university offered courses in Japanese language, history, and culture. Nakamura also edited and published a monthly called *Kaigai no Nippon* [Japan Overseas]. He traveled regularly to the United States lecturing to *dōhō* audiences on the West Coast and in Hawaii. A Hawaii tour in June 1940 evoked an enthusiastic response from the *issei* community. Hundreds turned out to hear him lecture in Honolulu, Kahului (Maui), and Hilo (island of Hawaii). Nakamura used his peripatetic energies to instill among scattered *nikkeijin* in the United States an appreciation of Japanese culture and pride in their Japanese ancestry. His services were officially recognized in 1941 when Minister of Colonization Kiyoshi Akita commended Nakamura for cementing the solidarity between the empire and its overseas *dōhō*.

In addition to Nakamura, there were three Hawaii *issei* who came to play important roles as educators of Hawaii *nisei* in Japan during the late 1930s and early 1940s: George Tadao Kunitomo,

Colbert Naoya Kurokawa, and Sōen Yamashita. During the war, all three (plus Nakamura) published visions of Hawaii under Japanese rule. One of them drew up political and economic guidelines for the occupation of the islands.

George Kunitomo was born in 1893 in Kurume, a city in Fukuoka Prefecture of Kyūshū, the southernmost main island of the Japanese archipelago. He studied at Waseda University and Aoyama Gakuin. From 1918 until 1920 he served with the Japanese Expeditionary Force in Siberia doing, in his own words, "pacification work." After his discharge from the army, Kunitomo came to the United States and enrolled in Oberlin College, from which he was graduated in 1923. He then moved to Hawaii and was hired as the first Japanese language instructor at Honolulu's McKinley High School (locally nicknamed "Tokyo High" because of the number of Japanese-American students). In 1929 Kunitomo joined the faculty of the University of Hawaii and taught Japanese language courses. Taking a leave of absence in 1935 to return to Japan, he received in 1937 a stipend from the Foreign Ministry to conduct research at Tokyo Imperial University. In 1939, Kunitomo submitted his resignation from the University of Hawaii to become a director of the *Kokusai gakuyūkai* (International Student Friendship Society), an organ sponsored by the Foreign Ministry for the assistance of foreign students in Japan.

Colbert Kurokawa came from a village in Chiba Prefecture (east of Tokyo) where he was born in 1890. Raised to enter the Buddhist priesthood, he ran away from a temple at the age of fourteen, having been infected by the excitement sweeping the country upon Japan's victory over Russia in 1905. The ex-acolyte boarded a steamer for Hawaii and arrived in Honolulu with fifty cents in his pocket. Fortunately for young Kurokawa, he had an uncle in Haleiwa on Oahu's north shore.

During the next twenty-five years, Kurokawa built a successful career in community service. He won a scholarship to Honolulu's Mid-Pacific Institute and went on to attend Dickinson College (Carlisle, Pennsylvania) from which he graduated in 1922. Meanwhile he had converted to Christianity, preached for Hawaii's Methodist Mission, and became educational secretary for the Nuuanu YMCA and the Pan Pacific Union (forerunner of the Pacific and Asian Affairs Council). As one of the first Japanese members of the Honolulu Lions Club, he campaigned successfully to have the word "white" removed from national membership requirements at the Lions International Convention in San Francisco in 1926.

As Kurokawa's career developed so did his ties with Japan. From around 1922 he began acting as interpreter for the local Japanese consul general. At the request of the consulate he served as interpreter for a succession of visiting officers of the Imperial Navy, among them two chiefs of naval intelligence: Kichisaburō Nomura and Ryōzō Nakamura. In 1935 Kurokawa returned to Japan with his family and assumed the post of lecturer in English at Kyoto's Dōshisha University. The following year he became director of Hawaii Ryō, a dormitory for selected Dōshisha students and instructors, including a number of Hawaii *nisei*. He remained in this post until 1939, after which the exact nature of his activities becomes unclear. In 1943 his name appeared as the author of an in-house report on Hawaii, under the imprint of a Navy-sponsored research institute.

Sōen Yamashita was born in 1898 at Yasuura, a small town in Hiroshima Prefecture. In 1914, at the age of sixteen, he came to Hawaii in order to learn English, enrolling in Honolulu's Iolani School. Following graduation he joined the staff of *Nippu jiji* as a reporter. In 1933 he went to Japan as a *Nippu jiji* correspondent.

From 1933 until well into the Second World War, Yamashita devoted himself to encouraging and helping Hawaii *nisei* in Japan. In 1935 he brought out a handbook for and about Hawaii *nisei* in their ancestral country. This book contained a list of over five hundred Japanese who had a special interest in the islands. Among these were Hachirō Arita (acting consul general in Honolulu from 1913 to 1916, foreign minister in four cabinets between 1936 and 1940), Masamichi Rōyama (prominent Tokyo University professor of politics), and Yūsuke Tsurumi (Diet member, author, active in the Japan Committee of the Institute of Pacific Relations). All three men would make revealing wartime pronouncements about Hawaii. As for Yamashita, he eventually assumed the post of director in a *nisei*-coordinative agency (*Dai nisei rengōkai* [League of nisei organizations]) financed and supervised by the Foreign Ministry.

Notwithstanding the variations in their careers, Kunitomo, Kurokawa, and Yamashita shared certain convictions that led to analogous experiences. All three were born in Japan but lived in Hawaii for a considerable time (Kunitomo for fourteen years,

Kurokawa for thrity years, Yamashita for nineteen years). Each decided to return to Japan during the 1930s, and one can only speculate on the reasons for their decisions. Perhaps they felt some constraints to their professional hopes in Hawaii. Perhaps they were drawn by a sense of duty to their motherland which was mobilizing to achieve great aims in East Asia. Perhaps they simply preferred living in Japan to living in Hawaii. It is clear that all three shared a commitment to nurturing the bond between Hawaii *nisei* and Japan. This commitment seems to have sprung not just from patriotism but from a concern that in the process of Americanization *nisei* were losing something important, something that deserved to be fostered lest it vanish.

What motivated Kunitomo, Kurokawa, and Yamashita also attracted attention from Japanese officials, yet there does not appear to have been any unified or systematic government policy toward *nisei* during the 1930s. In their calls for *dōhō* contributions to the war effort, figures such as Diet member Harutsugu Tahara and General Kuniaki Koiso (minister of colonization, 1939–1940; prime minister, 1944–1945) sounded as if they regarded *nisei* as Imperial subjects with all the attendant obligations. On the other hand, there were officials who shared the view of former Prime Minister Reijirō Wakatsuki and Admiral Kenwa Kanna who asserted that *nisei* were Americans and as such owed primary loyalty to the United States.

Judging from available evidence, most officials seem to have fallen between these two polar perspectives. In practice, each ministry followed its own policies toward *nisei*. The Foreign Ministry assisted *nisei* through the sponsorship of educational organizations. The armed forces drafted eligible *nisei* recruits. No one, however, mounted a coordinated drive to mobilize Hawaii *dōhō* in Japan during the 1930s.

This state of affairs changed in 1940. The shift seems to have occurred as a result of a complex interplay between international and domestic forces converging on Japan after the outbreak of war in Europe. Breathtaking German victories on the continent, coupled with the prospect of a British collapse, presented Tokyo with an unprecedented opportunity to move into resource-rich Southeast Asia, where Dutch, French, and British colonies—cut off from Europe—hovered like ripe fruit ready to be plucked. At the same time, a serious deterioration of relations with the United States

confronted Tokyo with the specter of a Pacific war. The conver-
gence of opportunities and risks, coming on top of a war in China
that showed no sign of ending, brewed a sense of tense expectancy
among many of Japan's leaders. This expectancy manifested itself
in a bolder policy toward overseas *dōhō*.

The year 1940 witnessed a series of events that encapsulated the
millenarian, now-or-never psychology pervading Japan. In March
Japan set up a puppet Chinese government in Nanking. In June
Diet members formed a League for the Prosecution of the Holy
War and called for the abolition of all political parties. In July the
government made a decision to move south whether or not Imperial forces met resistance. In August Foreign Minister Yōsuke Matsuoka unveiled a new phrase at a press conference: Greater East
Asia Co-Prosperity Sphere. In September Japan signed the Tripartite Agreement with Germany and Italy. In October, after the
country's political parties had abolished themselves, an Imperial
Rule Assistance Association was created and hailed as a great all-
embracing organization that by subsuming hitherto competing
interest groups would consolidate national unity, accelerate national mobilization, and promote the construction of a New Order
in East Asia.

Amid the swirl of international tumult and domestic exalta-
tion, Japan celebrated in 1940 the empire's 2,600th birthday.*
Speeches and literature on the occasion of this celebration stressed
that the Japanese Imperial line and the Japanese people were
bound by links analogous to those within a family. Using this currently widespread concept of a familial state, the government
staged a Grand Congress of Overseas Compatriots—an impressive
display of solidarity with overseas *dōhō* in November 1940 that
would have been unthinkable ten years earlier.

The congress was held between 4 and 11 November in Tokyo's
Hibiya Hall. Convened under the auspices of the Foreign Ministry
and the Ministry of Colonization, the congress was managed by a

---

*Japan's Imperial line was noted by eighth century chronicles as dating from the
ascension of the first emperor, Jimmu, on the eleventh day of the second (lunar)
month of 660 B.C. Both the date and the emperor were extrapolated from genea-
logical records by imaginative A.D. seventh- or eighth-century scribes attempting
to legitimize the Yamato clan's imperial claims by a veneer of spurious antiquity.
Although educated people in 1940 were aware of this, the government treated
the anniversary as a historic fact.

committee of civil and military officials: Mannosuke Yamaoka of the Foreign Ministry, Lieutenant General Yoshiyuki Suzuki of the Army, Vice-Admiral Yoshijirō Hamada of the Navy, and Diet member Harutsugu Tahara, who in 1938 had estimated that Japanese-Americans could contribute half of their assets to support Japan's war in China. Sōen Yamashita headed the Hawaii section of this Tokyo-based committee.

Hawaii occupied a prominent position in the congress. The islands were described as the first destination of Japanese emigration after the Meiji Restoration. Hawaii also sent one of the largest and most prestigious delegations to Tokyo.

Of nineteen-hundred *dōhō* delegates from twenty-seven countries at the Tokyo congress, 188 came from Hawaii (276 had applied but for one reason or another not all could attend). The Hawaii delegation was officially headed by a seventy-seven-year-old Honolulu physician, Iga Mōri. However, younger men played a major role as organizers. These were: Shōzō Kawakami, fifty-one, and Kōichi Iida, fifty-two, both Honolulu businessmen; Katsuichi Miho, fifty-seven, a Kahului, Maui innkeeper; Koshirō Tōfukuji, sixty-five, a Maui physician; and Kaiun Mikami, forty-four, a Buddhist priest from Maui. Also on the Hawaii delegation, albeit in a less prominent role, was Kuwaichi Nōnin, who had toured military hospitals and divisional headquarters in Japan and China during 1938.

As a whole, the Hawaii delegation was younger than the age of its leaders. The average age was 42.9. A quarter of the delegates were under thirty, and a quarter (not necessarily the same people) were *nisei*. Most members were *issei* in their thirties, forties, and fifties. Residents of Oahu and Hawaii (the Big Island) made up three-quarters of the delegation.

The congress opened with *dōhō* delegations walking along the Imperial Palace grounds to Hibiya Hall. The route was lined with schoolchildren waving rising sun flags and shouting *banzai*. One Hawaii participant noted that the scene reminded him of troops being sent off to the front. Another recalled that he had cried with emotion. Kaiun Mikami explained this emotion as follows: "Because the Japanese in Hawaii are separated from the homeland, their patriotism burns all the more." A remark by Mannosuke Yamaoka, the congress's co-organizer, also throws light on the emotional atmosphere. "The greater the past afflictions, the more

intense the overseas compatriot's attachment and love for the ancestral land."

When the procession reached Hibiya Hall, the delegates found a
glittering assemblage of government leaders and royalty waiting
for them: Prime Minister Fumimaro Konoe, Foreign Minister Yōsuke Matsuoka, Army Minister Hideki Tōjō, Minister of Colonization Kiyoshi Akita, together with the Home, Agriculture, Health,
and Postal ministers. The Navy Minister, Admiral Koshirō Oikawa, being unable to attend, sent a staff officer in his place. Representing the emperor was his uncle Prince Higashikuni, who was
seated behind an Imperial dias in the center of the stage. About a
dozen ranking civil and military officials flanked these dignitaries.
A huge rising-sun flag, a map of Asia and Oceania, and a twenty-
foot calligraphic banner proclaiming the name of the congress
hung above the stage. Another banner to the left of the stage bore
the slogan: *kokuryoku sōdōin* (total mobilization of national
power).

According to Sōen Yamashita the scene made a deep impression
upon the Hawaii delegation. Yamashita's assessment, judging from
subsequent pronouncements by delegates themselves, was certainly no overstatement. After the delegates had assembled within
the hall, all bowed toward the Imperial palace, sang Japan's national anthem, and—still standing—prayed silently to the Kasuga
Shrine, the Meiji Shrine, to members of the Imperial armed forces
who had fallen in combat, and finally to those *dōhō* who had
passed away in foreign countries. At this juncture, a song com-
memorating the 2,600th anniversary of the foundation of the Japanese Empire was sung.*

After introductory remarks by Diet member Harutsugu Tahara,
each member of the cabinet made a short speech welcoming the
delegates. Yōsuke Matsuoka was characteristically forthright. Describing himself as a former emigrant to the United States (he
came to America at the age of thirteen and graduated from the

---

*Three songs were regularly sung during the course of the congress. One, entitled
the "2,600-Year Overseas *Dōhō* Hymn," included the following verse:

Our honor is to be the advance guard
Of the rising Co-Prosperity Sphere in Asia
Lending our efforts to national glory
Our blood throbs as we make our pledge.

University of Oregon in 1900), the foreign minister hailed overseas *dōhō* as the "first line of overseas expansion."

At the conclusion of the welcoming ceremony, the delegates adopted a number of resolutions thanking the government and pledging support for Japan. The final resolution, adopted unanimously, was addressed to the Imperial Army:

> On the occasion of the Tokyo Congress of Overseas Compatriots celebrating the 2,600th anniversary [of Japan's foundation], we reverently express sincere gratitude to the honorable labor of Imperial soldiers, heroically struggling in a holy war for the establishment of the Greater East Asia Co-Prosperity Sphere, for the construction of a New Order in East Asia.

It is difficult to say whether Hawaii delegates suspected that the Greater East Asia Co-Prosperity Sphere might encompass Hawaii. The term was still quite new, amorphous, and fraught with vague connotations of economic cooperation. Until mid-1941, Hawaii was not publicly included within the Sphere.

After the opening ceremony, congress activities assumed an increasingly military coloration. On 5 November the delegates attended lectures by officers of the armed forces. Colonel Hideitsu Matsumura, chief of the Army Information Section, talked to the *dōhō* about "constructing a new order in East Asia." Captain Yuzuru Ōkuma, chief of the First Section of the Navy's Military Affairs Information Bureau, spoke on the Imperial Navy's role in Asia and the Pacific. Unfortunately, texts of these lectures are not available.

On 6 November the delegates were taken on a tour of the Army Air Base at Tachikawa in Tokyo's western suburbs. Hawaii delegate Shōzō Kawakami delivered a speech of thanks to the base commander, saying that he had been "moved to tears" by the army's hospitality and that he would share his admiration and excitement with other *dōhō* upon his return to Hawaii.

On 7 November the Hawaii delegation was taken to the Yokosuka Naval Base south of Tokyo, escorted by Vice Admiral Hamada of the congress's organizing committee. Base commander Admiral Kōichi Shiozawa greeted the guests with the following words:

An unseverable relationship binds overseas compatriots and the [Imperial] Navy. We are thankful for your warm hospitality whenever our training squadrons enter your ports. We are also grateful for your warm support since the Incident [Sino-Japanese war]. Since the conclusion of the Japan-Germany-Italy alliance, the international situation has become more complicated, but the Imperial Navy remains ready day and night. Your hearts can be at rest.

In reply, Hawaii delegate Takashi Isobe, a forty-eight-year-old Honolulu Shinto priest, thanked the navy for its hospitality in Japan and in China where Hawaiian "comfort delegations" had traveled. Isobe went on to pledge Hawaii *dōhō* support for Japan: "Linked by the Pacific, our Navy* and Hawaii *dōhō* have a relationship which is not shallow. . . . We emigrant warriors deeply feel our responsibilities and are firmly resolved that we must achieve Eight Corners and Co-Prosperity.†"

The military connection continued after the congress, as the army conducted some Hawaii delegates on a three-week tour of Manchuria and North China. The tour was led by Lieutenant General Yoshiyuki Suzuki, who had dual qualifications. In addition to being one of the congress organizers, he had previously served as the chief of Army Intelligence in Mukden, a city in southern Manchuria.

How some Hawaii delegates reacted to their experiences at the Tokyo congress can be gauged by statements made during the remaining days of 1940 and the first weeks of 1941. In a telephone call from Tokyo to the *Nippu jiji* editor on 6 November Honolulu businessman Shichirō Haga, fifty-one, exclaimed:

The economic strength of our ancestral land is so powerful as to be beyond the grasp of the imagination. Attending the celebration of the 2,600th anniversary, our eyes are struck by the extraordinary development of Japan's politics, economy, and culture. But especially when beholding the unwavering power of the Army and Navy

*"Our Navy" here refers to the Imperial Japanese Navy. Interestingly, in some of the papers prepared by Hawaii delegates at the congress, non-Japanese residents of Hawaii are referred to as *gaijin* ("foreigners").

†Abbreviations for "Eight Corners of the World Under One Roof" and Greater East Asia Co-Prosperity Sphere. The former phrase is Confucian in origin and denotes the ideal of universal harmony. As used in the 1930s and early 1940s, it connoted harmony—under Japanese leadership.

do our hearts feel an ineffable excitement, and our breasts are filled with palpitations.

In a broadcast from Tokyo to Honolulu on 23 January 1941, Yoshihiro Sugamura, the fifty-eight-year-old director of the Kona Hospital on the island of Hawaii, asserted: "Japan is going to win. The day is coming when the New Order in East Asia will be completed. . . . Hawaii listeners! Please explain to Americans the determination of Japan to construct a new world order."

Encouraged by the success of the Tokyo congress, its organizers proposed and gained official backing for the creation of a permanent organ that would coordinate overseas *dōhō* relations with Japan. The new body was formally created on 9 April 1941 and called *Kaigai dōhō chūō kai* (Central society for overseas compatriots). Its offices were located in the Tōtaku Building close to government ministries in Tokyo's Uchisaiwai-chō district.

In the largely honorary role of president of the society was Prime Minister Konoe. Army Minister Tōjō, Navy Minister Oikawa, Foreign Minister Matsuoka, and Colonization Minister Akita held the position of "honorary advisers." The organizers selected as chairman of the society Toshio Shiratori, a senior diplomat with outspokenly pro-Axis views and a frank proponent of Japanese domination of the Pacific. Active, as opposed to "honorary," advisers included senior officials with long-standing interest in overseas *dōhō*: Hachirō Arita, General Kuniaki Koiso, Admiral Kichisaburō Nomura (Japan's ambassador to the United States), and Mitsuru Tōyama, a godfather of superpatriots. On the society's board of directors were two individuals whose special interest in Hawaii has already been noted: Lieutenant General Yoshiyuki Suzuki and Diet member Yūsuke Tsurumi.

In the summer of 1941, the society inaugurated publication of a monthly journal called *Kaigai dōhō* [Overseas compatriot]. Unfortunately, not a single copy of this journal can be located in the National Diet Library or in other major Japanese repositories. Published until the end of World War II, it doubtless constitutes an excellent source from which to glean a sense of wartime Japanese perceptions of Hawaii.

On the eve of World War II, the Japanese government was taking concrete steps to organize Japanese abroad for support of national aims in Asia and the Pacific. But to what extent before 7

December 1941 did Hawaii actually figure in Japanese plans for a new order in East Asia, for the Greater East Asia Co-Prosperity Sphere? To deal with that question, it is first necessary to examine the phenomenon of public fantasizing about the invasion and occupation of Hawaii that took place on both sides of the Pacific in the three decades before Pearl Harbor.

CHAPTER IV

Invasion Scenarios, 1909–1941

During the first four decades of the twentieth century, scores of people, among them Vladimir Lenin and H. G. Wells, predicted a Japanese-American war for control of the Pacific. A number of these predictions took the form of books and articles about how such a war might start and end. Written by Japanese and Americans, by military officers and civilians, these publications reached an international audience. The quality of these scenarios varied. Some were not only realistic but prescient. Others quickly betrayed themselves as products of overheated and untutored imaginations.

Whether realistic or whimsical, Pacific war forecasting more often than not featured descriptions of a Japanese invasion of, or uprising within, the Hawaiian Islands. The Hawaii scenarios taken collectively offer two notable insights. First, they reflect ways in which people on both sides of the Pacific envisioned Japan's conquest of (or liberation of) Hawaii. Secondly, they came up with methods of seizing the islands that in some cases anticipated plans developed by the Imperial Navy in 1941 and 1942.

The earliest scenarios grew out of Hawaii and West Coast opposition to Japanese immigration in the 1890s and early 1900s. By the mid-1890s, Japanese immigrants constituted the largest ethnic group in the Islands and were perceived as a political threat by elements of the dominant white propertied class. This "threat" was depicted as having an internal (local Japanese) and external (Imperial Army and Navy) dimension. It was invoked by island and mainland proponents of annexation, among them Alfred Thayer

Mahan, doyen naval strategist of the age. In the spring of 1897, Mahan wrote Theodore Roosevelt (then Assistant Secretary of the Navy) that the government should "take the islands first and solve the [Japanese] problem afterwards."*

American annexation of Hawaii in 1898 only temporarily stilled agitation against the supposed dangers of a Japanese takeover. In the wake of the Russo-Japanese War, Japanese immigrants arrived in unprecedented numbers, some thirty thousand in 1906 alone. Complaints began to be heard in Hawaii and on the West Coast that the islands were being swamped. A rumor circulated that Tokyo was infiltrating war veterans into Hawaii. In June 1907 Massachusetts Senator Henry Cabot Lodge expressed misgivings that the Japanese might "hoist their flag in Hawaii overnight."

Two fictionalized accounts of a seizure of Hawaii, appearing in 1909, mirrored contemporary fears of a takeover of the islands from within: *The Conflict of Nations* by Ernest Hugh Fitzpatrick, and *The Valor of Ignorance* by Homer Lea. Lea described how Japanese army veterans infiltrated the islands as immigrants and, as soon as they had gained numerical ascendancy, how they annihilated the "solitary United States battalion" within twenty-four hours. Fitzpatrick conjured up thirty Imperial Army regiments whose men, disguised as "coolies," slipped into Hawaii and seized control. Both authors made Hawaii a launching site for a Japanese invasion of the American mainland. Lea's book has all the accoutrements of a Baedeker guide to the conquest of California. Detailed topographical maps help the reader follow Japanese columns as they converge on the Bay Area.

A five-foot three-inch eighty-eight-pound hunchback from Cripple Creek, Colorado, Lea was not inexperienced in military matters. After leaving Stanford University he went to China in 1899 "to topple the Manchus from their ancient Dragon Throne." He returned to Los Angeles two years later wearing the uniform of a "Chinese general" and boasting of close ties to Sun Yat-sen.

For all his eccentricities, Lea had no shortage of admirers. *Valor of Ignorance* sold widely in German and Japanese translations. Kaiser Wilhelm advised his officers to read it and invited Lea to visit him in 1911. Death overtook Lea before he could go to Ger-

---

*Curiously, Mahan had written an article in 1893 about Hawaii in which he identified China as a threat to the islands but made no mention of Japan.

many, but Hitler paid him a posthumous compliment by making use of passages from *Valor of Ignorance* in *Mein Kampf*. *Valor of Ignorance* was reissued in the United States during World War II with a foreword by Clare Boothe [Luce].

In *Conflict of Nations*, Fitzpatrick spun a grandiose plot resulting in an uneven admixture of wild fantasy with flashes of accurate forecasting. After seizing Hawaii, Japan transports 250,000 troops to the West Coast, whose cities have already been softened up by Honolulu-style coups by local immigrants. The American Army retreats to the Rockies while the U.S. Atlantic Fleet rushes to join the Pacific Fleet. Both fleets are destroyed off Panama by a Japanese squadron, which shrouds the American battleships in a cloud of smoke and then sinks the blinded behemoths with torpedoes. Japan demands the cession of Washington, Oregon, and California together with a $1.5 billion indemnity. When the Americans refuse, the Japanese increase their forces on the West Coast to one and a half million men. Meanwhile, Mexico signs an alliance with Japan and allows Marshal Nogi (the hero of Port Arthur) to lead his divisions across Sonora in a *blitzkrieg* thrust into Texas. The tide finally turns when Japan offends England by occupying Panama. London thereupon declares war upon Tokyo (after repudiating the 1902 Anglo-Japanese Alliance) and dispatches a British expeditionary force to Louisiana, reinforced by contingents from Australia, New Zealand, and South Africa. At this juncture, a Birmingham chemist discovers how to dispel smoke bombs, enabling a British armada to annihilate Japan's battle fleet off California. In a desperate gamble, General Yoritomo strikes out from California toward Montana, only to be crushed by the Anglo-Americans at China Point in eastern Idaho. The allies recapture Hawaii and prepare for a general assault on Japan. Tokyo, recognizing the inevitable, surrenders and agrees to an Anglo-American occupation. The post-war occupation turns out to be a success, evoking a favorable response from Japanese themselves. The emperor system is preserved, political and economic reforms implemented, and a joint security agreement concluded wherein England and the United States underwrite Japan's national defense.

Whereas Fitzpatrick and Lea dwelt upon a Japanese invasion of the United States, their most celebrated successor in this particular literary-journalistic genre concentrated upon naval engagements in the Pacific. In 1925 Hector C. Bywater brought out *The Great*

Pacific War: A History of the American-Japanese Campaign of 1931–33 which attracted as much attention in Japan as it did in the United States.

Bywater followed his predecessors to the extent of having the Imperial Navy destroy an American fleet at the war's outbreak, opening the way for seizure of the Philippines. Hawaii, however, was to experience a different fate. As described by Bywater, the invasion of Hawaii is timed so as to coincide with an uprising among the Islands' 140,000 Japanese. Lack of intelligence data leads Tokyo to cancel the invasion at the last moment. Nevertheless Imperial Army veterans in Hawaii proceed with their own plans on 17 May 1932. Except for some smuggled arms, the mother country gives no assistance.

The insurgents get off to a promising start by capitalizing upon the element of surprise. They capture a supply of weapons in a pre-dawn raid on an army training barracks just outside Honolulu. Equipped with small arms, several thousand Japanese, led by Imperial Army reserve officers, move toward Honolulu. En route they disrupt communications between the city and outlying military bases by tearing up railroad tracks and cutting telephone and telegraph lines. Downtown Honolulu is quickly occupied, and the more solid buildings are turned into strongpoints. Insurgent units surround two United States Army garrisons within the city: Fort Armstrong at the harbor entrance and Fort De Russy in Waikiki. The besieged garrisons manage to send a courier to Pearl Harbor, but attempts to sortie are repulsed by a withering crossfire from the occupied buildings in the business district.

The Americans begin to gain the upper hand during the afternoon. Naval units from Pearl Harbor start shelling the downtown area. Relief columns arrive from Schofield Barracks and Fort Shafter. Finally, the timely arrival of a shipment of light tanks and their crews from the mainland allows the Americans to clear the business district. The Japanese light fires to cover their retreat, turning the central section of Honolulu into a charred rubble.

Surviving insurgents then regroup for an assault on an ammunition depot located on the slopes of Mount Konahuanui, five miles northeast of the city. The attempt is frustrated by an American lieutenant who ignites a powder magazine, evaporating himself and the attackers. Sporadic guerrilla activity continues for a few weeks, but reinforcements from the mainland eventually mop up the last pockets of resistance. Except for some rioting in Hilo, the neighbor islands remain calm throughout the fighting on Oahu.

Bywater concludes his treatment of this episode by having a court of inquiry set up at Pearl Harbor to investigate the causes of the uprising. Although some captured ringleaders claim to have acted on Tokyo's orders, no direct evidence of Imperial complicity is uncovered. Only several months later does an Imperial Navy officer reveal Tokyo's involvement. Meanwhile, all Japanese captured with weapons are deported to Panama as canal laborers. The rest remain at liberty in Hawaii, but under surveillance.

Japanese assaults on Hawaii figured in war games of the U.S. Pacific Fleet during the 1930s, but Hector Bywater's *The Great Pacific War* turned out to be the last example of this type of fantasy to appear in the United States before World War II. Japan, however, provided a rich harvest of this genre.

Japanese scenarios of a Hawaii invasion were generally episodes within books about imaginary wars with the United States. Such scenarios surfaced in 1913 and appeared from time to time until 1941. Japanese fantasies about a Pacific War, like analogous works appearing in the United States, grew out of deepening tensions and distrust between the two countries after 1905. Offended by anti-Japanese prejudice in California, frustrated by American obstacles to peaceful expansion in the Pacific, writers conjured up consoling victories in the realm of fantasy.

The earliest scenarios, written by authors innocent of technical knowledge about naval warfare, have a whimsical quality. Among these is *Nichi-Bei kaisen yume monogatari* [Fantasy on the outbreak of a Japanese-American war], which appeared in 1913 under the editorship of the National Military Affairs Association (to all appearances a private group). The book opens with the destruction of the American fleet by a Japanese squadron between Luzon and Taiwan. Japanese forces then take the Philippines and occupy Hawaii (the author noted that Hawaii presented fewer obstacles than did the Philippines). Hawaii's fall prompts the Kaiser, Tsar, and president of France to mediate a peace settlement. The United States cedes Hawaii to Japan, and the islands are incorporated "forever" into the Empire. This book conveys two perceptions that thereafter crop up regularly in Japanese literature about Hawaii: Hawaii is a natural part of Japan, and Americans are not terribly disturbed about losing the Islands.

In 1914 Yoshikatsu Ōto brought out a similar fantasy entitled *Nichi-Bei moshi kaisen seba* [If Japan and America fight] with a preface by a retired admiral, Seijirō Kawashima. Ōto echoed the theme of Hawaii belonging to Japan, adding that this was so because *dōhō* had developed the local economy. He even suggested that *dōhō* already held *de facto* political power in the Islands. Like the author of the earlier fantasy, Ōto assured readers that Hawaii could be captured more easily than could the Philippines. About forty thousand troops, he estimated, should be able to land on Oahu's north shore and deal with the fifteen thousand American defenders. The book then proceeds to describe a successful Japanese assault, followed by formal acquisition in the peace treaty.

A more extravagant scenario unfolded in *Nichi-Bei sensō yume monogatari* [Japanese-America war fantasy] (1921) by Kōjirō Satō, a retired army general. Satō portrayed the destruction of the U.S. Pacific Fleet after it has been lured to Midway, an uncanny forerunner of Admiral Isoroku Yamamoto's ill-fated plan twenty-one years later. Japan then seizes Hawaii and from its mid-Pacific base strikes San Francisco. Building air bases in California, Imperial forces launch bombing missions across the Rocky Mountains into the Midwest. Allies materialize from among American minorities. Ten million blacks revolt, led by Marcus Garvey.* Jews and German-Americans also rise up against the Anglo-Saxons. Eager to rectify past injustices, Mexico invades Texas. Satō brought his tale to a climax with a grand finale in New York at 9:00 A.M. Sunday morning ("when people are still asleep"). Japanese commandos blow up the Brooklyn Bridge and—using dirigibles—land on the Woolworth Building. Washington sues for peace, and Lothrop Stoddard† joins the surrender negotiations.

Naval officers eventually participated in the avocation of producing invasion fantasies. In 1933 Kyōsuke Fukunaga, a lieutenant commander in the naval reserve, published a novel called *Nichi-Bei sen miraiki* [Account of a future Japanese-American war]. Otherwise larded with already familiar literary baggage (destruction of the U.S. Pacific Fleet, seizure of Hawaii, uprising of

---

*Marcus Garvey (1887–1940). Jamaica-born black nationalist who lived in New York from 1916 until his deportation to Jamaica in 1927.

†Lothrop Stoddard (1883–1950). Author of a notorious racist tract, *The Rising Tide of Color Against White World Supremacy* (1920).

American minorities, and so forth), this book was distinguished
from its predecessors by what seems to have been intended as
forays into humor. For example, two Imperial Navy officers have
the following conversation about Hawaii *dōhō*:

Hawaii? Hmmmm. Yeah, where they got bananas, pineapple,
sugar, and where there's more Japanese than people from any other
country.

You know, they'd be a real help. If we could stir them up, we
could hit the Americans from inside as well as outside.

Sure, but it's not all that easy. However much [Hawaii's] Japanese
get aroused, they got no weapons.

Weapons? Why they can use sharpened bamboo!

At another juncture of this remarkable volume, an officer sur-
veying Diamond Head Crater through the periscope of a submarine off Waikiki exclaims: "Let's hurry up and take this island! I'm
dying to eat some of those bananas!"

Lest readers were tempted to dismiss Lieutenant Commander
Fukunaga's novel as entirely facetious, the book carried porten-
tous forewords by Admiral Kanji Katō (who had expressed regret
that Japan did not intervene in Hawaii during the 1893 revolution) and Vice Admiral Nobumasa Suetsugu, commander in chief
of the Combined Fleet. Admiral Suetsugu recommended the novel
as "an important book for laymen and professional officers alike,"
adding that "it would be simply splendid if the war turned out as
Fukunaga imagines."

As Mark Peattie has observed: "Books like these, in which
descriptions of Japanese naval glories are substituted for meaning-
ful analysis of strategy or tactics, were obviously less intended to
inform the Japanese public of the strategic and material requirements for victory than to provide them with satisfying visions of
Japanese expansive power and military ardor."

Yet not all Japanese scenarios were as whimsical as those of Ōto,
Satō, and Fukunaga. As early as 1924, Imperial naval officers
were publicly discussing how to take Hawaii by invasion. Such
discussions reflected new strains in Japanese-American relations
which surfaced after World War I. In the aftermath of the Washington Naval Conference (1921–1922), which had established a

five-five-three ratio for American, British, and Japanese capital ships, discontent at what was perceived as strategic inequality turned to bitter indignation when in 1924 Congress passed the Exclusion Act barring Japanese immigration to the United States and its territories. In this inauspicious atmosphere Admiral Seijirō Kawashima (who it will be recalled wrote a foreword to Ōto's 1914 war scenario) delivered a lecture to a Tokyo audience in which an invasion of Hawaii was openly discussed.

Published in 1924, Kawashima's lecture ("The Japanese-American Problem from a Naval Perspective") called for an assault on Hawaii in the event of war with the United States. The rationale for such an operation, according to the retired admiral, was that naval facilities* at Pearl Harbor posed a strategic threat to Japan and could not be left in American hands. Admiral Kawashima's plan to take Hawaii reflected the influence of Ōto's 1914 fantasy. The Imperial Navy should first destroy the U.S. Pacific Fleet. With access to the islands cleared, Japan could then transport troops across nearly four thousand miles of ocean for landings on Oahu's north shore.

> Hawaii is difficult to assault frontally. This is because at the entrance to Pearl Harbor are forts with 12-inch and 14-inch guns, together with coral reefs. But for some twenty miles along Oahu's north-west shore runs a wide, shallow beach which can serve as a landing site. Forty, sixty, or even a hundred thousand Japanese troops can land here and occupy the island. The Americans have only about fifteen or sixteen thousand troops. In this case, we can get Hawaii.

Kawashima went on to dismiss as baseless the idea that Japan would foment an uprising of Hawaii *dōhō*. He also discounted the role played by airplanes in any Hawaii operation, a point which sharply differentiated him from subsequent naval planners.

By the 1930s, several circumstances led to the appearance of more refined public scenarios of the conquest of Hawaii. The bravado of the 1910s and 1920s gave way to a more sober appre-

---

*By naval facilities, Kawashima was referring to dry docks, fuel storage tanks, and submarine pens. The U.S. Pacific Fleet was not based at Pearl Harbor until 1941 but was expected to proceed there upon the outbreak of war.

ciation of America's industrial might. Most observers by then recognized the dangers of a war of attrition with the United States. Attention was drawn to the opportunities offered by aircraft carriers and naval air power, opportunities that Japan might exploit to help offset American material superiority in general and to expedite seizure of Hawaii in particular.

In this context, Commander Hironori Mizuno, superintendant of the Naval Archives, published a book in 1932 that contained the boldest public statements to date about Hawaii made by a naval officer on active duty. Mizuno bluntly declared Hawaii to be the key to the outcome of a Japanese-American war: "Hawaii is the Tennōzan,* the Waterloo, the Verdun which will determine victory or defeat in a Japanese-American war. . . . Because America occupies Hawaii, America can attack Japan. But if Japan were to seize Hawaii, it could attack America."

In Mizuno's estimation, Hawaii had far greater strategic importance than any other American outpost in the Pacific. Its loss would entail a profound national reaction (here he differed from those who said Americans did not have a visceral attachment to Hawaii). "If America loses Guam or the Philippines, national morale may suffer but national security would not be endangered. However, if Hawaii is lost, America's national fate will be affected, because the Pacific Coast will be exposed to bombardment by squadrons of the Rising Sun."

Hawaii was also, according to Mizuno, of supreme importance for Japan. "If Japan can seize Hawaii, it will mean it has destroyed the American Fleet and can control the waters of the Pacific, winning the war. Conversely, if Japan does not succeed in seizing Hawaii, it means that the war will be prolonged and that Japan will not be able to win."

Mizuno conceded that capturing Hawaii would be difficult, but he maintained that Japan could do it with verve and imagination. Assault by surface forces, the approach favored by Admiral Kawashima, would in Mizuno's opinion be suicidal. He preferred to use air power and take the islands from the skies: bombardment and strafing by carrier-based planes, then massive parachute drops of

*A hill between Kyoto and Osaka which figured in the campaigns of sixteenth-century *daimyo*. It was said that possession of Tennōzan enabled Toyotomi Hideyoshi to defeat a rival in 1582 and thereby to secure mastery over the country.

troops. Mizuno recognized that once Hawaii had been secured, it would have to be supplied and defended. For these twin tasks, he assigned an important role to the Marshall and Caroline islands in Micronesia, urging their development as support bases.

Mizuno dismissed the notion of a *dōhō* insurrection as having no more utility than a "children's movie." *Dōhō* lacked training and weapons. Besides, the Americans would probably ship out local Japanese men at the outset of the war.

By highlighting Hawaii's strategic and symbolic importance, Mizuno anticipated operational priorities in the central Pacific as perceived a decade later by the Combined Fleet. Yet even more prescience can be found in the writings of a naval critic named Chūkō Ikezaki.

An accomplished novelist before he turned to the study of naval affairs in 1925, Ikezaki authored a series of books and articles in the late 1920s and the 1930s that won international respect. His principal concern in these publications was to identify Japan's strategic goals and to assess Japan's chances in the event of a showdown with the United States. Unlike most scenario writers, he approached the prospect of a Japanese-American war (which he regarded as inevitable) with cold realism and dispassionate objectivity. He neither exaggerated American strengths nor denigrated American fighting abilities. A solid grasp of both countries' naval histories, strategies, and technological levels enabled him to speak with more authority than those who let faith in "Japanese spirit" obscure better judgment.

Ikezaki distilled his basic concepts in a book entitled *Taiheiyō senryaku ron* [Discourse on Pacific strategy] published in 1932. He bluntly stated that total victory over the United States, a victory which had inflamed the imaginations of so many scenario writers, was illusory. At the same time, he pointed out that a draw with the United States that left Japan with freedom of action in East Asia and with control over the Western Pacific would in effect be a significant—and adequate—victory. To want more would be unrealistic. To accept less would imperil Japan's security.

Ikezaki prescribed a specific series of steps necessary to achieve such a draw. First, Japan must take the initiative in hostilities. Second, Japan must inflict a rapid succession of painful defeats on the Americans. Third, taking advantage of American demoralization, Japan must seek peace, negotiating a settlement which would legitimize limited but vital strategic gains made during the first few weeks of the war. Ikezaki meant by taking the initiative an attack on Pearl Harbor that would destroy dry docks and fuel storage facilities. As to the rapid succession of military blows, he specified mauling the U.S. Pacific Fleet, seizing Guam and the Philippines, and invading Hawaii.

An invasion of the Hawaiian Islands, warned Ikezaki (thereby sharply differing from his predecessors), would be much more difficult than taking the Philippines. But the operation was essential for political as well as military reasons. Militarily, with Hawaii under the Rising Sun, Japan could blockade the West Coast, cripple American trade in the Pacific, and threaten the Panama Canal. Politically, Hawaii's loss would so demoralize Washington that it would afford Japan an opening to bring the war to an end through a negotiated peace.

Ikezaki's tactical formula for taking Hawaii was eclectic. Like Mizuno, he foresaw a major role for air power. Like Kawashima, he selected Oahu's north shore for amphibious assaults. But unlike either, he envisioned ex-servicemen among Hawaii's Japanese as helping the invaders by staging an uprising just before the landings.

Admiral Kanji Katō, well known spokesman for a forward naval strategy in the Pacific, heartily approved of Ikezaki's plans for Hawaii. In a letter to the author of *Taiheiyō senryaku ron*, the admiral said that the sections about Hawaii were the finest part of the book, adding that as long as the islands remained in American hands they would be "a cancer in the Pacific."

For the remainder of the decade little was added to the public commentary on a Hawaii invasion. Talk about Hawaii revived in 1940, however, stimulated by Japanese moves into Southeast Asia, conclusion of the Tripartite Pact, souring relations with Washington, and heady rhetoric about building a Greater East Asia Co-Prosperity Sphere.

Late in 1940 a journalist by the name of Kinoaki Matsuo discussed the possibility of a Hawaiian invasion in a book entitled *Sangoku dōmei to Nichi-Bei sen* [The Tripartite Alliance and a Japanese-American War]. Matsuo began by stating that Hawaii should belong to Japan, because as long as it remained part of the United States the Americans would use it to dominate the Pacific. Conversely, a Japanese Hawaii would forestall United States designs on the western Pacific and ensure Japan freedom of action in China. Moreover, loss of the islands would probably force the Americans to the peace table.

Matsuo asserted that any invasion of Hawaii must follow, not precede, annihilation of the U.S. Pacific Fleet. Before Honolulu and Pearl Harbor were assaulted, it would first be necessary to acquire Midway as a base. The main attack would concentrate on Oahu's north shore after air and naval bombardment had eliminated fortified positions and rendered airfields unusable.

Matsuo conceded that landings on Oahu even if successful would cost Japan heavily in human lives ("many more than the German Army would lose taking London"). Moreoever, supplying the islands from Japan would put a strain on shipping capabilities.

But there were compensating factors. The Americans, Matsuo estimated, would need sixty thousand troops to repel an invasion, yet they had deployed only twenty thousand on Oahu. Second, Hawaii *dōhō* could help. Once they had heard reports of their ancestral land's victories around Asia and in the western Pacific (including how the Imperial Navy had dealt with the U.S. Pacific Fleet), *dōhō* would form a volunteer army *(giyūgun)* which would go into action behind American lines simultaneously with the north shore landings. Matsuo cautioned against a premature *dōhō* uprising, which, he said, would jeopardize not only the whole invasion but the lives of all members of Hawaii's Japanese community. Third, Matsuo guessed that the United States might not make a determined effort to defend Hawaii after having lost part or all of its Pacific Fleet. Washington would concentrate on strengthening the West Coast leaving Hawaii's garrison to fend for itself.

Taking difficulties and compensating factors into consideration, Matsuo estimated that the Oahu campaign would last one week. With Oahu in Japanese hands, the neighbor islands, weakly defended and isolated, would fall without a struggle.

Matsuo appears to have been the first Japanese to comment in print about post-invasion occupation policies in Hawaii. His words to this effect were brief and somewhat enigmatic. The imprisoned local *dōhō* (Matsuo, like most Japanese commentators, foresaw mass internments following the outbreak of war) would be released, and all Hawaii Japanese would be allowed to resume daily work. The local community would play an important role supplying the Imperial Army with food supplies and thereby reducing dependency on imports from Japan.

A less optimistic scenario, the last published in Japan before 7 December 1941, appeared several months before the Pearl Harbor attack. Called *Taiheiyō senryaku joron* [Prologue to Pacific strategy], the book was written by Chū Saitō, a journalist with naval connections. While recognizing Hawaii's importance to Japan (he rated Singapore as secondary compared with Pearl Harbor), Saitō enumerated obstacles to an assault on Oahu: coastal fortifications, naval bases and airfields bristling with equipment and well supplied with fuel, coral reefs, an unpredictable surf, and distance from Japan. In a significant departure from previous scenario writers, he recommended that an invasion bypass Oahu in favor of the island of Hawaii: it was thinly defended, and Hilo could be turned into a base for the final drive on Oahu. Hilo, according to Saitō, was not ideal for the harbor faced open sea and was vulnerable to torpedo attacks. Still, the Big Island route to Oahu promised to achieve the same end with less loss of life. Saitō's suggestion surfaced one year later as a key ingredient in the Combined Fleet's plans for Hawaii.

Hawaii invasion scenarios that were published in Japan and the United States between 1909 and 1941 reveal similar evolutionary patterns. The earlier works (1909–1921) treated Hawaii as but a stepping-stone to the American mainland. Later scenarios recognized that Japan did not have the resources to mount an invasion of the American continent, and consequently that a Japanese-American war would be fought in the Pacific. This recognition, together with a growing awareness of the possibilities and implications of naval air power, significantly promoted Hawaii's strategic importance in public literature. One writer even regarded Hawaii as the key not only to a Japanese-American war but to the entire power configuration of the Pacific Basin.

American and Japanese scenarios also revealed interesting differences. American writers stressed the internal threat of a Japanese takeover, that is the threat of an uprising by local Hawaii Japanese. Yet only two Japanese writers gave this idea serious consideration. Ironically, Americans feared Hawaii *dōhō* more than Japanese valued them as tactical instruments.

The high proportion of naval officers among Japanese scenario

writers raises questions about attitudes toward Hawaii within the
Imperial Navy. That a commander in chief of the Combined Fleet
would contribute a laudatory preface to a novel about an invasion
of Hawaii suggests that such a vision animated the hearts of some
senior officers. To what extent these scenarios reflected actual planning, can be gleaned from an examination of Hawaii's role in prewar Imperial naval strategy.

CHAPTER V

Hawaii in
Imperial Naval Strategy

Insofar as Hawaii figured in Japan's prewar strategic planning, it did so largely within the confines of the Imperial Navy. After 1907 the Navy consistently regarded the United States as a potential adversary. Hawaii was the most important American naval base between the Philippines and California, a base from which, in the event of war with Japan, the American Battle Fleet was expected to advance into the Western Pacific. Under such conditions, the Imperial Navy could not afford to ignore Hawaii.

The Imperial Army, in contrast, showed little interest in Hawaii until the eve of the Pacific War. Army planners focused their attention on China and Russia. This continental orientation was reinforced by experience: the Sino-Japanese War (1894–1895), the Russo-Japanese War (1904–1905), the seizure of Tsingtao (1914), intervention in Siberia (1918–1922), occupation of Manchuria and Inner Mongolia (1931–1933), hostilities with China after 1937, and border clashes with the Soviet Union throughout the 1930s. From an army perspective it was Russia, not the United States, that posed the greatest threat to Japan's security and the most stubborn obstacle to Japan's aims in East Asia. After 1917 anti-communism added an ideological impetus to an army tradition of seeing Russia as the ultimate enemy.

Only in the summer of 1940, when Japan decided to move into Southeast Asia, a decision which augured a collision with the United States, did army strategists begin to include Hawaii in long-term plans. But after Pearl Harbor, army leaders opposed an invasion of Hawaii on the grounds that such an undertaking was operationally too risky, logistically too demanding, and—most important—that it would entail the redeployment of army units from continental assignments.

Army indifference to Hawaii left the navy free to assess the islands' strategic significance and to fit them into war contingency plans. Yet freedom to plan operations did not in this case mean that such operations could be implemented. In practice, the Imperial Navy operated under manifold external and internal constraints. A Hawaii invasion was unthinkable without army cooperation. In addition to divergent strategic objectives, the army and navy were competitors for status and budgetary appropriations, making cooperation difficult to attain. Although the Meiji Constitution (1889) made the armed forces accountable directly to the emperor rather than to the cabinet, the navy was dependent upon budgetary allowances voted in the Diet. Finally, divisions within the navy complicated strategic priorities in general and planning for Hawaii in particular.

Three overlapping sets of internal tensions plagued the navy during the 1920s and 1930s. The first involved a division between the so-called administrative group and the command group. The former consisted of high- and medium-ranking officers whose careers had advanced largely on the basis of political and administrative abilities. The latter were "warrior types" who valued operational skills and leadership in combat. During the 1920s the administrative group dominated the Navy Ministry while the command group held sway in the Navy General Staff. This functional division left the administrative group in a more influential position, for in peacetime the Navy Ministry not only formulated naval policy and decided on personnel matters but also exercised command over all naval units. In 1933, however, as a result of bureaucratic maneuvering, the Navy General Staff acquired control over naval operations. Thereafter, the ministry's role in strategic planning shrank, although it did not disappear.

The second set of tensions grew from disagreements over naval limitations. Specifically, naval leaders split over the ratio of American and Japanese capital ship tonnage (five to three) established by a naval treaty concluded during the Washington Conference of 1921–1922. Administrative group officers, led by Navy Minister Tomosaburō Katō, aware of Japan's weakness vis à vis the United States, saw political accommodation as essential. This group supported the Washington treaty and later endorsed the London Naval Treaty of 1930, both of which held Japan to lower tonnage ceilings on capital ships than those of the United States and Britain. Opposed to these treaties were leaders of the command group, notably admirals Kanji Katō (Chief of Navy Staff, 1929–1930) and Nobumasa Suetsugu (Vice Chief of Navy Staff, 1928–1930, Commander in Chief of the Combined Fleet, 1933–1934). These men and their followers embraced a narrow military approach to the United States. Their views were heavily laden with nationalist and ethnic (superiority of Japanese "spirit") overtones. Katō and Suetsugu denounced naval limitations as an Anglo-American ploy to condemn Japan to permanent strategic inferiority. They proclaimed their confidence in Japan's ability to defeat the United States in a Pacific War, if only the Imperial Navy were given free rein to build a powerful fleet centered about "big-gun" battleships.

The third locus of tension arose between those officers favoring an Anglo-American orientation and those seeking closer ties with Germany. Older officers, whose careers spanned the Anglo-Japanese Alliance (1902–1922), tended to retain a high regard for Britain and by extension were less willing to contemplate hostilities with the United States. In addition to Admiral Suetsugu, the German faction included a number of junior officers who had fallen under the spell of the Third Reich while serving as naval attachés in Berlin. These younger officers, impatient with the caution of their elders, admired the vigor with which Germany was challenging the "old order" in Europe. They urged that Japan do the same in East Asia.

Making allowance for a degree of fluidity between them, these three sets of tensions tended to create two opposing camps within the Imperial Navy, led respectively by Admiral Mitsumasa Yonai (Navy Minister, 1937–1939) and by Admiral Suetsugu. Yonai, widely regarded as an administrative group officer although he had commanded the Combined Fleet in 1936–1937, was a supporter of the Washington system. He also strove for improved relations with the United States and opposed closer ties with Germany. Suetsugu, on the other hand, denounced naval limitations, harangued against Britain and the United States, and favored an alliance with the Third Reich. Personal feelings ran so high between Yonai and Suetsugu that the two men are said to have refused even to speak to each other.

One would expect that the idea of a Hawaii invasion would take root in the anti-American, anti-naval limitation, pro-German, command group. To be sure, as mentioned in the previous chapter, admirals Kanji Katō and Nobumasa Suetsugu did write laudatory forewords to a 1933 novel that featured a Hawaii assault. Yet the Katō-Suetsugu strategic concepts, which dominated naval planning from the mid-1920s until 1941, paid very little attention to Hawaii. For all their public bellicosity, Katō and Suetsugu adhered to a conservative tradition when it came to planning for the contingency of a Japanese-American war.

The Imperial Navy's earliest plan for a Pacific war was completed in 1909, two years after the United States was first named as a hypothetical enemy. At this time, hypothetical enemy largely meant a "budgetary enemy" used periodically as a device to extract more appropriations from the Diet. Although British and German military circles in 1907 gave Japan a five-to-four chance of besting the United States in a naval war, naval planners in Tokyo rated American capabilities very highly. Projected operations were based on the twin assumptions of American superiority in firepower and Japanese superiority in maneuverability.

The basic plan called for luring the American Fleet into the Western Pacific and annihilating it off Japan's coast. This strategy envisioned Japan picking the time and the place for a decisive engagement. It also assumed that the issue would be decided by capital ships. The model toward which planners looked was the Battle of Tsushima (27–28 May 1905), in which Admiral Tōgō ambushed a large but unwieldy Russian fleet that had sailed from the Gulf of Finland around the Cape of Good Hope only to meet its nemesis on Japan's doorstep.

Admiral Suetsugu refined this strategy from 1923 to 1925 while heading the First Section of the First Department, that part of the Navy General Staff in charge of operational planning. Called *yō-geki sakusen* (interceptive operations), Suetsugu's strategy retained the traditional concept of a decisive battle in Japanese waters but added a new element, submarines. High-speed submarines would harass the American Fleet as it steamed across the Pacific, gradually reducing its combat abilities by an estimated 30 percent. Arriving in a depleted state in the western Pacific, the American forces would be destroyed in a decisive battle by Japanese battleships. *Yōgeki sakusen*, essentially a strategy of attrition, became naval orthodoxy during the 1930s.

From 1925 until 1941, Japan's "mainstream" naval strategy, as reflected in the Navy General Staff's plans, changed very little. Every year, some ten staff officers of the First Section (Planning) of the First Division (Operations) would draw up a war plan for the forthcoming twelve months, covering the period 1 April to 31 March. After consultation with the Army General Staff, this plan was submitted to the emperor for approval. The basic plan changed very little from year to year, with the exception of 1936 when Great Britain was added as a hypothetical enemy.

The strategy of attrition did not rule out assaults on American territory. As early as 1923, Guam and the Philippines were marked for landings. Their seizure remained integral to the Navy General Staff's annual plans for the next eighteen years. Hawaii, however, was not once mentioned as a target.

In looking for the roots of Hawaii invasion plans, one will find little or nothing in "mainstream" strategic thinking within the Imperial Navy. Rather, the idea germinated and matured in the minds of officers who entertained doubts about the conventional wisdom of interceptive operations, about the battleship as an ultimate weapon. These officers came to recognize that technological innovations allowed, indeed required, Japan to consider bolder options in planning for a Pacific War.

Ironically, the naval officer who first called an invasion of Hawaii a strategic necessity if Japan and America were to fight, and who eventually supervised the planning for such an invasion, was a man who regarded Suetsugu as needlessly bellicose, who counted himself a follower of Admiral Yonai, who accepted the Washington system and opposed an alliance with Germany, who appreciated American industrial might, and who respected America's fighting potential. This man was Isoroku Yamamoto, Japan's most celebrated naval strategist, known internationally as the architect of the Pearl Harbor attack.

The association of Yamamoto with a Hawaii invasion plan may be ironic, but it is not contradictory. Over the course of fourteen years, the idea of invading Hawaii gestated in Yamamoto's brain, emerging in 1942 as a bold but essentially defensive gamble born of an acute awareness of Japanese weakness and American power. By 1942 Yamamoto saw the seizure of Hawaii as a political as well as a military act, a stroke through which Japan could extricate herself, via a negotiated peace, from a war that could prove ruinous if it were not terminated quickly.

Yamamoto's background equipped him with a rare appreciation of political and economic as well as military matters. He was born in 1884 into a schoolmaster's family in Nagaoka, a castle town near the Japan Sea coast of Niigata Prefecture. After graduating from the Naval Academy in 1904, during the Russo-Japanese War, he served under Admiral Tōgō and lost two fingers in the epochal Battle of Tsushima. Following several fleet assignments, Yamamoto studied at the Naval Torpedo School and the Naval War College. In 1919 he was sent to Harvard University as a language student. During the next two years, he took advantage of the opportunity to attend lectures on American history and diplomacy.

Yamamoto's knowledge of the United States deepened during the 1920s. He toured the country in 1923 and 1924 and served as naval attaché at the Japanese embassy in Washington from 1925 until 1928. What he saw convinced him that Japan was no match for the United States in a drawn-out war of attrition.

Between 1919 and 1924 Yamamoto conceived a deep interest in air power. He may well have been influenced by the outspoken General William "Billy" Mitchell, who was claiming that aircraft, properly armed, could sink anything that floated and that planes, not battleships, were the ultimate naval weapon. Between his American assignments, Yamamoto commanded the naval air base at Kasumigaura, where he had the opportunity to observe and evaluate aircraft performance. Returning from Washington in 1928, he declared that aircraft would someday become the strategic mainstay of the Imperial Navy.

It was also in 1928 that Yamamoto made his earliest recorded statement about an invasion of Hawaii. The reference occurred during a lecture at his alma mater, the Navy Torpedo School: "In operations against America, we must take positive actions such as an invasion of Hawaii."

The timing of Yamamoto's remarks about air power and Hawaii was not coincidental. His appreciation of the former led to a recognition of the importance of the latter. In an air age, Hawaii was an unsinkable aircraft carrier anchored in the middle of the Pacific Ocean. From Hawaii, planes could attack and destroy battleships cruising within a range of hundreds of miles. More ominously, carrier strike forces based on Hawaii could move directly against Japan.

In 1928 Yamamoto's views carried little weight in the Navy

General Staff, where Admiral Suetsugu's *yōgeki sakusen* doctrine reigned supreme. But starting in the mid-1930s, a combination of events gradually obliged senior naval officers to take cognizance of Hawaii.

For one thing Hawaii assumed a new significance as the implications of air power made themselves felt in all branches of the Imperial Navy. Improvements in speed, payload, and flight range opened dramatic new possiblities for offensive operations. In 1935 Pan American Airways inaugurated trans-Pacific service with flying clippers connecting California and Shanghai via Hawaii, Wake, Guam, and Manila. Imperial Navy observers could not help but note that the clipper's flight route passed uncomfortably close to Japan's Micronesian mandate. Moreover, Pan American's island hopping demonstrated that atolls could serve as stepping-stones for air assaults on Japan. It also did not escape the notice of astute observers that the Hawaiian Islands were the only stepping-stones between Micronesia and the American West Coast.

Second, the American Navy built up its presence in and around the Hawaiian Islands. During the 1920s and early 1930s Pearl Harbor was used as a base only for submarines. Capital ships were stationed along the West Coast at Puget Sound, San Francisco, San Pedro, and San Diego. In 1935, however, the fleet assembled at Pearl Harbor for its annual maneuvers. It then proceeded from Hawaii westward to Midway Island in a simulated offensive against Japan in which Pearl Harbor represented Manila and Midway stood for one of the Ryukyu Islands. Although Japanese naval observers had long anticipated such an exercise, the spectacle of American capital ships maneuvering west of Hawaii unsettled the Navy General Staff. Hawaii as in the past was not mentioned in the 1935–1936 war plan, but it did figure in a study completed by the Navy War College in 1936. Entitled "Strategy and Tactics in Operations against the United States," the War College paper suggested that if the American Fleet was berthed in Hawaii, Japan should open hostilities by a surprise attack on Pearl Harbor.

The 1938 American Fleet maneuvers offered Japanese planners more food for thought about Hawaii. Conducted between 15 March and 28 April, they centered around an imaginary attack on Hawaii by a "Blue" fleet. "Blue" carrier-based planes succeeded in knocking out Oahu's airfields and caused considerable damage to ships anchored in Pearl Harbor. A defending "Red" carrier, cruising off Waikiki Beach, survived the air assault, but its planes failed to locate "Blue" carriers or to prevent "Blue" transports from landing troops on Oahu and Maui. The 1938 maneuvers in effect left the impression that Japan could invade and occupy the Hawaiian Islands. A German professor of Soviet and Asian history at the University of Hawaii, Klaus Mehnert, wrote an article on these maneuvers, adding his own commentary about Hawaii's special vulnerabilities (dependence upon food imports and uncertain behavior of the local Japanese population). Dr. Mehnert sent the article to Berlin where it appeared in the July issue of *Zeitschrift für Geopolitik,* a well-known journal of geopolitics edited by Karl Haushofer. According to the testimony of a former German naval officer then serving in Tokyo, the Mehnert article stimulated discussion in Japan's naval circles.

Third, shifts in personnel gradually placed officers with an appreciation of Hawaii's strategic significance in positions where they could influence war plans. Yamamoto, a captain in 1928, had by 1935 risen to the rank of vice admiral in charge of Naval Aviation Headquarters, where he could put into practice some of his ideas about air power. He was supported by another aviation enthusiast, Rear Admiral Shigeyoshi Inoue, who in 1937 moved into the post of chief of the Navy Ministry's Naval Affairs Bureau. In the General Staff, the First Department (Operations) in 1938 came under the leadership of Rear Admiral Matome Ugaki, who had a keen interest in Hawaii and eventually became a forceful proponent for an invasion.

Together with these trends that collectively lifted Hawaii's profile, there occurred a functional shift within the Imperial Navy. The initiative for strategic planning started to move from the Navy General Staff to the Combined Fleet. The timing of this shift is difficult to pinpoint, but the appointment of Yamamoto to command the Combined Fleet (30 August 1939) helped set forces in motion.

Yamamoto's appointment coincided with the outbreak of World War II in Europe. Within months Japan was veering toward a showdown with the United States. The approach of war, together with Yamamoto's prestige within the navy, gave the Combined Fleet an unprecedented role in strategic planning. The Navy General Staff retained the prerogative of formulating strategy, but in practice war planning after 1940 evolved into a complex interaction of initiatives and compromises between the General Staff in

Tokyo and the Combined Fleet, whose commander set up headquarters on the battleship *Nagato*, which normally rode at anchor at Hashirajima in Hiroshima Bay.

Upon assuming the responsibilities of commanding Japan's naval forces, Yamamoto gathered about him a staff of about a dozen officers. Most were in their thirties and forties with the rank of commander or captain. These officers were directed by a chief of staff with the rank of rear admiral. Yamamoto was served by three successive chiefs of staff before the outbreak of the Pacific War. The third, Matome Ugaki, joined the Combined Fleet on 11 August 1941 and remained with it until the middle of 1943. Born in 1890 Ugaki had broad experience in his many assignments. His most important post, at which he worked from 1938 until 1941, was to head the First (Operations) Department of the Navy General Staff. It will be recalled that this department contained the First Section which was responsible for long-term strategic planning.

In addition to Ugaki, four younger staff officers deserve mention for their subsequent contributions to the Hawaii invasion plan. Captain Kameto Kuroshima was forty-six when he joined Yamamoto's staff as vice chief in October 1939. A brilliant if somewhat eccentric officer prone to wearing *kimono* on duty, Kuroshima had served in the Navy Ministry's Naval Affairs Bureau and in a number of squadrons as a staff officer. Captain Yoshitake Miwa, Yamamoto's operations officer, was born in 1899 and had worked as an assistant naval attaché under Yamamoto in Washington from 1926 to 1928. His subsequent career had led through assignments with air units, the War College, and the First Section of the Navy General Staff's First Department. Commander Shigeru Fujii, born in 1900, had served in the Fifth Section (United States) of the General Staff's Third Department (Intelligence). He had traveled extensively in the United States and in Europe. Youngest in this group was Commander Yasuji Watanabe, thirty-eight, a logistics expert. Despite his youth, Watanabe came as close to the commander in chief as anyone on the *Nagato*. Yamamoto and Watanabe regularly played *shōgi* (Japanese chess), a game in which regular opponents can learn much about each other's approach to strategy. Yamamoto put Watanabe in charge of the staff's planning section.

Within eight months of Yamamoto's appointment to the Combined Fleet, Japan's political and military leaders took a series of steps which made a confrontation with the United States difficult to avoid. German conquests in Europe during April, May, and June of 1940 created a psychological atmosphere in Tokyo that Japan had a providential opportunity to achieve an unassailable position in Asia and the Pacific. British, French, and Dutch colonies in Southeast Asia, deprived of strong defenses because their mother countries were occupied or struggling to survive, offered Tokyo attractive targets. Southeast Asia's natural resources (Malayan rubber, Dutch East Indies petroleum) held out to Japan a vision of self-sufficiency that would enable the empire to prepare for a showdown with the United States and eventually with the Soviet Union. Accordingly, on 4 July 1940 leading officers of the army and navy ministries and general staffs reached a consensus on the overriding importance of southern expansion. On 27 July a liaison conference between Imperial Headquarters* and government leaders resulted in a decision to occupy the northern part of French Indochina. Japanese forces started moving into the area on 23 September prompting the United Stated to retaliate by imposing an embargo on scrap metal exports to Japan on 16 October.

Japan's 1940 southern orientation gave birth to a new vocabulary of national goals. Since November 1938 Tokyo had proclaimed the empire's mission to be the construction of a "new order in East Asia." The boundaries of the New Order were generally understood to include Japan and its colonies (southern Sakhalin, Taiwan, Korea, Kwantung Territory, Micronesian mandate), Manchukuo (a puppet state created in 1932), and a "reformed" China (i.e., a China without communists or Chiang Kai-shek, a China friendly and subservient to Japan). In the summer of 1940, however, a new and grandiose phrase began to appear in the news media: Greater East Asia Co-Prosperity Sphere *(Dai Tōa kyōeiken)*.

Who coined the slogan "Greater East Asia Co-Prosperity Sphere" cannot be said with certainty. The phrase is commonly attributed to the ebulliently mercurial foreign minister Yōsuke Matsuoka, who aired it at a press conference on 1 August 1940. A reliable academic source, however, says that the concept was

---

*The highest organ coordinating military leadership. Created in 1893, it functioned only in wartime (1894–1895, 1904–1905). Revived after the outbreak of the China Incident in 1937 it consisted of leaders of the army and navy general staffs.

in fact broached by Matsuoka's predecessor Hachirō Arita two months earlier in private conversations with colleagues. At any rate, by October it was cropping up regularly in liaison conferences between the cabinet and Imperial Headquarters. In November the government proclaimed the establishment of the Sphere as a fundamental objective of Imperial foreign policy. Prime Minister Konoe stressed its basic importance in an address to the Diet on 21 January 1941.

Publicly the Sphere's geographical scope and political structure remained nebulous. The addition of "Greater" to "East Asia" strongly implied that the Sphere encompassed more than the new order. Such public vagueness was probably deliberate, for it reduced the risk of offending countries with which Japan was then at peace, yet it left open options for including those same countries (or parts of them) in the event of war.

Most observers in 1940 and early 1941 understood the Sphere to include East and Southeast Asia. The Philippines, then an American possession, raised a delicate point. Tokyo University professor Masamichi Rōyama, a member of Prime Minister Konoe's "brain trust," cryptically noted in January 1941 that the Sphere "overlapped" with American interests in the Pacific. Konoe himself seems to have hoped that the Sphere could be established without resorting to war with the United States. The prime minister was thinking possibly of some components of the Sphere having an economic relationship with Japan without being subjected to political control from Tokyo.

A secret planning paper produced by the Navy General Staff's Research Section, however, left no doubt about one conception of the Sphere's scope. Dated 29 November 1940 the paper was entitled "Draft Outline for the Establishment of the Greater East Asia Co-Prosperity Sphere." This paper throws light upon how some planners viewed Hawaii's future disposition.

The "Draft Outline" envisioned the Sphere as a sort of onion with multiple layers enveloping a core. Each layer had a distinct relationship to Japan (the core). For general purposes, the Sphere was to be divided into three layers. The innermost was to consist of the Japanese archipelago, Taiwan, Korea, and Manchukuo. The second would include most of China, all of Micronesia, and Hawaii. The third was defined as "those outlying areas necessary for the achievement of absolute economic self-sufficiency."

In characterizing types of political relationships within the Sphere, the "Draft Outline" proposed four categories: (1) territories to be incorporated into the Japanese Empire; (2) autonomous regions under Japanese protection; (3) independent countries closely tied to Japan by economic and defense agreements; and (4) independent countries linked to Japan by only economic ties. Hawaii and the Philippine island of Mindanao (which had a significant local Japanese population) were to be annexed and treated as Imperial possessions falling into the first category.

Although the "Draft Outline" identified Hawaii as a target for annexation, the Planning Section of the Navy General Staff's First Department paid little attention to the possiblity of mounting an invasion of the islands. The 1940 war plan rested upon the same basic assumptions that had governed its predecessors for over ten years: a Japanese-American conflict would be decided by an engagement between battleships after submarines had weakened the advancing American fleet through a strategy of attrition. The only significant innovation of the 1940 plan was that the projected "decisive battle" was moved two thousand miles eastward from the Marianas to the Marshalls.

Within the Combined Fleet, however, Hawaii by 1940 and 1941 was attracting serious interest as both a tactical and a strategic objective. Ironically, this interest derived largely from the commander in chief's awareness of Japan's basic weakness.

By the fall of 1940, Admiral Yamamoto was more certain than ever that Japan could not win a war of attrition with the United States. Japan, in his opinion, could not sustain a drawn-out struggle even if it managed to seize the raw materials of Southeast Asia. The Tripartite Alliance, which some younger naval officers hailed as a deterrent against American belligerency in the Pacific, Yamamoto wrote off as a dangerous liability. If Japan could not win a long war, the admiral reasoned, it should not fight the United States. If it were driven to fight the United States, then that war must be a short one. Only in a short conflict could Japan hold its initial advantage. As the commander in chief bluntly told Prime Minister Konoe in September 1940: "If I am told to fight regardless of consequences, I shall run wild for the first six months or a year, but I have utterly no confidence for the second or third years."

Hawaii would play a key role in the Combined Fleet's ability to "run wild" for the first six months. When Yamamoto spoke to Konoe, he was already thinking about a surprise attack on Pearl Harbor with carrier-based dive bombers, torpedo planes, and fighters.

Rear Admiral Shigeru Fukudome, Yamamoto's chief of staff from November 1939 until April 1941, later recalled that the commander in chief began seriously considering a Pearl Harbor attack in April 1940. There is some evidence that Yamamoto had the idea in the back of his mind since 1928 when he read a paper prepared by an officer at the Kasumigaura air base outlining the ingredients of a Pearl Harbor strike.* Yamamoto broached the idea of a Hawaii raid to Navy Minister Koshirō Oikawa in a letter dated 7 January 1941. Throughout the spring and summer, he periodically informed the Navy General Staff that by hitting the Americans in Hawaii, where the enemy would not be expecting it, Japan could immobilize part of the Pacific Fleet† and gain valuable time to consolidate control over Malaya, the Philippines, and the Dutch East Indies.

The Navy Ministry and General Staff reacted negatively to Yamamoto's arguments. The senior officers in Tokyo considered a Hawaii raid too complicated and too risky. Moreover, they favored concentrating fleet action in Southeast Asia, where the army was insistently calling for support and protection. Yamamoto's concern for Hawaii and the Navy General Staff's orientation toward Southeast Asia and the southwestern Pacific constituted a divergence in strategic priorities that widened after the outbreak of the war.

Meanwhile some members of the Combined Fleet staff went further than Yamamoto and were contemplating not just an attack *(kōgeki)* on Pearl Harbor but an invasion *(kōryaku)* of Hawaii. During the summer of 1941, Captain Kuroshima and Commander Watanabe studied the feasibility of amphibious landings on Oahu, Maui, and the Big Island. They came to a tentative conclusion that the chances for success of such an operation were good, provided that the landings took place immediately after the Pearl Harbor

*The paper was authored by Lieutenant Commander Ryūnosuke Kusaka who in 1938 headed the planning section of the Navy General Staff and who in 1944 was appointed chief of staff for the Combined Fleet.

†The Pacific Fleet moved its headquarters from San Diego to Pearl Harbor in July 1941, adding weight to Yamamoto's argument.

strike. Assuming that the Pacific Fleet would be severely damaged at Pearl Harbor, Kuroshima and Watanabe calculated that troop transports would be able to reach assigned beaches without undue difficulties. Resistance was not likely to be strong because of the element of surprise. Once Japanese infantry and armor established beachheads, they could move inland and annihilate enemy units before they could regroup.

When the Navy General Staff got wind of Hawaii invasion talk within the Combined Fleet, it was not pleased. On 7 August heated words were exchanged between Kuroshima and Captain Sadatoshi Tomioka, chief of the First Section (Planning) of the Staff's First Department. Tomioka complained that "the Combined Fleet thinks too much about Hawaii," and it needed to take a broader view of strategic possibilities and constraints.

Smoldering differences between Combined Fleet and General Staff planners over Hawaii came to a head during 5–17 September 1941 when the Imperial Navy held its final prewar war games in Tokyo at the Army War College auditorium (navy facilities proved inadequate to accommodate the large number of officers in attendance). The Pearl Harbor attack was rehearsed and judged feasible on 13 September, although the results suggested that the task force carrying out the operation would suffer heavy losses: two carriers sunk, two carriers damaged, and 127 aircraft destroyed.

During the rehearsal, Captain Kuroshima and Rear Admiral Seiichi Itō, vice chief of Navy General Staff, heatedly argued the pros and cons of amphibious landings on Oahu immediately after the raid. Kuroshima asserted that even a modest assault would succeed, for the Americans, reeling from air attacks, would not have time to regroup. Itō demurred, noting that a double operation *(kōgeki* and *kōryaku)* was too complex and too risky. Moreover tankers and troopships were badly needed for operations in Southeast Asia. A long discussion ensued, involving several officers.

Yamamoto listened to the debate in silence and then came to a decision. He opted for Itō's caution over Kuroshima's daring. A gambler himself, as the Pearl Harbor operation eloquently testified, Yamamoto was not reckless. He sensed that Itō was right in arguing that an invasion of Hawaii in December 1941 would be trying to do too much at once with too few resources. Itō had formerly served as Yamamoto's chief of staff and the commander in chief respected his judgment.

On 13 September 1941 Yamamoto rejected a Pearl Harbor "encore", but did he still keep open the possibility of an invasion at some other time? The evidence is not clear. One account of the 13 September discussion reported that the commander in chief discounted the possibility of any landings on Hawaii even should transports become available a month or so after a successful Pearl Harbor attack. By that time, Yamamoto is said to have remarked, the Americans would have recovered and be on the alert. Japanese troop convoys would become vulnerable targets for submarines. Finally, once in Japanese hands, Hawaii would confront the Imperial Navy with an enormous logistic problem. Yet in the light of subsequent events, one suspects that the commander in chief never completely banished the idea of a Hawaii invasion from his thoughts.

The Pearl Harbor operation finally won the Navy General Staff's reluctant approval on 19 October 1941. By that time Japanese-American negotiations in Washington were heading toward the final impasse. Orders had already been approved by a liaison conference for hostilities to commence early in December. Torpedo pilots were undergoing intensive training in Kagoshima Bay, a simulated Pearl Harbor.

As the date of the attack approached, intelligence on Hawaii became critically important. The navy had one agent stationed in Honolulu, Ensign Takeo Yoshikawa, who served in the local Japanese consulate under the assumed name of Tadashi Morimura. It is likely that the navy had other sources of information in Hawaii. Some of these could well have been Japanese nationals working in Honolulu branches of Japanese corporations. In December 1940 Tokyo had instructed its Washington embassy to recruit Japanese bank officials in the United States for espionage. There were branches of the Yokohama Specie Bank and Sumitomo Bank in Honolulu, but to what extent—if at all—their officers provided information to the navy is not known.

Tokyo does not appear to have recruited actively within Hawaii's local Japanese community. In a directive to the Washington embassy dated 30 January 1941, Foreign Minister Matsuoka advised that the "utmost caution" be used in utilizing "our second generation . . . in view of the fact that if there is any slip in this phase our people in the United States will be subject to considerable persecution." No evidence is available that the navy successfully recruited Japanese-American agents in Hawaii, although one former officer in the Navy General Staff's Third Department (Intelligence) recalled that some *kibei* were approached in Japan. The self-confessed spy, Ensign Yoshikawa, claimed that he did not trust local Japanese and hence did not attempt to use them. Admiral Fukudome echoed Yoshikawa's doubts, adding that the utility of Hawaii *dōhō* was limited by their being under suspicion by American authorities.

Hawaii *dōhō* did, however, unwittingly render valuable service to Japanese Naval Intelligence on the eve of Pearl Harbor. The occasion was early in November, when two officers visited Honolulu posing as a doctor and an assistant purser on the passenger liner *Taiyō-maru*. The Navy General Staff had sent them to gather the latest information on the location of American warships and submarine nets (thought to be strung across the entrance of Pearl Harbor). One of the officers was Lieutenant Commander Suguru Suzuki, an aviation expert and scion of a distinguished military family.* Suzuki had previously worked in the Fifth Section (United States) of Naval Intelligence, where he had collected sackfuls of mail from patriotic Hawaii *dōhō*. During the week that the *Taiyō-maru* lay at anchor in Honolulu harbor (1–8 November 1941), neither Suzuki nor the other officer were permitted to go ashore, for the ship was guarded by a contingent of Marines who had orders to keep all Japanese nationals except passengers bound for Hawaii aboard. However, Japanese consular agents managed to smuggle aboard intelligence data gathered by Yoshikawa (Morimura).

One piece of intelligence that had eluded Yoshikawa was whether American warships, particularly aircraft carriers, were off Lahaina, a settlement on the west coast of Maui. Lahaina roads had been used as a fleet anchorage in the past, and Japanese planners were intensely interested to know whether it would be necessary to attack it as well as Pearl Harbor. While the *Taiyō-maru* steamed

---

*Son of General Takao Suzuki (director of Yasukuni Shrine and of Dai Nippon seishōnendan, a patriotic youth league), nephew of Admiral Kantarō Suzuki (prime minister in 1945), and son-in-law of Admiral Keisuke Okada (prime minister, 1934–1936).

toward Yokohama, Suzuki befriended some *dōhō* who had opted for repatriation to Japan. Over drinks he learned that no ships were at Lahaina. This piece of information enabled the task force on 7 December to concentrate on Oahu, without diverting planes to Maui.

Upon his return to Japan, Suzuki immediately met with Matome Ugaki, Yamamoto's chief of staff, and presented an oral report on conditions in Hawaii. This meeting occurred on 17 November, just nine days before the task force embarked from its assembly point at Hitokappu Bay in the southern Kurile Islands. After describing American ship deployments, Suzuki volunteered the suggestion that Japan had an excellent opportunity to invade Hawaii. The lieutenant commander estimated that two Imperial Army divisions would suffice to seize Oahu. Local *nikkeijin*, he added, would most likely cooperate in the occupation.

Ugaki listened to Suzuki's proposal attentively but dismissed it as impractical. He agreed that the Hawaiian Islands could be seized with two divisions. But could they be retained? How would Japan keep its Hawaii garrisons supplied across thousands of miles of ocean prowled by enemy submarines? How would Japan feed Hawaii's civilian population, which relied upon imports for most of its food supply? And would Japan be able to repel an American counterattack?

The Suzuki-Ugaki conversation of 17 November 1941 turned out to be the last known occasion when a Hawaii invasion was discussed within the Imperial Navy prior to 7 December. The subject would loom up again immediately after the attack, when Yamamoto realized that by not assaulting Hawaii, Japan had missed a strategic opportunity that was not likely to present itself again.

In historical hindsight, it is remarkable how little long-term planning was done by the Imperial Navy as it prepared for war with the United States. At the outbreak of hostilities Japan's military leaders had formulated only a vague set of strategic war aims. These fell into two projected stages: stage one called for the elimination of American, British, and Dutch forces from Southeast Asia and the western Pacific, enabling Japan to secure the resources of Malaya and the East Indies. In stage two, Japan was to destroy the "main part" of the U.S. Pacific Fleet and to strengthen its ability to conduct a protracted conflict. Nothing was mentioned about an invasion of Hawaii, although the possibility was left open for submarines to interdict Hawaii's maritime supply lines with the West Coast.

In short, Japan went to war without spelling out its strategic objectives in any detail. There was a vague notion that once stage two had been reached, the Americans would lose their will to fight and would accede to a negotiated peace, leaving Japan in control of the western Pacific and Southeast Asia.

One reason why the Imperial Navy went to war without a long-term strategic plan was that its leaders were unwilling to contemplate the prospects of a drawn-out war of attrition. On 6 September 1941 Chief of Navy Staff Admiral Osami Nagano told a liaison conference that the navy could do well against the Americans for about two years. Chief of the Naval Air Corps Admiral Shigeyoshi Inoue asserted on another occasion that Japan could not maintain momentum in a war with the United States for more than a year. Admiral Yamamoto as mentioned earlier gave Japan six months to a year for "running wild" in the Pacific but could not predict with any confidence what would ensue.

The vagueness of the Imperial Navy's war plans was not peculiar to that branch of the armed services nor was it confined to military circles. The prospect of a showdown with the United States left Japan's leaders prey to self-delusion, pride, and fatalism. In the charged atmosphere reigning during the six months before December, there was little cold analysis of the realities of power.

American power was—on the surface—so much greater than that of Japan in 1941 that any strategic planner looking dispassionately at the statistics would be forced to conclude that war with the United States was a hopeless undertaking. In 1941 the United States was, with the exception of chrome and rubber, self-sufficient in raw materials indispensable to sustain a major effort. American industrial production in crucial sectors (steel, oil, coal, aircraft construction) ranged from two to one hundred times that of Japan. Even before the outbreak of hostilities, President Roosevelt was putting the country on a war footing. On 3 December 1941 the *New York Times* reported that the United States Navy was launching one major warship every day. Planned aircraft carrier construction was triple that of Japan. Japan was overshadowed in terms of manpower as well as in resources and industrial potential. A major part of the empire's forces were tied down on the Asian continent, locked in a stalemate with Chiang Kai-shek in China and girding for a collision with the Soviet Union in Manchuria.

No Japanese leader in 1941 was unaware of the material superiority of the United States. Yet many convinced themselves that special circumstances compensated for Japan's disadvantages. The rich resources of Southeast Asia were expected to enable the empire to achieve self-sufficiency in strategic materials within two years. The spiritual qualities of the Japanese people in general and of the armed forces in particular were thought to more than make up for material shortages. Some publicists claimed that America's wealth promoted softness and emasculated its national will.

Wishful thinking about Germany also colored Japan's war plans —or the lack thereof. The mirage of a German victory in Europe and the Middle East shimmered over Tokyo after Hitler's blitzkrieg triumphs in the spring of 1940. Not every Japanese leader succumbed to the myth of an invincible Third Reich, but the palpable rewards of German boldness in Europe eroded caution in Tokyo, tipping the balance in many minds toward a willingness to risk war with the United States.

In November 1941, the German offensive in the USSR was losing momentum, but Tokyo expected its Tripartite partner at least to compel the United States to think twice before becoming involved in a two-front, two-ocean war. Ironically, the Wehrmacht suffered its first major setback, outside Moscow, one day before the Pearl Harbor attack.

Pride also prevented Japan's leaders from weighing the full implications of war with the United States. The army, which held the American soldier in low esteem, would not even consider Washington's demand that Japan withdraw its forces from Indochina and China as a precondition for lifting the embargos imposed in 1940 and 1941. Senior naval officers were too proud to admit to army counterparts that the Imperial Navy might not be up to the task of handling the U.S. Pacific Fleet. Consequently, at liaison conferences during the summer and fall of 1941, naval spokesmen made bold pronouncements about its preparedness for war. These statements led the army to assume (incorrectly) that the navy could take care of the Pacific theater of operations by itself.

Finally fatalism and a sort of quiet desperation unbalanced

even sober minds during the summer and fall of 1941. Tokyo became obsessed with the specter of "ABCD encirclement"* strangling Japan's economic lifelines. American demands for withdrawals from Indochina and China appeared to confront the empire with a stark choice of war or ruinous humiliation. An all-or-nothing psychology, coupled with a sense of resignation, gradually crowded out other options and made confrontation appear to be the sole hope for national survival.

Yamamoto's thoughts on the eve of Pearl Harbor are difficult to fathom. It has been alleged that he reconciled himself to war after the Navy General Staff had grudgingly sanctioned his Pearl Harbor strike plan on 19 October 1941. Yet judging from views conveyed in his letters and conversations with relatives, friends, and colleagues, it seems likely that he never jettisoned doubts about Japan's long-term prospects.

The Hawaii operation, for which Yamamoto had argued so tenaciously and for which he had threatened to resign should it fail to win Navy General Staff approval, was but the prologue to an unpredictable drama. The commander in chief hoped that damage inflicted on American warships in Pearl Harbor would give Japan breathing space to take over Southeast Asia and to gird for a decisive showdown with the U.S. Pacific Fleet. Yamamoto hoped that in the longer run a string of Japanese tactical victories would deprive the American public of the will to fight and convince Roosevelt to accede to peace negotiations.

Yamamoto's prognosis did not materialize in either the short or long term. While tactically successful beyond expectations in some ways, the Pearl Harbor operation had unforeseen consequences, consequences which forced the commander in chief to take the first concrete steps toward launching an invasion of Hawaii.

*ABCD denoted Americans, British, Chinese, and Dutch.

CHAPTER VI

The Birth Pangs of
"Eastern Operation"

As planes from Admiral Chūichi Nagumo's six-carrier task force approached Pearl Harbor in the early hours of 7 December (Hawaii time), the commander in chief of the Combined Fleet assembled his staff in the operations room of his flagship, the aging battleship *Nagato*, to wait for news of the attack. The *Nagato* lay at anchor off Hashirajima in Hiroshima Bay, nearly four thousand miles from Oahu. Yet the dozen officers gathered in the operations room felt the islands loom around them with suffocating immediacy. Every man knew that the strike on "America's Gibralter" (as Nagumo called it in a predawn address to aviators) would trigger a showdown with the world's greatest industrial power. Every man was aware that the outcome of the Hawaii operation would shape the whole course of the war which in turn would determine the empire's fate.

At 3:19 A.M. on 8 December (Japan time), Yamamoto was handed a wireless message from the task force, tersely stating that the first wave of planes had reached the skies over Oahu without opposition and that the attack on Pearl Harbor was about to begin. In the next few minutes bulletins trickled, then streamed, into the *Nagato*'s operations room. The contents were exhilarating. Complete surprise had been achieved. Colossal damage had been inflicted on battleships and land-based aircraft. Enemy resistance was weak and disorganized.

The assembled officers beamed in jubilation and relief. It had worked. The Hawaii gamble, opposed by the Navy General Staff until just a few weeks earlier, was succeeding beyond everybody's expectations. Elated, the staff exchanged warm congratulations.

Yamamoto alone remained impassive amid the excitement that swirled around him. He listened to each incoming report without comment. As the final attack wave headed back toward the task force, the commander in chief turned to his staff and in an even tone remarked: *"Sa, kore kara dō suru ka kangaero."* (Well, let's think about what we're going to do from now on).

When Yamamoto uttered these words, he already knew that the Pearl Harbor operation, soon to be hailed throughout the Japanese Empire as a monumental victory, was in fact seriously flawed. It had bequeathed two major disappointments, one resulting from bad luck, the other from miscalculation.

First, the attackers had found no aircraft carriers in Pearl Harbor. The *Enterprise, Lexington,* and *Saratoga*—the core of the U.S. Pacific Fleet air power—escaped destruction. No one even knew where they were. This disturbed the commander in chief, for he acutely appreciated the strategic significance of naval air power. As long as those carriers remained at large, they could deny the Imperial Navy control of the western Pacific and could harass Japan's insular outposts and maritime communications. If allowed to increase in numbers, American carriers could spearhead a counteroffensive against Japan's home islands. The absence of three carriers from Pearl Harbor that morning did more than spoil Yamamoto's satisfaction with an otherwise brilliantly executed operation. It was a bad omen.

The second disappointment stemmed, ironically, from the ease with which the attack on Pearl Harbor had been carried out. Upon being told that American resistance was unexpectedly weak, the admiral realized that Nagumo could have seized Oahu had he been prepared to do so, that is if the task force had included troopships with men trained and equipped for amphibious landings. A golden opportunity to deprive the United States of its most important base in the Pacific had slipped by. Yamamoto now realized that his operations officer, Captain Kuroshima, had been right on 13 September when he had argued for seizing Oahu while the Americans were still paralyzed with confusion from the Pearl Harbor attack. The commander in chief had rejected Kuroshima's proposal as too risky. Now, on 8 December he had occasion to ponder the consequences of that decision.

It is not recorded that Yamamoto communicated any expressions of regrets to his staff on that historic morning. But shortly thereafter, he did refer to the subject in a letter to a close friend: "If we had known that air units alone could achieve so much in the Hawaii operation, we wouldn't have used just air units . . . but we didn't know that at the time, and it can't be helped."

These twin disappointments heightened Yamamoto's appreciation of the Hawaiian Islands. There was now no question but that the carriers which had eluded Nagumo's task force would use Pearl Harbor as a base for a counteroffensive against Japan. Hawaii's short-term vulnerability made the islands tempting targets. But could an assault be launched before the Americans shored up insular defenses?

By nature, Admiral Yamamoto was not a garrulous man. He rarely shared his innermost thoughts with even close associates. To his staff, he habitually cloaked ideas about strategic options in nebulous phrases. This was apparently a tactic to give himself sufficient room to maneuver in negotiations between the Combined Fleet and the Navy General Staff. Consequently, the admiral's staff officers—Ugaki, Kuroshima, Miwa, Fujii, Watanabe—were often hard put to fathom their commander's true intentions. Yamamoto revealed his strategic thinking by actions more than by words. Yet on the eve of the war, Yamamoto was dropping hints about a Hawaiian invasion to members of his staff. He talked about the prospect several times just before Pearl Harbor with his operations officer, Captain Kuroshima. He asked his planning officer, Commander Watanabe, whether there was not some way that Hawaii could be seized.

Instructions to Nagumo's task force also contain a hint of the commander in chief's thinking about a Hawaii invasion. The war diary of the Fifth Air Corps contains the following entry, describing a contingency operation to be carried out upon receipt of a coded signal as the task force returned from Hawaii to Japan: "From point L, in cooperation with the Fourth Fleet, strike Wake, then attack Midway, Johnston, Palmyra islands. Destroy the bases and air units [there] in preparation for an invasion of Hawaii."

This evidence strongly suggests that despite his decision not to support Captain Kuroshima's Hawaii *kōryaku* proposal of 13 September, Yamamoto had not dismissed the idea from his mind before 7 December.

The impact of the Pearl Harbor operation upon Yamamoto's thinking can be gauged from his behavior after 8 December 1941.

His staff noticed that he started talking "repeatedly" about invading Hawaii. On 9 December he instructed his chief of staff, Admiral Ugaki, to draw up a plan for a Hawaii invasion. Ugaki, it will
be recalled, had only three weeks earlier expressed skepticism
about a Hawaii assault to an intelligence officer (Suguru Suzuki)
who had just returned from a reconnaissance mission to Honolulu
and reported that the islands could be taken with two divisions.
Pearl Harbor seems to have affected Ugaki as strongly as it did
Yamamoto. From 9 December the Combined Fleet's chief of staff
turned into a vociferous champion of a Hawaii invasion, code-
named "Eastern Operation" *(Tōhō sakusen).*

Yamamoto's support of a Hawaii invasion derived from an appreciation of strategic realities. He wanted above all to avoid a
war of attrition with the United States, a war that Japan could not
hope to win. The longer hostilities continued, the more the Americans would mobilize their overwhelming industrial power. Yamamoto doubted that the resources of Southeast Asia would enable
Japan to build an "impregnable" sphere in Greater East Asia (as
the army was wont to intone). Nor did he put much faith in the
Navy General Staff's strategy of waiting for an American trans-
Pacific offensive.

In Yamamoto's view, Japan's only hope against such a formidable adversary lay in bold military action followed by skillful diplomacy. Japan must seize certain strategic advantages and then
quickly bring hostilities to a close through a negotiated peace. But
how would the Americans be convinced that a negotiated peace
would serve their interests more than the prolongation of war?
Yamamoto believed that Washington could be made to feel that
war would be too costly to continue if Japan kept hitting American
forces so hard that the loss of life would arouse American public
opinion. For this tactic to work, speed was essential. Japan must
retain the initiative that she had seized in the Hawaiian and Southeast Asian operations. These strikes must be immediately followed
by aggressive action in all directions that would keep the Americans off balance and allow Japan to continue enlarging the perimeter until Washington sued for peace. Yamamoto dubbed this strategy *happō yabure* (strike on all sides). He had three targets in
mind: Ceylon, Australia, and Hawaii. Of these Hawaii was the
most important for it sheltered the most serious strategic threat
against Japan: carriers of the U.S. Pacific Fleet.

If Hawaii in American hands posed a threat to Japan, Hawaii as an invasion target held out the prospect of becoming America's achilles' heel. Yamamoto grasped that the islands could be used both militarily and politically against the United States. Militarily they would serve as bait to trap the Pacific Fleet; politically they would become the lever that Tokyo would use to exert pressure on Washington to end the war.

Yamamoto assumed that Washington could not stand idly by and let the Imperial Navy capture Hawaii's western sentinels such as Midway. Lured out into battle before it could fully recover from the Pearl Harbor debacle, the Pacific Fleet would be obliterated, opening the way for an invasion of Hawaii. With Hawaii in Japanese hands, calculated Yamamoto, Tokyo would be in a strong position to push for a peace settlement. Imperial Navy squadrons based in Pearl Harbor would raise the specter of Japanese attacks along the West Coast. The spectacle of 400,000 Americans living under Japanese rule would come as such a "spiritual blow" *(seishinteki dageki)* to the American public that it would force Roosevelt to open negotiations.

According to the recollections of Captain Kuroshima, Yamamoto did not envision a Japanese annexation of Hawaii. Rather, the islands would be used as a bargaining tool to secure a peace treaty that left Japan in control of the western Pacific. Their ultimate disposition would be left up to diplomats and politicians. Annexation was but one of several options, including the establishment of a protectorate, the creation of an independent state, or even retrocession to the United States.

Yamamoto apparently did not think that Japan's conquest of Hawaii might backfire by galvanizing American determination to avenge such a humiliating loss. It seems that the admiral assumed that Americans in general saw Hawaii as expendable. After all, the islands in 1942 were still a territory, not a state. The opponents of statehood in Congress and in various strata of American society had already made known their views about "alien" and "colored" peoples in Hawaii, and these views had not escaped notice in Japan. It was not an uncommon perception in Japan that the Americans regarded Hawaii as a colony rather than as an integral part of the United States. From such an assumption, it was logical to deduce that Americans could be reconciled to Hawaii's loss. This impression may have been reinforced by a *Fortune* magazine poll, published in the summer of 1940, revealing that if Hawaii were invaded by a foreign power only 55 percent of the respondents wanted the United States to come to its rescue.

Hawaii's Japanese community did not loom prominently in Yamamoto's calculations. But others in the Imperial Navy may have thought otherwise. According to Commander Suzuki, who worked in the Navy Ministry after his return from Honolulu late in 1941, the presence of 160,000 *nikkeijin* on the islands definitely added an element of attractiveness *(miryoku)* to the idea of an invasion.

While Yamamoto pondered grand strategy, Ugaki got down to the practical task of working out the details of an assault on Hawaii. Being also charged with responsibility for preparing invasion plans for Ceylon and Australia, the chief of staff at first delegated the Hawaii project to subordinates. But on 27 December, concerned that the preparatory work was not moving ahead fast enough and convinced that Hawaii must be hit before the Pearl Harbor damage could be repaired, Ugaki assumed personal control over the details of "Eastern Operation." By this time, Ugaki had come to regard the islands as having the highest strategic priority.

Ugaki faced awesome difficulties in putting together a blueprint of "Eastern Operation" on such short notice. His immediate problem was the lack of up-to-date intelligence. Without agents in the islands after 7 December, the Imperial Navy was forced to rely upon informants from neutral countries (notably Portugal, Spain, Sweden), radio monitoring, and by surveillance through submarine periscopes.

Unfortunately for Ugaki, heavy demands for submarines in the southwestern Pacific reduced the number of vessels operating in Hawaiian waters from twenty-five on 8 December to three one month later. Moreover, anti-submarine patrols kept remaining vessels at a respectful distance from Oahu.

Planes launched from submarines did manage to make reconnaissance flights over Pearl Harbor on 16 December 1941 and 4 January 1942. Their reports were not encouraging. Reconstruction work was in full swing around the clock. Reinforcements were arriving from the American mainland by sea and air.

Completion of a plan on paper was only the first of many hurdles which Yamamoto and Ugaki had to clear before a Hawaii invasion could be launched. However much the Combined Fleet staff recognized Hawaii as a top strategic priority, nothing could be done without the approval of the Navy General Staff and the Army General Staff, for an invasion would require extensive cooperation by both services. The prospects for getting this cooperation in late 1941 and early 1942 were dim.

Relations between the army and navy, never cordial, grew strained after the outbreak of the Pacific War. Sensitivity to prestige led each service to arrogate to itself the leading role in the war effort. Competition over budgetary allocations spilled over into an unseemly scramble for scarce ordnance, ranging from aviaton fuel to copper wire. Each service showed reluctance to help the other, particularly if such help meant diverting more than token resources. Each service, while ready to tell the other how to conduct operations, resented unsolicited advice. Rudeness intruded into formal meetings at the highest level. At a joint staffs meeting in February 1942, during an appeal by Prime Minister (concurrently Army Minister) Tōjō for navy cooperation in the Timor campaign, Navy Chief of Staff Nagano pointedly fell (or pretended to fall) asleep.

Poor army-navy relations had consequences beyond the coordination of tactics. They prevented the armed services from sharing a strategic vision of the war. To be sure, a general plan existed on paper. But such documents were largely of symbolic significance. Each general staff drew up its own war objectives. Liaison officers met and discussed—but did not integrate—their respective plans. After a series of consultations, a document was drawn up accommodating both the army and navy viewpoints in vague language. The document was then presented to the emperor for approval. Subsequently each service interpreted the "imperial instructions" as it saw fit.

Japan's general war plan as of 8 December 1941 was outlined in "Plan for Prosecution of the War against the United States, Britain, Holland, China." In this document, strategic objectives were to be achieved in two stages. In stage one, Japan was to destroy enemy naval forces in the western and southwestern Pacific, occupy most of Southeast Asia, and establish a defensive perimeter through the central Pacific. Specifically, this meant annihilating the U.S. Asiatic Fleet (based in Manila), British naval units based in Hong Kong, Shanghai, and Singapore, and Dutch units based in

Batavia. Guam, the Philippines, Hong Kong, Singapore, Malaya, and the Dutch East Indies were to be seized. Finally, the Imperial Navy would establish an insular perimeter running from north to south starting in the Kuriles and proceeding through Wake, the Marshalls, and the Gilberts, to the Bismarcks.

In stage two, the aforementioned gains were to be consolidated. This would be done by exploiting the natural resources of Southeast Asia, by strengthening the continental and insular periphery, and by intercepting and destroying enemy attempts to penetrate Japan's newly won sphere.

The unexpected ease with which Imperial forces, both army and navy, advanced in December 1941 made this war plan out of date almost from the first few weeks of hostilities. Stage one had been carried out more quickly than anticipated. Destruction of part of the U.S. Pacific Fleet at Pearl Harbor was seen as a partial fulfillment of stage two. Yet the details of stage two had not yet been adequately researched. Therefore a revised stage two would have to be drawn up and agreed upon by both services.

The need to adjust the empire's basic war plan to reflect dizzying ongoing changes on several fronts gave rise to interservice and intraservice deliberations starting within days of the Pearl Harbor attack. The immediate issue was how Japan should capitalize upon unforeseen success. A consensus was slow in coming. Each service had different priorities. The Army General Staff opposed any expansion of the Pacific perimeter. It wanted the navy to consolidate in the Pacific and concentrate on eliminating British naval forces in the Indian Ocean. Mainstream thinking within the Navy General Staff placed emphasis on preserving the Combined Fleet for the anticipated "decisive battle" with the Pacific Fleet. Navy General Staff planners therefore did not look favorably upon offensive operations that might prematurely jeopardize the Combined Fleet. They favored a strike against Fiji and Samoa, a relatively risk-free venture that could be justified as a means to sever communications between the United States and Australia. In the Combined Fleet, however, there was little enthusiasm for either Indian Ocean or Fiji-Samoa options. A Hawaii invasion was accorded top priority, insofar as it promised to force a confrontation with the Pacific Fleet and to open the way for a quick end to the war.

Discussion between the Army General Staff, the Navy General Staff, and the Combined Fleet's staff about long-term strategy started in mid-December 1941 and continued for three months, without a consensus being reached. During those three months "Eastern Operation" came under heavy criticism and seemed at times on the verge of being discarded. But Ugaki, Kuroshima, and others kept the idea perpetually in the forefront of the interservice and intraservice negotiations.

The first recorded instance of a Hawaii invasion figuring in intraservice discussions occurred on 16 December when Captain Sadatoshi Tomioka, chief of the Navy General Staff's Planning Section, flew from Tokyo to Hashirajima and met with Yamamoto and his staff on board the *Nagato*. On the instructions of his superior, First Department (Operations) chief Rear Admiral Shigeru Fukudome, Tomioka was to inform Yamamoto of the General Staff's revised stage two plans and to sound out Combined Fleet thoughts about upcoming operations.

After boarding the *Nagato* and making his presentation to the assembled Combined Fleet staff, Tomioka found himself listening to Yamamoto's operations officer, Captain Kuroshima, outline plans for another strike in the mid-Pacific. It will be recalled that in August 1941 Tomioka and Kuroshima had clashed over the feasibility of a Hawaii invasion. Now, however, Tomioka raised no objections to Kuroshima's recommendations. It was not that Tomioka had changed his mind about Hawaii, rather, he did not grasp the implications of what Kuroshima was saying.

Tomioka heard Kuroshima propose the seizure of Palmyra Island (an atoll 1,100 miles southwest of Honolulu). If it were intended as a means to hamper communications between the United States and Australia, a Palmyra operation was consistent with Navy General Staff strategic thinking on stage two. Tomioka interpreted it that way and consequently did not question Kuroshima closely. For his part, Kuroshima did not volunteer to elaborate. To speak of deliberate concealment may do Kuroshima an injustice, but the vagueness that permeated his presentation of the Palmyra plan does not seem to have been entirely accidental.

As a result of the 16 December consultations on the *Nagato*, a misunderstanding developed between the Navy General Staff and the Combined Fleet. Tomioka went back to Tokyo assuming that Yamamoto would support a Fiji-Samoa strategy. He did not suspect that a strike on Palmyra was an overture to "Eastern Operation." Meanwhile, Ugaki and Kuroshima chose to infer that Tomioka's failure to object to a Palmyra operation signified that the Navy General Staff was tacitly acquiescing to an eventual assault on Hawaii. "Eastern Operation" seemed to have a green light.

Upon returning to Tokyo, Tomioka communicated what he had heard on the *Nagato* to Admiral Fukudome and to Major-General Shin'ichi Tanaka, Operations Section chief in the Army General Staff. Tanaka had already picked up rumors that there was talk of a Hawaii invasion in the Combined Fleet. This talk disturbed him. Just before meeting with Tomioka, Tanaka had jotted in his diary: ". . . problem of Hawaii assault . . . a Hawaii invasion could endanger the foundations of war leadership." Tanaka's misgivings were not allayed when Tomioka said that the Combined Fleet was only planning to move on Palmyra and no farther.

Tanaka's doubts about invading Hawaii were typical of army thinking about the war. With few exceptions,* army leaders and planners saw the war as being decided in China and Southeast Asia; the Pacific was a secondary theater. The navy's main task, from an army point of view, was to clear the Indian Ocean of British forces and to protect Japan's maritime supply lines.

The Army General Staff regarded any enlargement of the Pacific perimeter as unnecessary and dangerous. It was unnecessary because the Americans were seen as incapable of posing any threat that could not be handled by the navy alone. At the same time overextension in the Pacific would incur dangerous risks. By drawing off men and supplies it would detract from vital commitments in Southeast Asia. By requiring the participation of army units in Manchuria it weakened Japan's defenses against the Soviet Union. At the very least it sapped the ability of both services to respond to unforeseen crises in widely separated theaters. The army staff wanted the navy to put a halt to further expansion in the Pacific in favor of making the existing perimeter "impregnable."

Tanaka conveyed these views bluntly to Captain Tomioka on 23 December. On that same day Japanese forces completed the occupation of Wake Island.

On 27 December, Captain Yoshitake Miwa, a Combined Fleet

*General Kanji Ishiwara, co-architect of the 1931 Manchurian Incident, and Major General Kenryō Satō, Army General Staff section chief, accorded strategic significance to Hawaii. Their views carried little weight among army colleagues in December 1941.

staff officer, arrived in Tokyo to update the Navy General Staff about "Eastern Operation." Upon hearing Miwa's report, Tomioka suddenly realized that he had not grasped the import of Kuroshima's briefing about Palmyra eleven days earlier. Nonetheless, he kept this discovery to himself for the time being, leaving Miwa with the impression that Navy General Staff had nothing against further planning for a Hawaii assault.

Tomioka reflected on the matter over the New Year holiday and then took two steps. On 4 January 1942 he informed his army counterpart Tanaka about the Combined Fleet's invasion plans for Hawaii. Tanaka, who had already suspected as much, stated that such an operation went beyond agreed-upon war plans. Rather than communicating this directly to Yamamoto, Tomioka decided first to gather his own evidence about "Eastern Operation's" feasibility. He ordered a subordinate in the Planning Section, Captain Shigenori Kami, to prepare within a week a study on whether Hawaii could be successfully invaded and, if it could, what would be needed to retain the islands.

Kami completed his study punctually on 11 January. He concluded that Hawaii could be captured but supplying it would pose great difficulties because of a shortage of shipping tonnage. Kami estimated that Japan would have to feed nearly half a million Americans in addition to its own garrison. Most of the food would have to be carried across 4,000 miles of submarine-infested ocean. Hawaii, according to Kami, produced 84 percent of its fruit, but percentages of other foodstuffs that could be grown locally were low: rice (10%), dairy products (28%), fish (30%), eggs (40%), meat (41%), and vegetables (46%). He noted that 2,900,000 tons of supplies had been shipped to Hawaii from American ports in 1941. This worked out to about twenty-five ships monthly. Under Japanese occupation, given the swollen population, the figure would be higher: 3,000,000 tons annually, brought in by thirty ships a month. An additional thirty ships per month would be required to transport military equipment. Kami concluded that Japan's merchant marine, already stretched to the limit in carrying vital resources from Southeast Asia to the home islands, could not fulfill this task.

Kami's report confirmed Tomioka's doubts about the feasibility of taking Hawaii. It also provided him with statistical ammunition for sinking "Eastern Operation" when the proper occasion arose.

Meanwhile obstacles to a Hawaii invasion were cropping up at the highest levels. During a 10 January liaison conference, Army Chief of Staff Sugiyama and Navy Chief of Staff Nagano found themselves in rare agreement, chorusing their opposition to an assault on Hawaii. Sugiyama did, however, show understanding toward the navy staff's preferences for stage two operations: seizing Fiji and Samoa. Although a Fiji-Samoa invasion constituted an expansion of the Pacific perimeter, Sugiyama did not oppose it on the understanding that little if any army support would be required.

Unaware of the army-navy *modus vivendi* on Fiji-Samoa, Commander Akira Sasaki of the Combined Fleet arrived in Tokyo on 13 January to report that Ugaki's "Eastern Operation" preliminary planning had been completed. To his surprise, Sasaki was told that the army and navy leadership absolutely opposed an assault on Hawaii. Moreover, both staffs had just reached a provisional agreement designating Fiji and Samoa as the next major targets in the Pacific.

This unexpected turn of events shocked and disappointed Ugaki, who had until then been unaware of any serious opposition to "Eastern Operation." On 14 January Ugaki wrote in his diary that Japan must seize Midway, Palmyra, Johnston, and Hawaii. "Eastern Operation" must be carried out, and the sooner the better, for time favored the enemy.

Faced with Tokyo's disapproval of "Eastern Operation," Yamamoto ordered Ugaki to prepare additional options to present to the Navy General Staff. Both men had every intention of keeping the Hawaii plan alive, but they knew that the Combined Fleet could not ignore other possibilities. Besides, the more that the Combined Fleet staff knew about all the alternatives, the more convincingly it could argue in support of its favorite plan of action.

Ugaki and his team worked uninterruptedly throughout the last half of January drawing up plans for an assault on Ceylon, an invasion of Australia, support for the Army in Burma, and for the seizure of Fiji and Samoa. Of all these options, the Fiji-Samoa operation evoked the least enthusiasm, for it served no vital strategic purpose and left the U.S. Pacific Fleet untouched.

Meanwhile, a flicker of interest in "Eastern Operation" flashed momentarily within the Navy General Staff. At an army-navy staff officers' conference on 23 January, Tomioka's assistant, Commander Yūji Yamamoto (no relation to the admiral), spoke up and declared that a Hawaii invasion deserved serious consideration. His remark prompted one army officer present to conclude that the Navy General Staff was being infected by Combined Fleet adventurism. Five days later, General Tanaka noted in his diary that the two services had fundamentally different ideals about how the war should be prosecuted: the navy was looking for a decisive battle that would end hostilities; the army wanted to build up an impregnable sphere for a prolonged war.

Strategic differences notwithstanding, the services did work out a *modus vivendi* for the record on 26 January. At this meeting, army and navy staff officers agreed to give top priority to Fiji and Samoa, thus confirming the Sugiyama-Nagano understanding of 10 January. Yūji Yamamoto immediately flew to Hashirajima to convey the bad news to Ugaki. Upon his return to Tokyo several days later, he reported to Captain Tomioka that the Combined Fleet was preparing several operational options. Both men knew that for all the "options," Ugaki and his men still had their sights on Hawaii.

Hawaii's strategic significance was suddenly made clear on 1 February, when the Americans carried out the first of a series of carrier-launched air raids on the Marshall Islands, Japan's mid-Pacific outposts. The Japanese press denigraded the action as "guerrilla tactics," but Yamamoto and Ugaki were impressed and disturbed by the reach of Hawaii-based naval air power. Ugaki immediately sent Captain Shigeru Fujii to Tokyo on 2 February to reiterate to the Navy Staff the urgency of "Eastern Operation."

Like his predecessors, Fujii's advocacy of a Hawaii invasion fell upon unreceptive ears. Tomioka stolidly repeated that Hawaii was logistically beyond Japan's reach. He added that the Americans probably now had three divisions deployed on Oahu. It would take several divisions to dislodge them, and the Imperial Army was not going to be talked into diverting that many men to the middle of the Pacific. Fujii returned to Hashirajima empty-handed.

As differences between the Navy General Staff and the Combined Fleet deepened during January and February of 1942, so did army-navy disagreements over the issue of perimeter expansion. These impasses were manifestly delaying the implementation of a revised stage two. And delays were costing Japan opportunities to exploit the momentum of those early victories, opportunities that were not likely to repeat themselves. Prime Minister Tōjō recognized this danger and was disturbed by it. At a liaison conference on 2 February, he exhorted both services to clarify their war aims for the sake of the whole nation. "How is the war going to be waged from now on? This question must be researched, not only from the point of view of [army-navy] command relations but from the point of view of the nation." Tōjō's plea notwithstanding, the services did little to resolve their differences or to improve operational coordination. Paying nominal obeisance to cooperation by composing vaguely phrased general plans, the army and navy continued in practice to act more or less independently.

The lack of interservice cooperation naturally had a direct impact upon the chances of "Eastern Operation" ever taking place. Without army participation, any invasion of Hawaii was out of the question. Therefore, both the Navy General Staff and the Combined Fleet staff found themselves thinking in terms of operations that could be conducted purely with naval units. An operation that under other circumstances would have a low priority might be adopted because it could be carried out by the navy alone or because it aroused no strong opposition within the navy itself.

An attack on Ceylon was just such an operation—secondary in strategic importance, low in controversial potential. Although they had no intention of invading Ceylon in 1942, army leaders raised no objections to a navy raid on the island, for such an operation would get part of the Combined Fleet into the Indian Ocean where it could indirectly support the Burma campaign and clear the way for an anticipated link-up with the Germans advancing across North Africa and the Caucasus. The Navy General Staff accepted a Ceylon raid as a low-risk way to knock the British off balance while preserving the Combined Fleet for a decisive battle with the Americans at some time in the future. Admiral Yamamoto was not enthusiastic about a Ceylon operation, but he recognized that it was the next best alternative to "Eastern Operation," which at least for the time being had foundered on Army and Navy General Staff intransigence. Besides, Ceylon could be construed as a stepping-stone to Hawaii. If Nagumo destroyed British naval forces in the Indian Ocean, the Combined Fleet would be able to concentrate its carriers in the Pacific without worrying about an unguarded rear.

Ugaki preferred to go straight for Hawaii without making a detour to Ceylon. He knew that time was working against Japan. With each passing day, the Americans were not only strengthening Hawaii's defenses but were turning the islands into a springboard for sallies into the western Pacific. The 1 February raid on the Marshalls was just a foretaste of worse to come.

Only through vigorous self-discipline was Ugaki able to shelve "Eastern Operation" and turn his attention to the Indian Ocean during February. But before the month was out, he found an energetic ally within the Combined Fleet: Admiral Tamon Yamaguchi, commander of the Second Carrier Division. Like Yamamoto, Yamaguchi blended a firsthand knowledge of the United States with an outspoken advocacy of air power. He had studied at Princeton University (1921–1923) and served as naval attaché in Washington (1934–1936) before being appointed to lead the Navy's Second Air Corps late in 1940. Yamaguchi differed from Yamamoto, however, in one important respect. He refused to give weight to Japan's strategic weakness and instead favored bold offensive action at every opportunity.

Yamaguchi perceived one of these opportunities on 8 December 1941, on his flagship, the carrier *Hiryū*, as he watched planes returning from Pearl Harbor. He had assumed that Nagumo would order another strike on Pearl Harbor to destroy fuel tanks and dry docks. The failure of this order to materialize puzzled and disappointed him. Now, ten weeks later, Yamaguchi was going to take advantage of another opportunity and present his colleagues with a blueprint for victory.

The occasion was a mock-up rehearsal for the Ceylon operation that took place aboard Yamamoto's new flagship, the battleship *Yamato*, on 20–23 February 1942. In attendance were Rear Admiral Fukudome and Captain Tomioka from Navy General Staff, Colonel Kumao Iimoto from Army General Staff, and senior line officers of the Combined Fleet. During the rehearsal Yamaguchi distributed copies of his blueprint to half a dozen Combined Fleet and Navy General Staff officers (but not to the army representative). The blueprint included a plan for an invasion of Hawaii. But it differed from Ugaki's "Eastern Operation" in two respects. It put almost exclusive emphasis upon naval air power, and it envisioned Hawaii's capture as preparatory to strikes on the United States mainland.

The "Yamaguchi plan" was predicated upon a crash naval and air construction program that would propel a series of increasingly ambitious operations in the Indian and Pacific oceans starting in May 1942 and culminating in the autumn of 1943. There would be an invasion of Ceylon in May, during which British naval forces in the Indian Ocean would be destroyed. During June and July landings would be made on Fiji, Samoa, New Caledonia, New Zealand, and northern Australia. During August and September the Aleutians would be occupied, followed by Midway, Johnston, and Palmyra islands in November and December. The climactic assault on Hawaii would commence in December 1942 or January 1943.

A formidable armada was to subdue American resistance on and around Hawaii. Yamaguchi estimated that there would be three task forces comprising 14 carriers, 477 Zero fighters, 159 bombers, and 144 torpedo planes. In addition, there would be 100 long-range bombers, 200 Zero fighters, and 50 amphibious planes based on Midway, Johnston, and Palmyra. Some 300 large submarines capable of cruising 9,000 miles over a period of three months would converge on Hawaiian waters. The plan made no mention of infantry, tanks, or troop transports. Perhaps Yamaguchi intended to leave the question of army participation open for future negotiation. But it is also possible that he believed that the Imperial Navy could carry out the entire operation on its own.

Yamaguchi's tactics for subduing Hawaii consisted of seizing Midway, Johnston, and Palmyra, imposing a blockade, and gradually tightening a noose of air and sea power around Oahu. Midway, Johnston, and Palmyra would be turned into forward bases for supporting carrier task forces as they annihilated the U.S. Pacific Fleet. Specially equipped long-range bombers would make strikes on Hawaiian targets from these islands. Submarines would sever surface communications between Hawaii and the West Coast and would prey upon interisland traffic, isolating each garrison.

An assault on the island of Hawaii would be carried out first, because it was sparsely populated and weakly defended. Once secured, the Big Island would be transformed into a giant aircraft carrier. Airfields would be constructed on cleared canefields and over old lava flows to accommodate units based on Midway, Johnston, and Palmyra. From Hawaii, the Imperial Navy would wrest control of Oahu's skies. Isolated and pummeled, Oahu would eventually fall to an amphibious assault. With Oahu in Japanese hands, the remaining neighbor islands would capitulate.

Yamaguchi did not see peace negotiations opening after the conquest of Hawaii. He favored carrying the war to the West Coast, hitting the enemy in its homeland and denying it access to overseas supplies. Carrier task forces based at Pearl Harbor would stalk everything that floated between Anchorage and San Diego. The Panama Canal would be rendered unusable. California oilfields were to be seized, inferentially to provide fuel for Imperial forces operating in the eastern Pacific. Yamaguchi ended his proposal with references to expeditions in South America in conjunction with the Wehrmacht and Italian units.

Reactions to this document on the part of those officers who received copies of it on the *Yamato* are unfortunately not known. With the possible exception of Ugaki and Kuroshima, both the Navy General Staff and the Combined Fleet staff probably responded unenthusiastically. The army, however, appears to have gotten wind of the "Yamaguchi plan," and its reactions were unambiguous.

Without mentioning the "Yamaguchi plan" by name, General Tanaka came out strongly against a Hawaii invasion at the 27 February meeting of army-navy staff operations chiefs. After citing logistical obstacles and warning of the dangers of overextension, he stated that the army's equipment was not up to the task. Amphibious assaults against an entrenched defense were extremely difficult. The only way to take Oahu would be to throw large numbers of troops on the beaches, supported by heavy tanks. The army had not yet developed a heavy tank that could function in amphibious landings. One prototype had been built, but it turned out to be unsuitable. Tanaka concluded his remarks by an implied criticism of the Combined Fleet's political prognostications: the fall of Hawaii, he warned, would not in itself force America to the peace table. To think that it would was self-delusion.

These intra- and interservice disagreements about strategic priorities took place against a background of uninterrupted Japanese triumphs in the field during the first ten weeks of 1942. Manila was occupied on 2 January and Rabaul on 23 January. On 4 February an Anglo-American-Dutch squadron was mauled in the Battle of Java Sea. Singapore fell on 15 February, Batavia on 3 March, and Rangoon on 8 March. Tactical strikes were already being made well beyond the periphery: a devastating air raid on Port Darwin, Australia (19 February), a shelling of the California coast near Santa Barbara by submarine (23 February); and a night bombing sortie over Honolulu (4 March). Yet these exploits would prove evanescent unless they could be sustained and directed in accordance with a strategic vision shared by both services. Despite a dozen meetings, army and navy staff officers still had not found a workable consensus.

On 4 March 1942 key officers from the army and navy general staffs and ministries came together for yet another attempt to compose their differences. This time they managed to reach a consensus—of sorts. Present were Rear Admiral Takazumi Oka and Lieutenant General Akira Mutō, respective heads of the navy and army ministries' military affairs sections, and Tanaka and Fukudome from the army and navy general staffs' operations sections.

At this meeting, a wide range of topics came under discussion, among the most sensitive being the direction and scope of future operations. On this matter, compromise was reached. The navy committed itself to eliminating British forces in the Indian Ocean and undertook not to launch any major campaign beyond the Pacific perimeter in the near future (that is toward Fiji, Samoa, or Hawaii). The army, in turn, acquiesced to tactical operations by the navy beyond the Pacific perimeter ("as opportunities arise") and committed itself to making feasibility studies of invasions of Hawaii, Australia, and Ceylon that might be put into practice at some time in the future (when was left vague). These compromises were recorded in a document entitled: "Fundamental Outline of Recommendations for Future War Leadership."

The army-navy *modus vivendi* of 4 March formed the main item on the agenda of a liaison conference that convened on 7 March. After Army Vice Chief of Staff Lieutenant General Moritake Tanabe had read aloud the "Fundamental Outline," Finance Minister Okinori Kaya asked what was meant by "expanding the existing war achievements" *(kitoku no senka o kakudai)*. Tanabe answered that the phrase referred to possible "supplementary operations" such as invasions of Hawaii, Ceylon, and Australia, which the army and navy were studying. The discussion then shifted to China, but after a few minutes Navy Ministry Military Affairs Bureau Chief Oka reintroduced the subject of "supplementary operations." In a thinly veiled criticism of army caution, Oka averred that Japan could not win the war by being passive in the Pacific. It was, Oka said, vitally important to maintain momentum by launching offensives against targets like Hawaii and Australia, targets that the enemy were turning into springboards for counterattacks. Oka's innuendoes elicited no response from army officers in attendance, but it must have been clear to every listener that the "Fundamental Outline" had not resolved interservice rivalries.

On 11 March another liaison conference convened and formally ratified the "Fundamental Outline." The document was presented to the emperor on 13 March by Prime Minister Tōjō, Army Chief of Staff Sugiyama, and Navy Chief of Staff Nagano.

In some ways, the "Fundamental Outline" obscured rather than clarified Japan's war aims. Couched in nebulous language so as to accommodate both army and navy perspectives, the document lent itself to contradictory interpretations. For example, a passage calling for "more positive war leadership" *(issō sekkyokuteki naru senső shidō)* could mean almost anything. Indeed, a misunderstanding over this very phrase occurred one day after the "Fundamental Outline" was introduced at the 7 March liaison conference. On 8 March Captain Miwa of Combined Fleet staff met with Captain Kami of Navy General Staff Planning Section to discuss long-term operational plans. Kami told Miwa that the General Staff endorsed "more positive war leadership" and added that the invasion could be set for October. Miwa assumed that Kami was talking about Hawaii and rushed back to Hashirajima to tell Ugaki the good news. Their celebrations were cut short several days later when word came that Kami had been referring to Ceylon, not Hawaii.

On 9 March Admiral Yamamoto ordered Vice Admiral Nagumo to start preparation for a carrier task force attack on British forces in the Ceylon area. During the next month, the Imperial Navy gave the British a terrible beating in the Indian Ocean. But neither Yamamoto nor Ugaki had given up their preoccupation with Hawaii. In fact, while Nagumo's carriers prowled off Ceylon, the Combined Fleet staff was working on a new sortie in the mid-Pacific. To circumvent army opposition, this operation would be carried out without infantry or armor. To win support from the Navy General Staff, the operation was designed to lure the U.S. Pacific Fleet into a "decisive battle" at a point where the Imperial

Navy could use land-based as well as carrier planes against it. It was called "Midway Operation."

Midway is part of the Hawaiian archipelago. The Combined Fleet staff, conditioned to be circumspect after months of encountering obstacles in Tokyo's military bureaucracy, did not advertise this fact, but it is safe to assume that every officer involved in the planning for Midway knew that its big brother, "Eastern Operation," was still alive and well.

CHAPTER VII

Stillborn Invasion

Conceived and developed by Combined Fleet staff officers during March 1942, the Midway Operation was the child of expediency. The army's refusal during January and February to commit troops to a Hawaii invasion convinced Yamamoto and Ugaki that the next mid-Pacific offensive would have to be conducted without army participation. Differences between the Navy General Staff and the Combined Fleet on whether to give priority to Hawaii or to Fiji-Samoa prompted Yamamoto to look for a compromise. The compromise that he and Ugaki wanted was one that would serve the strategic objectives of "Eastern Operation" discreetly enough so that the Navy General Staff would not get alarmed yet substantially enough so that a Hawaii invasion could take place at the end of 1942 or in early 1943. Midway filled this prescription—or so Combined Fleet planners thought.

Midway's significance derived from its location rather than its size. Consisting of two islets that barely rise above sea level, surrounded by a barrier reef, the atoll occupies only a few acres. Midway's name reflects its mid-Pacific location, although it lies closer to Yokohama (2,250 miles) than to San Francisco (2,800 miles). Pearl Harbor is 1,135 miles to the southeast of Midway. Between Midway and Oahu the ocean is dotted with islets, atolls, reefs, seamounts, and one of the main islands of the Hawaiian chain, Kauai. In 1942 Midway had one airstrip, the only runway between Wake Island (renamed Ōtorijima after the Japanese occupation) and Kauai. Admiral Nagumo appropriately called Midway "the sentry for Hawaii."

Exactly when research on a Midway operation began cannot be determined, but it is a reasonable assumption to think in terms of the first week of March 1942, when the Ceylon attack was about to be launched and Combined Fleet planners started looking for a Pacific target consistent with an eventual Hawaii invasion yet palatable to the Navy General Staff. Midway promised to meet both requirements. As the western outpost of the Hawaiian archipelago (a 1942 Japanese study called it the "ninth inhabited Hawaiian Island"), it guarded the approaches to Pearl Harbor. In American hands, Midway was a forward base for submarines and carriers operating in the western Pacific. Under Japanese control, it could serve as a stepping-stone to the main Hawaiian islands.

Midway was to serve as bait for the U.S. Pacific Fleet. Yamamoto and Ugaki felt certain that the Americans valued the island too highly to let the Japanese seize it without sending out those carriers that had escaped destruction at Pearl Harbor on 7 December. As a lure to the U.S. Pacific Fleet, Midway would provide Japan with that "decisive battle" under circumstances favorable to the Combined Fleet.

Some postwar writers have stated that Yamamoto intended to urge his government to open peace negotiations with the United States if Japan had reaped a victory at Midway. This idea may have occurred to the commander in chief, but the preponderance of evidence suggests that he wanted to have Hawaii in hand before making any peace overtures.

Midway itself was but one step toward Hawaii, and a tenuous step at that, for even with Midway in Japanese hands the main Hawaiian islands could not be directly attacked. Apart from Army and Navy General Staff objections, there were formidable logistic obstacles. Midway lies over one thousand miles from Oahu. The Combined Fleet's main tactical fighter (the Zero) had a range of 600–700 miles. The only intermediate airfields were on Kauai, which lay in the shadow of American air power on Oahu.

Consequently the Midway Operation was aimed essentially at the U.S. Pacific Fleet. Following the anticipated destruction of American carriers which Midway's occupation would engender, the Combined Fleet would move on to Johnston Island, which would put Japanese land-based planes to within 710 miles of Honolulu. From Johnston, an assault on the Big Island would be launched. A Combined Fleet operations officer, Commander Yasuji

Watanabe, recalled after the war: "If we could, we wanted to go to Pearl Harbor; but it was not authorized, because it was too far. We intended to capture small islands between Midway and Pearl Harbor. If we captured these islands, the land-based planes could attack Pearl Harbor. We wanted to capture Pearl Harbor later."

Innocuously packaged, the Midway Operation nevertheless aroused suspicions in Tokyo as a Trojan horse concealing "Eastern Operation." As early as 13 March 1942, Navy General Staff planning officer Captain Tomioka shared his doubts about Midway with his army counterpart, Major General Tanaka. Tanaka caught the implications immediately and reported them to Chief of Army Staff Sugiyama. On 19 March Sugiyama expressed his opposition directly to the emperor, stating that whatever value a Hawaii invasion might have, the value was outweighed by the difficulties of holding such a remote group of islands.

Undeterred, Combined Fleet staff officers went ahead with calculations and projections. By 31 March they had completed a plan of operation for Yamamoto's inspection. It envisaged the following timetable: Midway and some of the Aleutians would be seized early in June, triggering a decisive battle with the U.S. Pacific Fleet. Johnston and Palmyra were to be occupied in August. The attack on the Big Island (Hawaii) would begin in October, culminating in an assault on Oahu in March 1943. As a gesture to win Navy General Staff acquiescence, the plan called for an attack on (but not occupation of) Fiji and Samoa in July 1942.

Captain Yoshitake Miwa, Ugaki's principal assistant, submitted the plan to Yamamoto on 1 April. The commander in chief approved it and ordered his operations officer, Watanabe, to take it to the Navy General Staff for approval.

Watanabe arrived in Tokyo on 3 April and immediately showed the plan to Commander Tatsukichi Miyo, a member of Captain Tomioka's Planning Section. Miyo reacted so negatively that according to one source Watanabe "was on the verge of angry tears." Tomioka then walked in and joined the two officers. Adding his disapproval to that of Miyo, Tomioka said that a Midway operation would put Japanese forces at the wrong place at the wrong time. Coming so close after the Pearl Harbor attack, the Americans would be on the alert around Hawaii. American carriers would not sortie to defend Midway. Instead, the Americans would reinforce Hawaii and mount air attacks against Midway, making the atoll impossible for the Japanese to retain. The Combined Fleet should think seriously about operations that had a better chance of success, with less risk.

Miyo and Tomioka failed to budge Watanabe. The young commander flatly stated that if the Navy General Staff did not approve the Midway operation, Yamamoto would resign as commander in chief of the Combined Fleet.

Intense, often heated, discussions continued during the following day. On 5 April the matter was referred to Tomioka's superior, Admiral Fukudome, who in turn talked with Navy Chief of Staff Nagano. Hearing of Yamamoto's threat to resign, Nagano decided to override the objections of his subordinates and approve the Midway operation. Nagano's action implied tentative Navy General Staff approval of a Hawaii invasion later in the year, for this was generally understood to be part of the Midway plan.

Now that the Combined Fleet had convinced the Navy General Staff about Midway/Hawaii, it was up to the Navy General Staff to sell the idea to the army. This was not an easy task for Tomioka. For one thing, he doubted the wisdom of the operation. For another, army officers were not going to be swayed by the threat of Yamamoto's resignation.

Tomioka met with Major General Tanaka on 12 April and gave him a tactfully diluted version of the Midway plan (that is, without mentioning Hawaii as a long-term objective). But Tanaka was too sharp not to catch the implications. He seems to have suspected all along that differences between the Navy General Staff and the Combined Fleet were more apparent than real, that Yamamoto could always have his way if he made a fuss. After listening to Tomioka's presentation, Tanaka remarked that Midway was nothing but the navy's stepping-stone to Hawaii. He then reminded his naval colleague that both constituted an unwarranted extension of Japan's perimeter. A Hawaii assault, he warned, would undermine Japan's entire war effort. The empire must concentrate on consolidating control of Southeast Asia and building an impregnable sphere in Greater East Asia. Tanaka concluded by categorically refusing to cooperate. The army would release no troops for either Midway or the Aleutians.

Despite Tanaka's rebuff, Tomioka went ahead and composed a report that outlined projected naval operations in the short-term and long-term future. Entitled "Imperial Navy Operational Plans for Stage Two of the Greater East Asia War," the document marked a significant departure from traditional Navy General Staff strategic thinking. It formalized acceptance of ideas that during the past four months had been championed by the Combined Fleet.

The contents of the report can be summarized as follows. The Indian Ocean, following the Ceylon operation, was to be relegated to a secondary status. So was the southwestern Pacific (Fiji and Samoa, the Navy General Staff's pet targets, were not even mentioned). Henceforth, the central Pacific would be given the highest strategic priority. Midway was to be seized and the U.S. Pacific Fleet destroyed. Naval forces alone (armed sailors trained in amphibious maneuvers) would make the landings on Midway. The achievement of these objectives would signal an end to revised stage two. In stage three, Johnston and Palmyra islands would be occupied. The invasion of Hawaii would take place in stage four. Notwithstanding Tanaka's refusal to release troops for Midway, the report stated that the projected Hawaii assault would be carried out "in cooperation with the Imperial Army."

On 16 April 1942, Chief of Navy Staff Nagano submitted this plan to the emperor. Chief of Army Staff Sugiyama would probably have lodged a protest, had not an unexpected incident occurred two days later that forced the army to revise radically its attitude to the Pacific in general and to Hawaii in particular. On 18 April sixteen B-25 bombers, launched from the carrier *Hornet*, flew over Tokyo, Yokohama, Nagoya, and Kobe. Although the *Hornet* had been sighted by a patrol boat that reported its position, the planes met virtually no resistance. After dropping some bombs, they flew unscathed across Japan to China and the USSR.

Japan suffered little physical destruction on 18 April. The press denounced what were portrayed as deliberate attacks on schools and hospitals. It disparagingly referred to the sortie as "do little," punning on the surname of the commander of the raid Colonel James Doolittle. The psychological effects of the Doolittle raid, however, were serious. Frustration gripped officers of the Imperial Navy, for the navy bore responsibility for guarding Japan's maritime approaches. It was a humiliation for the Combined Fleet. Hitherto undefeated and supposedly in control of the western Pacific, it had allowed a handful of enemy planes to penetrate the heart of the empire. Navy Chief of Staff Nagano, who was in Tokyo on 18 April and heard the explosions, is said to have muttered:

"Kore de wa naranu, kore de wa naranu ne" (This shouldn't happen. This simply should not happen).

Yamamoto reacted with mortification. He closeted himself in his cabin on the *Yamato* for hours, leaving Ugaki to deal with pursuit of the intruders.

For a few hours, it was not known from where Doolittle's planes had been launched. Although the *Hornet* had been sighted that morning, few intelligence officers believed that B-25's could take off from the deck of a carrier. There were speculations that the planes had come from Soviet bases in Kamchatka. Midway was also considered a possible launching site. After interrogation of captured pilots, it became clear that the *Hornet* had indeed brought B-25's to Japan's doorstep. And the *Hornet* had come from Hawaii.

Doolittle's raid confirmed Ugaki's worst fears. Since the war's outbreak, the Combined Fleet chief of staff had suspected that Hawaii-based carriers would sooner or later pose a direct threat to Japan. Ugaki's anxieties had not been shared by his subordinates, who doubted that the Americans were capable of recovering from the Pearl Harbor attack within six months. But Ugaki could not forget that no carriers had been destroyed on 7 December. His submarine monitors had informed him that carriers were coming and going to and from Pearl Harbor to unknown destinations. When carrier-launched planes raided the Marshalls in early February, Ugaki had hard evidence that the enemy was already probing Japan's perimeter. Further air attacks on Wake (4 February) and Rabaul (20 February) underlined the mobility of Hawaii-based carriers. When the Americans struck on 4 March at Marcus Island, a mere 1,000 miles from Tokyo, Ugaki sensed real danger to the home islands. Six weeks later his fears were confirmed.

And yet, the Doolittle raid had one salutary consequence from Ugaki's perspective. It accomplished what neither the Combined Fleet nor the Navy General Staff had been able to do. It convinced army leaders that the Pacific was an important theater. For the first time, the Army General Staff paid serious attention to the Pacific in general and to Hawaii in particular.

Major General Tanaka made an about-face. On 19 April one day after the Doolittle raid, he met with Tomioka and stated that he was reconsidering his reservations about expanding the Pacific perimeter. One day later, Tanaka formally notified Tomioka that the Army General Staff had decided to participate in the Midway operation. Troops would also be provided for an assault on Attu and Kiska in the Aleutians. Informally, he expressed an interest in learning more about "Eastern Operation."

Ironically, by opening the Imperial Army's eyes to Hawaii's strategic importance, the Doolittle raid prompted Tokyo to think seriously about seizing the archipelago. Major General Tanaka, who until 18 April had spearheaded army opposition to Combined Fleet strategies in the mid-Pacific, suddenly started to urge his superiors to support such strategies.

At first glance, Shin'ichi Tanaka made an unlikely champion for a "Hawaii-first" strategy. Both his career and his convictions until April 1942 were those of a typical army continentalist. Born in 1893 in Hokkaido, Tanaka had spent considerable time in the USSR, Germany, and Manchuria before his appointment as Army General Staff operations chief in November 1940. Between 8 December 1941 and 18 April 1942 he had argued consistently against expanding the Pacific perimeter. Again and again he told Tomioka that Japan must prepare itself for a long-term war by consolidating existing territories under its control and building an "impregnable" self-sufficient sphere in East and Southeast Asia.

After Doolittle, however, Tanaka began to sound more and more like a Combined Fleet strategist. He started talking about bold initiatives in the central Pacific so as to end the war quickly. By mid-May 1942, Tanaka was being described by another army staff officer as evincing *netsui* (enthusiasm) about "Eastern Operation."

Tanaka's conversion occurred more quickly than that of the Army General Staff as a whole. Lack of documentation and of surviving witnesses precludes a detailed reconstruction of discussions within the army leadership about whether it should provide troops only for the Midway operation or go all the way and commit itself to the conquest of Hawaii. The outcome of these discussions, however, is unambiguous. The army decided to seize Hawaii. A month after the Doolittle raid this decision was officially communicated to field commanders. Senior field officers learned of the Hawaii invasion plans upon receipt of an order dated 23 May 1942 issued by Imperial Headquarters to commanders of the northern and southern area armies. The order, which called for the training of certain units designated to carry out an assault on the Hawaiian Islands, read as follows:

Dairikushi* no. 1159

The following is ordered on the basis of *Dairikushi* no. 564.†

The commander of the Southern [Northern] Area Army shall expedite the training of the Second [Seventh] Division by the end of September 1942 in accordance with the following specifications.

   I. Proposed theater of operations
      1. Coastal configuration is divided into areas where mountains approach the sea, forming precipitous cliffs, and low-lying areas with relatively gentle slopes. Many coastal sections have coral reefs lying several hundred meters from shore. Inland areas are largely mountainous, but there is also flat land on which military units can operate without obstructions.
      2. Various obstacles deployed in the water and at the water's edge—mines, pillboxes, long-range artillery—form a strong coast defense. Fortified positions and permanent defense installations are in the interior.
      3. The enemy possesses superior air power.

  II. Division composition and equipment
      Wartime composition minus horses but supplemented by quick-firing guns, smoke-screen equipment, and flame-throwers. In addition, tank and heavy field artillery units will be placed under divisional command.

 III. Principal training objectives
      1. Main forces will land in coastal areas that have favorable configurations and overcome resistance by an entrenched enemy. Landings will be carried out under skies dominated by enemy air power. In landings, special emphasis will be placed on close cooperation of participating units and on the use of smokescreens.
      2. A part of our forces will conduct landings along difficult portions of the coast, break through local enemy defenders, and move into inland mountainous areas.
      3. There will be training for landings on coral reefs and coastal cliffs.

---

*An order issued without the Imperial Seal to field units.

†Order issued on 15 November 1941 relating to the seizure of certain areas in Southeast Asia and the southwestern Pacific.

4. After the landings, local enemy units shall be destroyed. Inland fortified positions shall be breached and occupied.

May 23, 1942

Imperial Headquarters specified only two divisions (the Second and the Seventh) in *Dairikushi* no. 1159, but additional units were soon designated for the Hawaii assault: an independent engineer regiment, one tank regiment, and the Fifty-Third Division. According to the recollections of former army staff officer Colonel Kumao Iimoto, orders to the Fifty-Third Division were issued through special channels so as to maximize secrecy about the total numbers of troops participating in the Hawaii invasion.

The choice of divisions that were to take part in the invasion raises some questions. None of the three were particularly well suited for a campaign in Hawaii. None had training in amphibious operations. Two were oriented toward the continent, and one lacked combat experience.

Take for example the Seventh Division. The Seventh, to be sure, was one of the finest fighting units in the Imperial Japanese Army. It boasted a proud tradition, including notable achievements during the Russo-Japanese War of 1904–1905. But the Seventh, to a degree unmatched by any other army unit, had its heart and soul in northern climes. Its home was Asahikawa on the island of Hokkaido. Its officers and men were trained to fight in cold regions and conditioned to regard the Soviet Union as their principal adversary. In May 1942, parts of the Seventh were deployed in Manchuria and parts in Karafuto (southern Sakhalin) and the Kurile Islands. The Seventh faced the Red Army, psychologically as well as physically. Hawaii was removed from the Seventh's experience and remote from the mainsprings of its morale.

The same can be said of the Second Division. Based in Sendai (in northern Honshū), the Second had a record of service on the continent. China, and more recently Southeast Asia, were its theaters of operations.

The Fifty-Third Division, based in Kyoto, existed as of May 1942 only on paper. It was in the process of being formed and—if popular prejudices are to be believed—formed from not the most promising material. Kyoto was universally respected as a cradle of traditional Japanese culture, but the fighting prowess of Kansai recruits received less flattering characterizations.

More appropriate divisions for a Hawaii invasion come to mind. For example, the Fifth was well trained in amphibious warfare. Moreover, based in Hiroshima, its rank and file consisted of troops who came from the same part of Japan as did a significant number of Hawaii *issei*. Common prefectural origins could have played a role in neutralizing resistance in Hawaii and enlisting civilian support for the occupation. The Sixth Division, based in Kumamoto (on the island of Kyushu), shared the same advantages as the Fifth.

Why were the Second, Seventh, and Fifty-Third selected and not the Fifth and Sixth? According to the noted military historian Ikuhiko Hata, the assignments for the Hawaii invasion were made on the basis of expediency. Although the Fifth and Sixth divisions may have been better suited for the campaign, they were either resting from major operations (the Fifth had taken part in the capture of Singapore) or were already engaged (the Sixth, in Central China, was soon to be transferred to the Solomon Islands). On the other hand, the Second Division was available, having been idle on Java after the conquest of that island in March. The Seventh was performing guard duty in Manchuria, Karafuto, and the Kuriles. Moreover, some units of the Seventh had been designated by the Army General Staff to take part in the Midway and Aleutian operations, scheduled for early June. Presumably, these units would form the nucleus of a Hawaii invasion force that would take shape incrementally as Johnston and Palmyra islands were subdued and occupied.

After months of resisting a Hawaii invasion as beyond its capabilities, the Army General Staff seemed to approach the task with a cavalier attitude. For example, *Dairikushi* no. 1159 assumes that landings will be carried out under enemy-controlled skies, a sharp departure from Ugaki's "Eastern Operation" and from the "Yamaguchi plan," both of which foresaw a step-by-step investment of the archipelago in order to ensure the local supremacy of Japanese air power at each stage. Furthermore, although the Army General Staff estimated on 2 April 1942 that the Americans had sixty-two thousand troops and eighty-nine hundred aircraft on Oahu and the neighbor islands, the projected invasion force would total no more than forty-five thousand men. That forty-five thousand infantrymen could cross reefs, wade ashore on beaches, and scale cliffs defended by superior numbers of entrenched enemy soldiers, under skies controlled by the enemy, suggests that the Army General Staff was, to say the least, confident.

Pride in the fighting prowess of Japanese soldiers may have led the Army General Staff to allocate so few troops to the Hawaii invasion. Moreover, despite fierce American resistance on Wake, Bataan, and Corregidor, there persisted in the Imperial Army a stereotype of the American soldier as "soft." The low regard with which many army officers held the American infantryman's combat ability continued until late 1942, when the Guadacanal campaign administered a painful lesson to those in a position to learn. It is also possible that the modest troop allocations designated in *Dairikushi* no. 1159 were preliminary. Additional units may have been earmarked for Hawaii, had the Midway operation succeeded.

After Imperial Headquarters had issued training orders to its field commanders, the Army General Staff turned its attention to putting together detailed studies of the intended target. On 3 June 1942, Tanaka instructed his subordinates in the Operations Section to prepare a feasibility study of an assault on Oahu. Two days later, an event occurred which made this study—together with all the Hawaii plans prepared within the Combined Fleet—superfluous.

On 5 June 1942 the Imperial Navy suffered an unprecedented defeat. The defeat was all the more stunning because it occurred at a moment when the Combined Fleet was expecting to reap a victory in the occupation of Midway Island. Midway's seizure was to have been bait to lure the U.S. Pacific Fleet to its doom in a "decisive battle." Instead, through a complex series of intelligence breakthroughs by the Americans, the Midway Task Force (led by Admiral Nagumo) walked into a deadly trap. Although bombed by Nagumo's planes, Midway Island was never assaulted, let alone occupied. The troopships retired after planes from three American carriers, whose presence in the area the Japanese did not suspect until it was too late, destroyed the four carriers comprising the core of Nagumo's force. At Midway the task force lost all of its carriers and 30 percent of its pilots, the cream of Japan's naval aviators. New carriers would eventually be built and young pilots trained, but they would never equal in quality what had been destroyed.

Admiral Tamon Yamaguchi, vociferous proponent of a Hawaii

invasion, also perished at Midway. He went down with his flagship, the carrier *Hiryū*. According to the recollections of Commander Watanabe, Yamaguchi, had he lived, would have eventually
succeeded Yamamoto as commander in chief of the Combined
Fleet.

Yamaguchi's death did more than deprive Japan of one of its
most daring commanders. It symbolized the fate of "Eastern Operation." On 8 June the Army General Staff issued *Dairikushi* no.
1176, which "postponed" training deadlines for the Second and
Seventh divisions. In fact their Hawaii assignments were terminated once and for all. Orders to the engineering and tank regiments were similarly cancelled. "Eastern Operation" died on 5
June 1942. Ugaki never mentioned it again. In abandoning a
Hawaii invasion, army and navy planners were recognizing realities. Japan no longer had the means to launch a transoceanic strike
of such magnitude. Without adequate carriers and trained pilots,
any attempt to take Hawaii would be suicidal.

Midway marked a turning point in Japanese naval strategy.
Despite the successful occupation of Attu and Kiska on 7 and 8
June, the Combined Fleet had lost the strategic initiative in the
Pacific once and for all when its four best carriers went up in
flames. Stung by the awesome suddenness of such a reverse, Yamamoto became obsessively cautious. Coralling his remaining carriers well within the perimeter, he shifted to a defensive posture.
After June 1942 the Combined Fleet launched tactical attacks and
in some cases even garnered local victories. But these were limited
and regional in character. They only served to postpone the inexo-
rable onslaught of a crushing American counteroffensive. As Yamamoto and Ugaki had foreseen and feared, Hawaii played a key
role in projecting American power across the Pacific to the very
shores of Japan.

Ironically, just as the army and navy discontinued planning for
a Hawaii invasion, civilian visions of Hawaii's impending "liberation" were becoming more graphic and extravagant. Indeed, most
civilian scenarios of Hawaii under Japanese rule were published
after Midway, when no possibility existed for their realization.

Several factors account for this paradox. First, strict military
censorship about the Midway disaster kept all but a handful of
Japanese ignorant of the strategic implications of that battle. Second, there were poor communications between the armed services'

operations sections and civilian agencies conducting research on areas scheduled to come under Japanese occupation. Third, the propensity of civilians, notably journalists, academics, and writers, to succumb to exhilarating speculations about the Greater East Asia Co-Prosperity Sphere ensured that Hawaii would animate imaginations long after any prospect for its capture had passed.

CHAPTER VIII

Victory Disease

To understand civilian writing about Hawaii during the Pacific War, it is necessary to bear in mind the psychological atmosphere that pervaded Japan during the year after Pearl Harbor. What may sound bombastic and whimsical in peacetime evoked in wartime Japan a genuine response from people (and there seems to have been many of them) who sincerely believed that a new age was dawning in Asia and the Pacific.

While Pearl Harbor outraged Americans, many Japanese reacted to the news by experiencing a deep sense of relief. Years of accumulated tensions suddenly found an exhilarating outlet. It was as if a stifling veil had been lifted, allowing people to breathe freely, to speak their minds, and to act without constraints. Dispelled at last was the agonizing uncertainty of whether Japan would accommodate or collide with the United States in Asia and the Pacific. In choosing war, the Imperial government had crossed the Rubicon. Millions of citizens sensed that their leaders had taken a fateful step, a step that might save *kokutai* (national polity) or that might destroy it. But regardless of the risks and the stakes, many citizens welcomed the end of temporizing diplomacy that seemed to lead only to slow national strangulation.

On the eve of 8 December the public mood in Japan was taut with frustration. Spiritually and materially mobilized for over three years, Japanese had watched an undeclared war in China drag on with no end in sight. Since 1939 Tokyo was convinced that Chiang Kai-shek's intransigence persisted only because of British and American aid. Washington was suspected of doing everything short of open hostilities to undermine Japan's position on the continent, a position built up through four decades of blood, sweat, and investments. Since 1940 the Americans were visibly trying to deny Japan access to the natural resources of Southeast Asia that had come to be regarded as vital to the empire's security and well-being. In the light of Uncle Sam's domination of Latin America, Washington's moralistic condemnation of Japanese activities in China looked infuriatingly hypocritical. When Franklin Roosevelt imposed an embargo on Japan in the summer of 1941, the country reacted to more than the specter of economic hardship. It was suffused with the visceral resentment of a weaker party humiliated —with impunity—by a stronger party. Past American behavior suddenly seemed to form a century-old pattern of pressures and insults: Commodore Perry's arrogance when "opening" Japan in 1853–1854; the "unequal treaties" of 1858; President Theodore Roosevelt's supposed cheating Japan out of the legitimate fruits of victory in the Russo-Japanese War; inferior naval ratios imposed on Japan by the Washington treaties; and the gratuitously insulting Exclusion Act (1924), which barred Japanese immigrants from the United States and its territories.

The announcement of war by Imperial Headquarters on the morning of 8 December released a torrent of pent-up emotions. The outbursts were so widespread and so intense that it would hardly be an exaggeration to say that Japan came close to undergoing a national catharsis. At last, the media exulted, the Yamato people would have it out with the arrogant Yankee and John Bull. Aware of America's wealth and of Britain's proud imperial tradition, citizens felt a special excitement and satisfaction upon hearing the initial war bulletins which without exception proclaimed spectacular, electrifying Japanese triumphs on fronts ranging from Hawaii to Malaya.

As reports of breathtaking military advances continued to reverberate through the press and radio during the remainder of 1941 and into the first months of 1942, some Japanese were caught up in a wave of euphoria. An uninterrupted succession of victories from Pearl Harbor through Guam, Wake, Hong Kong, Singapore, and Manila generated feelings of invincibility throughout the country. What before 8 December would have struck most people as whimsical was by February 1942 not just feasible but expected.

An upsurge of confidence in the "invincible" *(muteki)* Imperial

Army and Navy, together with what amounted to a national mystique of "Yamato spirit," spawned extravagant expectations of future conquests. After Japan's defeat in 1945, commentators dubbed the florid expectations of 1942 "victory disease" *(senshō-byō)*. In fact the expression was coined during the 1930s by Chūkō Ikezaki, the clairvoyant geopolitical strategist discussed in chapter 4.

"Victory disease" infected civilians and military personnel alike, but its most virulent symptoms showed up among politicians, journalists, writers, and academics. This can be explained in part by civilian ignorance about Japan's strategic weakness. Moreover, civilians were also prone to accept the stereotype of Americans as degenerate, selfish, and soft. Intellectuals in particular were wont to indulge in grand abstractions. Ecstatic over military triumphs, yet in 1942 still insulated from the battlefronts, their imaginations spun out exuberant fantasies.

Civilian rhetoric grew so extravagant early in 1942 that the prime minister, General Hideki Tōjō, felt compelled to caution elected officials and the public against overconfidence and to warn them that the struggle with America would be long and costly. Admiral Yamamoto also worried about the popular euphoria created by Japan's early victories. In a letter to his sister, the hero of Pearl Harbor somberly predicted that the war could last as long as ten years.

Such sober interjections notwithstanding, wildly optimistic prognoses continued to circulate in the media. True, some of these derived from propaganda disseminated by the army and navy information bureaux. But civilian commentators not infrequently interpolated their own visions, thereby inviting inflated public expectations and creating a gap between what informed military officers knew and what ordinary citizens believed.

Public commentary on the Pearl Harbor attack exaggerated the damage and minimized prospects for an American recovery. Radio Tokyo announced that 88 percent of army and navy personnel stationed in Hawaii on 8 December had been killed or wounded. In another broadcast, it was stated that the aircraft carrier *Enterprise* went down off Honolulu and that the *Lexington* was torpedoed shortly thereafter near Hawaii. Kaju Nakamura, director of Tokyo's Oriental Culture Summer University, asserted in the journal *Kaigai no Nippon* [Japan overseas] that all vessels at Pearl Harbor except for "minor cruisers" had been destroyed. A book on Hawaii which appeared early in 1942 affirmed that out of America's total of 388 warships, no less than 255 were in Pearl Harbor on 8 December.* Nor were naval vessels the only trophies. On 21 December, *Shūkan Asahi*, a popular weekly published by Japan's biggest and most prestigious newspaper, reported that Imperial Navy planes had obliterated the fuel storage tanks around Pearl Harbor. "The destruction of the Pacific Fleet at Pearl Harbor," confidently predicted economist Kichihiko Taniguchi early in 1942, "ruled out" an enemy counteroffensive.

Images of catastrophe in Hawaii spawned scenes of panic and confusion on the American mainland. Pundits described the United States as "paralyzed" and "gripped by fear" in the wake of Pearl Harbor. On 24 December, Radio Tokyo contrasted festively luminescent Ginza (Tokyo's fashionable shopping area) with the dark, empty streets of blacked-out American cities. After a Japanese submarine had lobbed a few salvoes in the direction of Santa Barbara, California, journalistic rhetoric soared. Radio Tokyo asserted on 24 January that the "bombardment" had inflicted "heavy damage in California" and had "unnerved the entire Pacific coast."

According to press reports, the United States was bracing itself for a siege. All shipping along the Pacific littoral had come to a halt. Roads near the shoreline of Washington, Oregon, and California were deserted except for an occasional tank. President Roosevelt had ordered the evacuation of West Coast factories to the Rocky Mountains. What afflicted the West Coast was not merely a regional emergency but a symptom of a national crisis. As Radio Tokyo intoned on 3 March 1942: "Sensible Americans know that the submarine shelling of the Pacific coast was a warning to the nation that the Paradise created by George Washington is on the verge of destruction."

Some commentators played up the ethnic tensions supposedly aggravated by the outbreak of hostilities with an Asian country. Racial minorities throughout the United States allegedly sensed that Japanese victories constituted blows against "Anglo-Saxon"† oppression. According to Masayoshi Murakami, a writer on Amer-

---

*Ninety-six ships were in Pearl Harbor on 7 December. Eighteen were sunk or heavily damaged.

†As used in Japan during World War II, "Anglo-Saxon" referred to a broader category of Caucasians than those of British nationality or ancestry.

ican affairs, news of Pearl Harbor electrified black communities from Harlem to Houston. By offering them hope, Japan was helping minorities in their struggle for social and economic justice. The educator Kaju Nakamura wrote that the upsurge of pro-Japanese sympathies among American minorities was strongest among Asian immigrants but that such sympathies were shared by other ethnic groups. "They [Asian-Americans] never felt so high an elation before, and we supposed that the same feeling was being shared by . . . colored races such as Negroes, American Indians, and Esquimaus [sic]".

The relocation of West Coast Japanese-Americans early in 1942 provoked not only expressions of concern and indignation, but it provided material for predictions of severe economic dislocation. An 18 June Radio Tokyo broadcast reported that "farms in California are facing total destruction since the Japanese have moved out." Some of those touched by "victory disease" supplemented predictions of America's disintegration with visions of a Pacific Ocean under Japanese control. By April 1942 the more outspoken commentators were talking as if the military requirements for this objective had already been achieved. The mercurial journalist Kōshin Murobuse* set the tone: "The western Pacific is in our hands. Our forces are almost in control of the entire Pacific. We have already won victories and we are continuing to win. It's no boast to state flatly that the final victory will be ours."

Going beyond Murobuse, Kaju Nakamura declared in the February 1942 issue of *Kaigai no Nippon* that the eastern Pacific was already under Japanese control. Radio Tokyo reinforced such misapprehensions in a 9 April broadcast that proclaimed that a recent submarine attack on the American West Coast had demonstrated that "the expanse of water between Hawaii and the United States is under control of Japanese warships."

The military propaganda organs helped to stoke the coals of such euphoria. A few days after the above Radio Tokyo broadcast,

*Murobuse (1892–1970) was a correspondent for *Asahi* and then for the journal *Kaizō* during the 1920s. His mercurial propensities revealed themselves during the 1930s and 1940s. In the 1930s, he gained prominence as an ultra-nationalist, editing the magazine *Nippon hyōron* [Japan review] from 1934 until 1945. After the war he made a political *volte-face*. In January 1946 at a Hibiya Park rally welcoming communist leader Sanzō Nosaka back from Yenan, China, Murobuse delivered a fiery speech denouncing Emperor Hirohito as a war criminal.

Captain Hideo Hiraide of the Naval Information Department, told reporters: "As the Imperial Navy now controls all the Pacific and Indian oceans, the day is imminent when these will be called the New Sea of Japan [*Shin Nipponkai*]."

Statements such as these almost certainly contributed to the heady speculations about the future of the Pacific by journalists and academics during 1942. In general these speculations envisioned reconstruction of the Pacific area under Japanese leadership. European and American influences were to be expunged. The Pacific was to be "restored" to its "natural unity" with Asia. Various reasons were given to justify Japan's leading role in this process. Ethnographic and geographic factors were commonly cited. "The Pacific Ocean is the *furusato* (native place) of the Japanese people," declared former Hawaii *Nippu jiji* reporter Sōen Yamashita in a 1942 book on Hawaii. Keio University sociologist Tetsuji Kada argued that all of the Pacific islands were "extensions" of the Japanese archipelago and as such should be treated as a single entity.

For rhetorical extravagance and originality, few proposals could equal those advanced by Kyoto Imperial University Professor Saneshige Komaki, the doyen of Japan's geopoliticians. In a series of academic and popular publications during 1942, Professor Komaki defined Japan's mission in apocalyptic terms. "The Pacific must become an Asian ocean," asserted Professor Komaki. It must be "restored" to its primeval condition in which nature and man, soil and culture, geography and history co-existed harmoniously. As the "greatest maritime people in the world," Japanese were uniquely qualified to carry out this task under the guiding principle of *kōdō* (imperial way).

Professor Komaki's first priority was to eliminate all "Anglo-Saxon" concepts that had intruded into the Pacific Basin during the past four centuries. One of these was the international dateline, which ran along the 180th meridian through the central part of the ocean. According to Komaki, the international dateline was a political instrument devised by Britain to create an artificial barrier between the eastern Pacific and Asia, to divide the Pacific between British and American spheres. "Anglo-Saxon" place names also constituted alien intrusions into the natural order of the Pacific and must be eliminated in favor of appellations reflecting the area's primordial Asian identity. The word "Pacific" fell into this category and would be discarded. To take its place, Komaki suggested—as did Captain Hiraide of the Naval Information Department—"New Sea of Japan" [*Shin Nipponkai*]. But Komaki felt that *Shin Nipponkai* should encompass more than just the Pacific, more than just the combined Pacific and Indian oceans. After all, the world's great oceans were connected. There was a world ocean, and *Shin Nipponkai* should be its name.

In the March 1942 issue of the political affairs journal *Seikai ōrai*, Professor Komaki gave "victory disease" an inspired expression: "Wherever imperial brilliance radiates, wherever imperial angry eagles fill the skies, wherever the Imperial Navy's flag advances, all these seas are an extension of Japan. All seas which are an extension of Japan are the *Shin Nipponkai*, the *Dai Nipponkai* [Great Sea of Japan]."

Professor Komaki did not neglect the world's land masses in his prescriptions for Asian nomenclatures. In the April 1942 issue of the academic journal *Chirigaku* [Geographical studies], he argued that the world's continents were geographically and historically extensions of Asia. Their names therefore should reflect this fact. Komaki suggested the following appellations as the most appropriate. Japan, China, Southeast Asia, India, and Siberia were to form the continent of "Asia"; Australia would be "South Asia"; North and South America, it followed, were "East Asia"; Africa—"Southwest Asia." And Europe? Not being a continent, Europe would have to be *"Ajia tairiku no hantō"* (a peninsula of the Asian continent).

In such an atmosphere, it would not be surprising if sooner or later someone proposed an invasion of the United States. Indeed, such talk did surface in the media. Proposals were made by journalists and educators who gave every appearance of acting on their own initiative. Occasionally, the idea of an invasion of the American mainland was stated obliquely, such as in the February 1942 issue of *Kaigai no Nippon*, where Kaju Nakamura predicted that Washington, D.C., and New York would soon come within range of Imperial bombers, inferentially from American mainland bases.

Other commentators advocated an invasion of the United States without mincing words. Hajime Mochizuki, military affairs reporter for the *Tokyo shinbun*, recommended that Japan occupy the mainland to the Rocky Mountains before opening peace negotiations. He calculated that the Americans would have no alternative but to accede to Japan's terms once Imperial forces had seized California, Oregon, and Washington, which collectively produced foodstuffs vital to national survival. Alternatively, continued Mochizuki, Japan might think about occupying the whole United States, from coast to coast. Whatever approach the empire adopted, the war would end with a triumphal entrance to a major American city. Mochizuki favored the following scenario:

> The Rising Sun flag flutters proudly over Rocky Mountain peaks. Following the fate of the Union Jack, the Stars and Stripes vanish forever from the globe. On this day, an imposing fleet steams toward New York City, the battleships shimmering on the Atlantic horizon. As the [Imperial] fleet enters New York harbor, huge crowds throng to the shoreline waving Rising Sun flags and screaming "Banzai!" On this stirring day, the Greater East Asia War comes to an end.

Another proposal for exploits on the North American continent emanated from the fertile imagination of Hideichi Noyori, editor of the Tokyo newspaper *Teitō nichinichi*. In the spring of 1942, Noyori brought out a collection of his own articles that had appeared in the paper from December 1941 until February 1942. Entitled *Bei-Ei gekimetsu* [Destroy America and England], the collection was prefaced with laudatory forewords by a former prime minister, two admirals, a general, a former minister of colonization, two Diet members, a business executive, a historian, and two prominent ultra-nationalists.* *Destroy America* dealt with, among other topics, operations in, and postwar disposition of, American territory. Noyori predicted that after seizing the Philippines and Hawaii, "landings on the American mainland must be considered as a matter of course." Estimating that Germany and Italy would strike the North American East Coast around May 1943 after settling with the USSR, Noyori opined that landings on the West Coast would not pose insuperable problems for Japan. What would Japan do with territories which she occupied? He favored

*General Senjūrō Hayashi, Admirals Naganori Ogasawara and Eisuke Yamamoto, General Kesago Nakajima, Kiyoshi Akita, Ichimin Tago, Chikubei Nakajima, Shingo Tsuda, Setsurei Miyake, Seigō Nakano, and Mitsuru Tōyama. Tago wrote an article for *Jitsugyō no Hawaii* in 1938. During the war, he served as speaker of the Lower House in the Diet.

annexation of Alaska and Hawaii. As for the forty-eight states, there were a number of options. One would be an equitable division of them among the Axis partners, or, Noyori suggested, Japan might consider balkanization.

> The time has come when it is feasible for Japan, Germany, and Italy to conduct operations on British and American home territories. This being the case, what contingencies can be anticipated for peace treaty negotiations? The annexation of Alaska, of Hawaii, of half of the United States, or setting up ten republics such as those of South America. . . . Japan's control sphere will be larger than the British Empire. More than half of humanity will realize its hopes of a new world under the rising sun of Japanese leadership.

Public discussion of operations on the American mainland was confined to a small circle of commentators, but talk of a Hawaii invasion was widespread during 1942. As the eminent philologist Yuzuru Shinmura put it in a tasteful understatement: "Events at Pearl Harbor seem to have stimulated a lively popular interest in Hawaii." This interest took several forms. Notable among them was the articulation of Hawaii's strategic importance for victory over the United States. The geographer Fusazō Motogawa stated this point succintly in the April 1942 issue of the journal *Chi-seigaku* [Geopolitics].

> Hawaii's strategic significance for Japan is immense. . . . In order to bring America to defeat, Japan will be thinking about options for achieving war aims: carrying out an invasion and occupation of Hawaii, using Hawaii as a base for striking the United States mainland, using Hawaii as a pivot for consolidating control of the South Pacific, and using Hawaii to interdict American military and commercial communications.

Sō Miyashiro, an economist working in the Research Department of the South Manchuria Railroad Company, graphically characterized Hawaii's importance for the United States—and by implication for Japan—in a 1942 book about the Islands. "If America loses Hawaii, it loses control of the Pacific. Hawaii is the nucleus of America's defenses. Who holds Hawaii holds the Pacific. Who loses Hawaii loses the Pacific. The day is not far off when America will lose Hawaii and be shut out from the Pacific."

If America was going to lose the Hawaiian Islands, it was only natural that Japan should acquire them. Acquisition was justified first of all by strategic necessity. Hawaii must be captured, propounded the sometime Marxist Yoshitarō Hirano, or the islands would always pose a security threat as stepping stones to Japan. "If only we could take Hawaii," wrote Miyashiro, "Japan would never again have to worry about the United States in the western and southern Pacific." Journalist Yōshi Kanda asserted that the whole problem of the Pacific could be solved once and for all by Japan taking Hawaii. *Tokyo shinbun* reporter Mochizuki expressed his anticipation poetically: "Hawaii's fate is like a lantern before the breeze." Professor Komaki preferred to put the matter in blunt prose: "Hawaii is a part of Japan."

In addition to strategic imperatives, geographical, ethnic, and historical reasons were adduced by Hawaii invasion advocates. One of Professor Komaki's students, Tsugio Murakami, spoke for a number of writers when he declared that it was Japan's duty to restore Hawaii to Asia, with which the islands were geographically, ethnically, and historically linked. Murakami conceded that Honolulu lay closer to San Francisco than to Tokyo, but he added that this spatial relationship was misleading. Hawaii in fact was an archipelago. Only open sea yawned between Hawaii and the American mainland, but between Hawaii and Japan the sea was sprinkled with islands, stepping-stones affording a geographical unity. Moreover, Hawaii formed an integral part of Japan's east-west axis (Manchuria-Hawaii) that intersected with Japan's north-south axis (Kurile Islands-Taiwan) in Tokyo.

Most writers mentioned that native Hawaiians, being Polynesians, were in fact Asians. Miyashiro, observing Hawaii from Japanese-occupied Manchuria, affirmed that the historical moment had come for Japan to "cleanse" Hawaii of the "pollution" incurred by nearly fifty years of alien rule.

Bolstered by notions of geographical propinquity, ethnic affinity, and historical justice, commentators often lapsed into sanguine speculations about Hawaii's liberation. Writing in the journal *Kaigai no Nippon*, Kaju Nakamura jubilated: "Hawaii is yet to be brought under the complete suzerainty of Japan, but it is expected that as Imperial Army operations progress, attacks upon American fortifications will be resumed with redoubled force."

Other commentators couched their expectations in rhetoric

common to much of wartime prose. Jihei Asai, a peripatetic geographer who had spent time in Hawaii before the war, wove a metaphor for invasion around a Hawaiian custom of departing visitors throwing their leis (garlands) overboard in the hope that by drifting ashore the leis would augur the visitors' return to the islands.

> Panicked at the surprise attack by Imperial forces, the American Navy won't have a chance to throw leis overboard as it departs. Even if the navy did throw leis, they would sink and turn to seaweed on the ocean floor. But the spirits of our young eagles [Imperial Navy personnel who perished on 7 December in midget submarines] who scattered cherry blossoms around the entrance of Pearl Harbor are awaiting the arrival of Imperial forces and shall help turn Hawaii into a forward base for our navy.

Humor as well as heroics occasionally surfaced in the symptoms of "victory disease." After he returned to Japan from the islands in October 1941, Sō Miyashiro produced a book on Hawaii in which he guessed how young island *dōhō* would someday joke about how a single salvo from the battleship *Mutsu* demolished the battery on Diamond Head, an extinct crater near Waikiki. Kichijirō Inoue, vice-chief of the culture department of the Osaka *Mainichi* newspaper, recalled how not long before Pearl Harbor he had been asked by a Japanese friend in Honolulu whether he would make a stopover in Hawaii while en route from California to Japan. "Only after we've occupied it," Inoue had laughingly answered. Writing about this incident in early 1942, Inoue mused that his joke had been prophetic.

Some writers offered suggestions about how to seize Hawaii. Most recommended blockade as an effective means to soften up the defenders. The most detailed public agenda for a Hawaii invasion came from Kyoto Imperial University's apprentice geopolitician Tsugio Murakami, a student of Professor Komaki. Murakami prefaced his recommendations with a forthright call to action. "We should not lose a moment in restoring Hawaii to its natural state, and our present task is to determine how it can be occupied."

While agreeing with other commentators about the utility of a blockade, Murakami warned that Hawaii was no easy target. First of all, the Americans also appreciated Hawaii's strategic importance. They knew that in Japanese hands Hawaii would expose the entire West Coast to attacks from the air and sea. Consequently, the Americans would resist any invasion fiercely. Second, Hawaii's location and environment posed substantial obstacles to invaders. The main islands were clustered at the eastern end of the archipelago, the part farthest from Japan and closest to California (one night's flying time). High surf and ubiquitous coral reefs made amphibious landings risky. Third, notwithstanding Pearl Harbor, the United States still had twenty-five thousand troops and many airfields on Oahu.

Murakami's prescription for dealing with these obstacles was to move step by step, consolidating each gain before moving further. Japan must first occupy Hawaii's sentinels: Midway, Johnston, Palmyra, Samoa, and the Aleutians. Using submarines Japan could then cast an iron net around the archipelago, cutting off the Hawaiian Islands not only from the American mainland but from each other. This tactic would put special pressure on Oahu, which had 60 percent of the population and imported 85 percent of its food supplies. Murakami studied the 1936–1937 shipping strike and noted that when the 100-day strike ended, Oahu had only a 14-day supply of food left.

Murakami thought it advisable for an invasion to be launched only when the above conditions had been fulfilled. Murakami's caution was shared by some but not all writers. Many expressed the opinion that Hawaii was like ripe fruit ready to fall into Japan's hands.

Within a month of the Pearl Harbor attack, Hawaii was publicly portrayed as already subjected to a crippling blockade. Retired Admiral Ryōzō Nakamura, writing in the January 1942 issue of *Taiheiyō* [Pacific Ocean], affirmed that the Americans were going to have great difficulty defending their Pacific island territories, because the Imperial Navy controlled the central Pacific. Radio Tokyo announced on 24 December 1941 that the Imperial Navy had cut fuel and food shipments from California to Hawaii. Another broadcast on 4 January 1942 reported that submarine shellings of Hilo and Kahului had inflicted "severe damage" on these Hawaiian towns. The announcer then evoked an image of wartime Hawaii that in the months ahead became a common stereotype: "Hawaii is under strict blockade by the Imperial Navy. How can it hold out for more than a couple of months? The planta-

tions are raising sugar and pineapple instead of the necessary vegetables."

Isolated and short of food, Hawaii seemed to be inching toward
internal collapse. A 10 January Radio Tokyo broadcast declared
that Hawaii's defenses were so poor that the military governor,
Lieutenant General Delos C. Emmons, had become "the laughing
stock of the people." On 30 January the Dōmei news agency
averred that Honolulu residents were thrown into "great confusion" by air raid sirens. A 5 February Radio Tokyo broadcast
announced that American authorities were evacuating women
and children to the West Coast or putting them into mountain
redoubts.

After the battle of Midway ("one of the greatest victories since
Pearl Harbor," according to Radio Tokyo), Hawaii's security was
said to have become even more precarious. The Imperial Army's
occupation of Attu (renamed "Atsuta"*) and Kiska ("Narukami")
in the Aleutians exposed Hawaii to direct bombing attacks, according to a 23 June broadcast. General Emmons, the announcer
continued, had ordered the evacuation of civilians in anticipation
of landings by Japanese forces.

"It is only a matter of time before the Hawaiian archipelago
falls into the hands of our Imperial Forces," predicted Pacific
affairs analyst Shinjirō Moriyasu in the summer of 1942. With
Hawaii's "liberation" a foregone conclusion, it was only natural
that a number of civilians began to give serious thought to how the
Islands should be treated under a Japanese occupation. One of
Japan's first tasks, however, would be to define Hawaii's role in the
Greater East Asia Co-Prosperity Sphere.

---

*A Shinto shrine in Nagoya.

CHAPTER IX

Hawaii in
Greater East Asia

On 12 December 1941 Japan's media announced that the four-day-old hostilities in the Pacific and Southeast Asia, together with the four-year-old China Incident, were henceforth to be referred to as the Greater East Asia War *(Dai Tōa sensō)*. During the next three and a half years, the word "Greater East Asia" reverberated through radio broadcasts, newspapers, magazines, academic monographs, Diet speeches, classrooms, and barracks. No other term so frequently surfaced in discussions of Japan's war aims. Imperial forces were waging a "holy war" to cleanse Greater East Asia of Chiang Kai-shek, communism, and Anglo-Saxons in order to build a Greater East Asia Co-Prosperity Sphere in which Asians could live and prosper under Imperial Japan's benevolent tutelage.

So closely was Greater East Asia identified with wartime propaganda that the term abruptly dropped out of sight in 1945 and has since been shunned. Japanese writers are loathe to employ something so tainted with emotional associations. Consequently, they have adopted the American nomenclatures: "World War II," and "Pacific War." Neither is very satisfactory. The former is too broad, because Japanese forces did not participate in the Soviet-German conflict, nor did they operate in Europe. The latter is too narrow, because it suggests that the war was basically oceanic and in doing so fails to reflect the major fighting that took place on the Asiatic continent. Despite its awkward connotations, "Greater East Asia War" remains the most accurate designation for a struggle that in Japan's perspective encompassed the Indian and Pacific oceans, East and Southeast Asia.

How far did the Greater East Asia Co-Prosperity Sphere extend? From the moment the term made its public debut at an August 1940 press conference called by Foreign Minister Yōsuke Matsuoka, its magnitude remained vaguely defined. Conceptions of the Sphere varied in accordance with individual inclinations and external circumstances. Available evidence clearly suggests, however, that the entire Hawaiian archipelago consistently fell within its envisioned boundaries, both before and after 7 December 1941.

Before 7 December public discussions about Greater East Asia usually referred to Hawaii indirectly through the term *Nan'yō* (South Seas). *Nan'yō*, which was said to lie within Japan's "lifeline" *(seimeisen)* and "life sphere" *(seimeiken)* had its nucleus in the Micronesian mandated islands, but at times was said to include Melanesia and Polynesia. Before 7 December mention of Hawaii as part of *Nan'yō* was usually done indirectly. For example, early in 1941 a book on Hawaii translated into Japanese by former University of Hawaii instructor George Tadao Kunitomo appeared in the "New Japan Sphere Series" [*Shin Nipponken sōsho*] of a Tokyo publisher. There were also, to be sure, more direct intimations of Hawaii's position. In a booklet published in September 1941 the retired army officer and ultranationalist Kingorō Hashimoto explicitly included Hawaii in the Greater East Asia Co-Prosperity Sphere.

Hashimoto's public identification of Hawaii with Greater East Asia was consistent with a classified study prepared several months earlier in the Research Section of Navy General Staff. Dated 29 November 1940 and entitled "Draft Outline for Construction of the Greater East Asia Co-Prosperity Sphere," this secret (it was stamped *gokuhi*) report cast Hawaii's future disposition in sharper focus than did any public document that appeared before the Pearl Harbor attack.

Authors of the "Draft Outline" stated that the objective for establishing a Sphere was: ". . . to create a new culture by the sharing of respect, by mutual good neighborliness, friendship, joint defense, and economic cooperation in an area with Japan [literally *"kōkoku"* or "imperial country"] as the nucleus and including [a list of nations] . . . Hawaii."

The Sphere was to be divided geographically into three concentric subspheres: inner, middle, and outer. The inner subsphere would consist of the Japanese archipelago, Korea, and Manchuria. The middle subsphere would be formed by most of China and all of *Nan'yo*, "including Hawaii." The third, outer subsphere, would include "such outer areas as are necessary for the complete economic self-sufficiency of Greater East Asia."

Defining political relationships within the Sphere, the document enumerated four categories: lands to be annexed outright by Japan; autonomous protectorates; independent states with "unbreakable" defense and economic ties with Japan; and independent states with close economic ties with Japan. Australia, New Zealand, and India fell into the final category. Hong Kong, Thailand, and the Philippines (with the exception of Mindanao, which had a Japanese population of twenty-six thousand) were put in the third category. Indochina and the Dutch East Indies were in the second category. The first category included Guam, Mindanao, and Hawaii. In other words, a Navy General Staff research report recommended, over a year before the outbreak of hostilities with the United States, that the Hawaiian Islands be incorporated into the Japanese Empire.

After 7 December 1941 there was no longer any need to exercise restraint in public discussions of the Pacific's role in the Co-Prosperity Sphere. Writing for the organ of the Japan Committee of the Institute of Pacific Relations,* Fumio Hanme set the tone by declaring that the final task of the Sphere would be the unification of the Pacific area. Pacific became synonomous with *Dai Nan'yō* (Greater South Seas) which, like so many hyperbolic neologisms, was coined during the euphoric aftermath of Pearl Harbor.

Grand visions of the Pacific were not confined to the military and to professional ultranationalists. They cropped up in scholarly discourse. The distinguished Waseda University historian Shinji Nishimura predicted early in 1942 that a "Greater South Seas Co-Prosperity Sphere" encompassing Micronesia, Melanesia, and Polynesia would soon take shape under Japanese leadership. Japan is eminently well qualified to unify all Pacific islands, argued Kyoto University Professor Saneshige Komaki, because the Japanese themselves are islanders. Keio University sociologist Tetsuji Kada

*Founded in Honolulu in 1925, the IPR International Council was located in New York in 1942.

(who had led a student group to Hawaii and California in 1937) wrote that the ultimate scope of the Sphere need not be delimited prematurely. Let the war take its course, he advised, and events would show how far the Sphere would extend.

Professor Kada's suggestions came close to opinions then being voiced in the highest official circles. At a liaison conference on 28 February 1942, Navy Minister Shigetarō Shimada proposed that the Sphere not exclude areas that were located outside of the existing perimeter controlled by Japanese forces. Shimada's view was conditionally endorsed by those present. It was agreed to continue deliberations on the Sphere's scope as war operations progressed. At another liaison conference on 18 March, Teiichi Suzuki, chief of the Cabinet Planning Board, relayed a recommendation by the Greater East Asia Deliberation Council* that the Sphere embrace all areas then occupied by Imperial forces "and such areas which may be occupied in the future." This elastic definition of the Sphere appears to have been accepted tacitly by the civilian and military leadership.

Whatever the ultimate scope of the Sphere, be it Greater East Asia, or Greater South Seas, the position of Hawaii was unambiguous. A wave of books and articles about the islands left little doubt about assumptions concerning Hawaii's future. Typical of the new tone was a prediction by the journalist Takeshi Haga, who authored a book on Hawaii in 1942: "Hawaii is geographically and historically part of the Greater East Asia Co-Prosperity Sphere and will soon enter a new life under its protective wings."

George Tadao Kunitomo echoed this sentiment in the preface to his 1943 translation of a history of Hawaii written by his former University of Hawaii colleague Ralph S. Kuykendall: "It is only a matter of time before the Hawaii Islands, a part of the Greater East Asia Co-Prosperity Sphere, make a new start under the Japanese flag."

Itsuko Kidō, a Hawaii *nisei* and author of a history of Hawaii with a foreword by Foreign Minister Masayuki Tani, made an analogous prediction in 1943: "The Philippines, Thailand, and Burma have already taken giant steps toward a heroic new life in the Greater East Asia Co-Prosperity Sphere. The time is coming

*Created early in March 1942 to advise the prime minister on problems relating to Greater East Asia.

when the Rising Sun flag will flutter over the islands, when Hawaii
will be restored again to Asia, when the spirits of nine gods* will
smile at the entrance to Pearl Harbor."

Using popular metaphors of the time, other writers described
Hawaii as "the first line of defense" and "the eastern anchor" of
the Co-Prosperity Sphere. At a round table discussion in Tokyo's
Marunouchi Hotel on 17 December 1941 Diet member Heigorō
Sakurai gave Hawaii high priority in the imminent "second stage"
of the Sphere's construction.

One of the more ringing characterizations of Hawaii turned out
to be a variation on an epithet dating from two decades before the
war when Kei (Takashi) Hara was prime minister. Taking a cue
from contemporary events in Russia, a critic in the Diet coined the
phrase "in the west Lenin, in the east Hara." In 1942 former Honolulu *Nippu jiji* reporter Sōen Yamashita celebrated Anglo-Saxon
expulsion from Asia with the phrase: "in the west Singapore, in the
east Hawaii."

Mellifluous slogans may have sufficed for proclaiming Hawaii's
association with Greater East Asia, but the archipelago's anticipated incorporation into the Japanese Empire called for a more
reasoned justification. Most writers were content to cite geographical proximity, ethnic ties (Japanese, it was repeatedly pointed out,
were the most populous group in the islands), and strategic imperatives. Others, however, felt the responsibility to educate Japanese
readers about Hawaii's past in order to prepare them for Japan's
role in Hawaii's future. As George Kunitomo remarked: "In the
not so distant future, the Hawaiian Islands will enter Japan's
power sphere. Because the Hawaiian Islands will have a new
meaning for Japanese . . . [we] must know their history." "Know
their history" in many cases meant becoming familiar with a version of Hawaii's past that portrayed Japanese rule as a natural cul-
mination of deep-seated historical forces.

Histories of Hawaii written in wartime Japan tended to divide
their subject into five stages: the Asian antecedents of Hawaiians,
the arrival of the Japanese, ties between the Hawaiian Kingdom
and the Japanese Empire, the American takeover and exploitation
of Hawaii, and the liberation of Hawaii.

---

*Nine Japanese crewmembers of midget submarines who perished in the early
hours of 7 December 1941 attempting to penetrate Pearl Harbor.

The Asian origin of Hawaiians was not so much demonstrated as proclaimed. During the 1930s and early 1940s Japanese propagandists (including a number of university academics) used cultural anthropology as an instrument to justify Japanese political goals in Korea, Manchuria, and southern Sakhalin. Wartime treatment of Hawaiian prehistory smacked strongly of this genre. The authors' logic was simple: Hawaiians are Polynesians; Polynesians are Asians; therefore, Hawaiians are Asians. George Kunitomo projected the repercussions of ethnic convergencies. "As Hawaiians are of the Asian race, the Hawaiian Islands will soon, with Japan's victory in the Greater East Asian War, shed America's immoral rule of money and return to East Asia."

As peoples of the Greater East Asia Co-Prosperity Sphere were said to share common blood, it was only natural that some writers should point out that Hawaiians and Japanese were related. Diet member Yūsuke Tsurumi, who before the war toured the United States lecturing on Japan's aims in Manchuria, took a step in this direction by declaration in a Foreign Ministry bulletin on 1 February 1942 that Hawaii was part of Greater East Asia because Polynesians are related to Japanese. Tsurumi's statement was soon being repeated by other writers. In his book on Hawaii, Takeshi Haga carried this line of thinking to an extreme by flatly stating that the Hawaiians are "an extension of the Japanese race." Haga attempted to prove his point by arguing that "Japan's relationship with Hawaii is older than Hawaii's relationship with any other country." Japanese arrived in Hawaii in the thirteenth century, five hundred years before Captain James Cook and two hundred years before Columbus discovered America. Moreover, asserted Haga, these Japanese intermarried with the aborigines and the offspring were consequently descendents of the Yamato race.

Haga was not the first to posit a thirteenth century Japanese presence in the Hawaiian islands. The hypothesis surfaced in 1893 in a book entitled *Japanese in the World* (reissued in 1942) by Shū-jirō Watanabe. As if anticipating the Greater East Asia Co-Prosperity Sphere, Watanabe averred that ancient Hawaiians felt a sense of kinship when they first beheld Japanese visitors. Visions of pre-Columbian links cropped up again in 1914 when the touring geographer-politician Shigetaka Shiga told a *dōhō* audience in Honolulu that Japanese fishermen had reached Hawaii in the twelfth century. Not everyone, however, accepted these allegations. A 1938 Japanese guidebook to Hawaii cautioned that the historicity of pre-Cook Hawaii-Japan contacts had yet to be established.

After 7 December 1941 if anyone was inclined to doubt the antiquity of Japan's roots in Hawaii, he or she remained silent. The post-Pearl Harbor euphoria produced not only historiographical unanimity but corroborative documentation. George Kunitomo wrote that ancient Hawaiian legends of "dark people" materializing on Maui were referring to "suntanned" Japanese fishermen. Historian Shigeru Ienaka identified exactly where these fishermen came ashore (at Wailuku, Maui) and what the Hawaiians called them ("Mamaru"). Sōen Yamashita revised and added to this discovery by revealing that the first Japanese in fact landed at Kahului, Maui (two miles from Wailuku), in 1270. A year later, Yamashita apparently discovered new data, for he wrote that the fishermen first set foot on Hawaiian territory at Makapuu Point, Oahu, in 1258. To leave open the possibility of further revelations, he added that "of course it's not difficult to imagine that others may have come earlier."

On 24 July 1942 Radio Tokyo distilled some of the implications of the aforementioned historical scholarship in the following words:

> You have been taught that Captain Cook discovered the Hawaiian islands. Actually, long before Captain Cook's time, there were Japanese fishermen who were blown to those shores by the storms. If this is true then the peoples of the Pacific race are part of the Japanese race, a part of the Asiatic race. It is very pleasant to think that there was such a race there in Hawaii where there are so many Japanese today.

In addition to identifying Hawaiians with Japanese ethnically and historically, writers underlined ties between the Hawaiian monarchy and Japan. Particular stress was placed upon King Kalakaua's visit to Japan in 1881 when the monarch proposed to Emperor Meiji a marriage alliance and the creation of a Japan-led federation of Asian nations including Hawaii. Kyoto University Professor Saneshige Komaki interpreted the marriage alliance proposal as reflecting not only Kalakaua's intention that a Japanese aristocrat succeed him, but also the king's hope that Japanese immigrants would intermarry with and reinvigorate the declining Hawaiian population. Yoshitarō Hirano hailed Kalakaua's Asian federation proposal as a forerunner of the Greater East Asia Co-Prosperity Sphere.

The achievements of Japanese immigrants to Hawaii were accorded considerable significance by wartime writers. They asserted that Hawaii's modern development was largely the result of the "blood and sweat" of local *dōhō*. Laudatory descriptions were interspersed with remarks whose objective seems to have been to prepare readers for Hawaii's forthcoming incorporation into the Japanese Empire. Sōen Yamashita pointed out that Hawaii was the first base of our Japanese overseas expansion. It would not, he added, have been unnatural had Hawaii become a Japanese possession. In explaining why "Japan's doorstep" had not already become part of the empire, writers blamed the Tokugawa shogunate's seclusion policy, delicately alluded to the caution of Meiji leaders, and denounced the United States.

American involvement in Hawaii was portrayed as a chronicle of aggression and exploitation. By annexing Hawaii in 1898 the United States violated the "historic unity" of Asia and the Pacific pronounced the journalist Gorō Matsumoto in a 1942 book. Building a formidable naval base at Pearl Harbor, Washington used Hawaii, together with Alaska and the Philippines, to encircle and threaten Japan. "Until the American takeover, Hawaii was very pro-Japanese," lamented Yamaguchi prefecture official Masahei Kawamura in 1944. Sōen Yamashita wrote that Hawaii had been turned from "Mark Twain's Pacific paradise" into a "Pacific Gibralter." Colbert Naoya Kurokawa, a former Honolulu YMCA official, paraphrased Admiral Kanji Katō and called Hawaii under American rule "a cancer to international peace." Acquisition and militarization of Hawaii by the United States, wrote Kurokawa, was "not only the shame of American history but a most unfortunate event for peace in the Pacific."

According to Itsuko Kidō, all Asia had reason to regret American rule in Hawaii: "This [Hawaii] is an Asian country. The United States seized it as part of a great plan to control East Asia. America destroyed a kingdom . . . brought in warships. Americans are glad to have succeeded in controlling this part of Asia, but for Asians there is decidedly nothing about which to rejoice."

Hand in hand with militarization of the Islands went the exploitation of Asian inhabitants, particularly Japanese. Japanese were excluded from the local political, economic, and social elites. Regardless of aptitudes and academic achievements, *nisei* could not find managerial jobs in the local "Big Five" corporations. The navy did not recruit *dōhō* or hire them to work at military installations. The Massie case* showed that justice was for Anglo-Saxons only. The infrequency of mixed marriages confirmed the depth of racial prejudice.

Perhaps the harshest published criticism of Americans in Hawaii that appeared in wartime Japan came from a twenty-six year old Hawaii-born *nisei*, Fred Noboru Miike. A member of the University of Hawaii class of 1939, Miike left for Japan just before the war. In 1942 he brought out a book entitled *My Native Hawaii*, which exuded the anger of a proud youth offended by the conditions in which he had grown up. Japanese, Miike wrote, have lived in Hawaii from prehistoric times, but Anglo-Saxons ignore this because they could not stand the idea that "yellow skins" preceded Captain Cook by five hundred years. Americans have "hated and suspected" Hawaii's Japanese, especially after the 1920 plantation strikes. Such feelings are reciprocated, not just by Japanese but by other Asian groups in Hawaii. Local youth occasionally beat up arrogant Anglo-Saxon sailors. Americans do not love Hawaii, because they have no roots in the islands. Most come temporarily to fulfill a stint of military service. With Americans, duty takes second place to debauchery. American soldiers and sailors are spiritually flaccid. Even during military exercises their minds are less on training than on "women embraced the previous night."

If disturbed by Hawaii's past, Miike was optimistic about its future: "With neither right nor reason [the United States] has taken away Hawaii's wealth produced by the sweat of Orientals, led by the Japanese. How long will they be able to prolong their control of Hawaii by force? As all history shows, their 'force' must soon raise the white flag to 'righteousness.' "

"Righteousness" in Miike's understanding as applied to Hawaii came to be identified with Japan's liberation of the islands from

---

*In 1932 four whites convicted of killing a Hawaiian accused of assaulting a white woman received sentences of ten years. The governor of Hawaii commuted the sentences to one hour.

the American yoke. The events of 7 December 1941 stirred in Miike a sense of "fierce excitement." He interpreted the Pearl Harbor attack as a blow against American haughtiness. Great changes were in store for the islands. As Hawaii was incapable of feeding its own inhabitants, a blockade would not take long in bringing the American defenders to their knees.

Japanese wartime accounts of Hawaii tended to portray Hawaii *dōhō* as reacting positively to the events of 7 December. Sō Miyashiro, who lived many years in the islands until October 1941, speculated how excited and moved "almost all" *dōhō* were as they saw their ancestral land's bombs raining down upon Pearl Harbor, a symbol of oppression and prejudice. Hawaii-born Itsuko Kidō proposed that "Remember Pearl Harbor" be a motto for all Japanese. Sōen Yamashita called Pearl Harbor a turning point in Hawaiian history, heralding the liberation of local *dōhō*. Kaju Nakamura affirmed that in the wake of Pearl Harbor, Hawaii's Japanese "are waiting for release from American domination." Summarizing the position of Japanese in Hawaii during the months after Pearl Harbor, the *South Seas Yearbook* concluded: "Hawaii *dōhō* saw with their own eyes the brilliant Japanese victory at Pearl Harbor on the first day of the war. Whatever persecution they may be subject to, they will faithfully await the day of their motherland's victory, the day when Imperial troops land on Hawaii."

The outbreak of the Great East Asia War immediately raised questions about the fate of over half a million overseas Japanese in enemy countries. Although of especially acute concern to relatives in Japan, the position of overseas *dōhō* gradually assumed significance in the media and in the government during 1942. Some 560,000 *dōhō* were residing in enemy nations: 279,000 in the United States (of whom 160,000 lived in Hawaii); 230,000 in Brazil; 23,000 in Canada; 20,000 in Peru; 6,000 in Mexico; 3,400 in Australia; 2,100 in India; and smaller numbers in Bolivia, Columbia, Venezuela, Equador, England, and New Zealand. Shortly after the war started, the Foreign Ministry set up an Emigrant's Office under the direction of Kyūman Suzuki. The office's first task was to gather information on and to open communications with overseas *dōhō*.

For the first few months of 1942, Tokyo was unable to obtain accurate information on the condition of Hawaii's Japanese. Interviews with *issei* and *nisei* who opted for repatriation on the eve of the war did not shed much light on the fate of those compatriots left behind. The fact that the war had started in Hawaii, moreover with such devastating consequences for the U.S. Pacific Fleet, created anxieties about how Hawaii's Japanese would fare in the hands of possibly vengeful American authorities.

During 1942 rumors and speculations circulated widely. Reports of violence against Japanese nationals on Mindanao (in the Philippines) prior to the island's occupation by Imperial forces led some observers to wonder aloud whether a similar fate did not await Hawaii *dōhō*. Fred Miike wrote: "It is certain that [U.S.] Army authorities are prepared to round up and shoot all suspicious Japanese."

Former San Francisco newspaperman Kazuo Ebina reported that Hawaii Japanese were already being rounded up en masse regardless of age or sex.* Some *dōhō*, he added, had already died in prison after undergoing torture. Kyoto University's Tsugio Murakami wrote that "many" *dōhō* in Hawaii had already been sent to mainland camps.† Kaju Nakamura asserted that Hawaii Japanese were receiving "the most inhuman treatment" of Japanese anywhere in the United States. Incarcerated in Fort Shafter,†† they were subjected to threats by guards made edgy by continuous Japanese victories in Southeast Asia and the Pacific.

In the spring of 1942 Tokyo began to receive more accurate information about the condition of *dōhō* on American territory. During 1942 some fifteen hundred Japanese returned home from North and South America on exchange ships. Among these were dozens from Hawaii (248 Hawaii Japanese, exclusive of consular personnel, opted for repatriation during the war). Repatriates provided Tokyo with firsthand accounts of conditions in Hawaii.

*In the weeks following 7 December, the FBI took into custody about 1,450 *dōhō* in the Territory of Hawaii, representing less than 1 percent of the combined Japanese and Japanese-American population in the Islands.

†Between the outbreak of the war and the end of 1943, 694 male and 8 female *dōhō* internees were transported from Hawaii to the mainland. During the war years (1941–1945) a total of 1,875 Hawaii *dōhō* were sent to the mainland for internment.

††Internment centers in the Territory were at Sand Island and Honouliuli on Oahu, Hilo on the island of Hawaii, Makaweli on Maui, and Kaleo on Kauai.

Additional channels of communication were set up through the International Red Cross Committee in Geneva and through Swedish and Spanish diplomats stationed in the United States. A Swedish diplomat visited a Honolulu internment center as early as 24 January 1942. His report reached the Foreign Ministry via Stockholm early in February. Using these intermediaries, relatives were able to exchange correspondence and Japan's foreign minister was permitted to send annual New Year's greetings to interned overseas *dōhō*.

With an improved knowledge of actual conditions in Hawaii, the foreign minister inaugurated specific measures to assist interned compatriots. Protests were filed with Spanish and Swedish authorities for transmission to Washington. The principal complaints were about internees being subjected to forced labor on Honolulu's Sand Island (digging trenches, fixing fences, moving timbers, all in the vicinity of unexploded anti-aircraft shells). Nor did Tokyo resort only to words. In an address to the Diet on 3 February 1943, Foreign Minister Masayuki Tani announced that during 1942 the government had allocated 2.53 million yen (about $1.2 million) to fund assistance to overseas *dōhō* through neutral countries. An additional 2 million yen was set aside for fiscal 1943 to assist relatives in Japan who before the war had been receiving remittances from overseas *dōhō* and who were now suffering hardships because these remittances had ceased.

Tokyo was also thinking seriously of making Washington accountable for the relocation of Japanese-Americans on the West Coast to inland camps. In his address to the Diet, Tani declared that the government was preparing postwar reparations claims against the United States to compensate *dōhō* for economic losses suffered as a result of forced relocation.

In addition to the Foreign Ministry, a blue-ribbon committee of prominent politicians, diplomats, and military figures involved itself in calling attention to the plight of overseas *dōhō*, particularly those in the United States. Starting in December 1942, the Committee for *Dōhō* in Enemy Countries held forums at Tokyo's Greater East Asia Hall to publicize and solicit support for their activities. The committee worked in conjunction with Kyūman Suzuki's Emigrant's Office in the Foreign Ministry and seems to have been instrumental in lobbying for government outlays for *dōhō* assistance. A number of the committee members knew

Hawaii from having worked in or visited the islands during the prewar years.*

Anxiety for the welfare of relatives and compatriots in Hawaii was probably not comforted by official confidence that the tribulations of island *dōhō* would end with the arrival of Imperial forces. George Kunitomo may have been serious, or he may have been whistling in the wind, when in 1943 he wrote: "Over 150,000 compatriots are now scattered throughout the Hawaiian Islands, detained under the enemy's fierce vigilance. But the sufferings of our compatriots will dissolve the moment that the Rising Sun flag unfurls high over the Hawaiian archipelago."

Two longtime Hawaii residents, Sōen Yamashita and Colbert Naoya Kurokawa, both predicted that the Greater East Asia War would end where it had started, in Hawaii. But what lay beyond liberation? What would a Japanese Hawaii be like in the postwar world? These questions occupied a number of analytic minds in Japan during 1942 and 1943, as the outlines of an occupation policy took shape.

*These included two former consul-generals in Honolulu (Hachirō Arita and Kazue Kuwashima), two admirals with Hawaii connections (Kichisaburō Nomura, Kenwa Kanna), a Diet member who in 1938 had suggested that Japanese-Americans contribute half of their income to buy Imperial war bonds (Harutsugu Tahara), and a future prime minister who had visited the islands in the 1930s (Hitoshi Ashida).

CHAPTER X

Hawaii Under
Japanese Rule

In contrast to the United States, Japan engaged in no systematic planning for postwar Asia and the Pacific. To be sure, the wartime media reverberated with grandiloquent discussions of the Greater East Asia Co-Prosperity Sphere. But these were largely rhetorical exercises at a high level of abstraction and a low level of substance. Academics published projections of growth potentials of various national economies in the Sphere. But these were disembodied, if occasionally sophisticated, visions of a postwar order. The government itself came up with no substantial statement of what the achievement of optimal peace terms would mean for areas under or expected to be under Japanese occupation when the war ended. Nor does it seem that any secret master plan existed.

The absence of comprehensive planning is not surprising. Before 7 December Tokyo had paid little attention to long-term political objectives in the Pacific. After the outbreak of hostilities with the United States, the government bureaucracy's efforts concentrated on the awesome task of mobilizing the empire's resources against a materially superior enemy.

Comprehensive planning was also inhibited by internal disunity. It is well known that Japan's war effort suffered from a chronic lack of coordination. The civil and military bureaucracies operated quasi-independently and sometimes at cross purposes. The Foreign Ministry resented the creation of the Greater East Asia Ministry* in November 1942 as an encroachment upon its

---

*An amalgamation of the Foreign Ministry's Asia Bureau, the Asia Development Board, and the Colonization Ministry.

traditional diplomatic prerogatives. The army and navy had fundamentally different ideas about how the war should be prosecuted. The two services competed for budgetary allocations and for scarce supplies. They bickered over operational responsibilities and blamed each other for delays or reverses in the field. The Navy General Staff and Combined Fleet were more often than not at variance about strategic priorities.

In view of such conditions, it is hardly surprising that no single agency was charged with responsibility for formulating occupation plans for Hawaii. Rather, various parts of the state bureaucracy and government-subsidized research institutes independently developed their own visions of Hawaii under Japanese rule. These separate studies were never brought together by a single coordinating authority. According to postwar testimony, liaison between groups preparing recommendations for Hawaii's administration and socioeconomic development was minimal. Tsugio Murakami recalled in 1979 how during the war his mentor, Kyoto University Professor Saneshige Komaki, had warned his assistants not to share information with outsiders, especially other academics who were working on similar topics.

If wartime research on Hawaii took place without central guidance, the results were nevertheless remarkably consistent. Visions of postwar Hawaii that emerged on paper in 1942 and 1943 shared many assumptions and recommendations, although the authors may not even have been aware of each other's existence. Whatever their institutional affiliation, planners tacitly assumed that in the initial occupation period Hawaii would be placed under military rule. Each service took preliminary steps to stake out its administrative prerogatives and purviews. It will be recalled that in November 1940 the Navy General Staff's Research Department recommended that Hawaii be annexed by Japan. On 8 December 1941 the Navy Ministry established a Southern Regions Affairs Department *(Nanpō seimubu)* under the direction of Rear Admiral Takazumi Oka, military affairs bureau chief. The new department was assigned the task of conducting research on how occupation personnel should be trained for existing or potential areas under naval administration. Although direct evidence is not available (destruction of naval files at the war's end was efficiently executed), it is logical to assume that this department included Hawaii in its plans no later than by mid-April 1942, when

the Navy General Staff dropped its opposition to "Eastern Operation."

Meanwhile, the Army Ministry also appears to have been giving
thought to the prospect of military rule in Hawaii, notwithstanding the Army General Staff's antipathy during 1941 and the first
three months of 1942 to any widening of the Pacific perimeter. In
December 1941 the ministry's research section prepared a "Land
Disposal Plan in the Greater East Asia Co-Prosperity Sphere" in
which Hawaii, together with other islands in Polynesia, were
grouped into a military "Government-General of the Eastern Pacific." It seems reasonable to assume that when the Army General
Staff did an about-face on "Eastern Operation" on 23 May 1942
and issued orders to three divisions to prepare for landings in
Hawaii, preliminary plans were initiated for postinvasion administration of the Islands. Unfortunately, these plans have been lost
or were destroyed.

A second general characteristic of thinking about Hawaii was
that planners studied and drew lessons from experiences in other
parts of Greater East Asia under Japanese occupation. Malaya,
under army control since General Tomoyuki Yamashita's forces
captured Singapore on 15 February 1942, served as a model for a
number of Hawaii occupation studies. Hawaii and Malaya both
had multiethnic societies, a condition that posed in each area analogous problems and opportunities.

Third, military and civilian planners alike studied the prospect
of enlisting local *dōhō* in the occupation. The idea of using overseas Japanese as instruments of Imperial strategy had occurred to
General Kuniaki Koiso before the war, when he was serving as
minister of colonization (16 January–16 July 1940). According to
the postwar historian Tōru Yano, Koiso prepared a plan to create
dōhō Fifth Columns throughout Greater East Asia. Presuming
that it existed, it does not appear that this plan was activated
before 7 December 1941, although the Tokyo Congress of Overseas *Dōhō* in November 1940 offered opportunities to approach
potentially cooperative individuals.

Events after 7 December showed that overseas *dōhō* in areas
under Japanese occupation were not only cooperative but useful
because of their knowledge of local conditions. Japanese forces in
the Philippines received a tempestuous welcome from resident
compatriots in Davao on Mindanao on 20 December 1941, and

the Macassar Japanese assisted Imperial Navy units occupying the Celebes in February 1942, volunteering as guides and interpreters.

On 3 June 1942 the Army General Staff issued a decree setting forth guidelines for using *dōhō* in the projected occupation of Fiji. These guidelines throw light upon parallel plans being prepared for Hawaii, although it should be pointed out that an important difference existed between the two areas. Fiji's Japanese (except those who were away from the islands on 8 December 1941) were rounded up after the outbreak of the war and sent to New Zealand for internment. Army planners therefore were obliged to think in terms of bringing back former Fijian *dōhō* who had returned to Japan before the war. In the words of the 3 June army decree:

> Under military rule, in each area resident compatriots are to cooperate in the management of administration and development. Priority is to be given to carefully selected compatriots who come to Fiji after the start of the war and to former residents [of Fiji] who went back to Japan and now will once again return to the area.

Unlike the Japanese community in Fiji, Hawaii's 160,000 *dōhō* remained for the most part untouched by arrest or relocation. Less than 1 percent of Hawaii Japanese was interned. Of these, about half were sent to the mainland. Therefore, it is likely that army and navy planners counted upon drawing from the reservoir of local human resources to support and to help administer occupation programs. No conclusive documentation has turned up in military archives, but wartime civilian sources strongly suggest that such expectations existed.

The need to set up military administrations in widely scattered areas throughout Greater East Asia led the army and navy to draw upon the expertise of civilian specialists in universities and research institutes. Historical, political, economic, and social information was collected, collated, and analyzed by these civilian consultants. Thousands of studies and reports were written, some of which contained policy recommendations. Much of this subcontracted research, being of a sensitive nature, circulated only within a restricted readership. But a significant portion came out in wartime books and articles. Professional journals in the fields of economics and geography carried abundant material of this nature between 1941 and 1944.

Government-subsidized research on Hawaii took place in three civilian centers during the war: the National Policy Research Society *(Kokusaku kenkyūkai)*; the South Seas Economic Research Center *(Nan'yō keizai kenkyūjo)*; and the Yoshida Research Center *(Yoshida kenkyūjo)*. In addition, individuals such as Takeshi Haga, George Kunitomo, Sōen Yamashita, Yōshi Kanda, and two Hawaii-born authors—Itsuko Kidō and Fred Noboru Miike—prognosticated about the Islands under Japanese rule.

Established in 1937 with headquarters in the Osaka Building at Uchisaiwai-cho near Tokyo's Hibiya Park, the National Policy Research Society (hereafter Policy Society) counted among its patrons powerful elements of Japan's political, military, and economic elites. Funds were provided by the Prime Minister's Secretariat, the Army Ministry, the Navy Ministry, and the Foreign Ministry. Corporate patrons included Mitsui, Mitsubishi, and the South Manchuria Railroad Company. The Policy Society's official function was to investigate and advise the government on problems critical to Japan's welfare and national security. Ties with the Army Ministry were particularly close. The late British historian G. R. Storry stated that the army "exercised a dominant influence on the policy of the society."

While the Policy Society's directors were venerable figures such as Baron Kimmochi Ōkura and Hachirō Ōhashi (chairman of the Japan Broadcasting Corporation), its guiding force was a relatively young, energetic, and well-connected political economist named Kazuo Yatsugi. Born in 1899, Yatsugi founded the precursor to the Policy Society in 1933. Thanks to his analytic astuteness and organizational talents, he was much in demand by various government organs during the 1930s. By 1940 he had become a member of the Cabinet Research Board, a councillor to the Imperial Rule Assistance Association, advisor to the Tokyo Chamber of Commerce, and an unofficial staff member *(shokutaku)* of the Army Ministry's Research Section.

In February 1942, under Yatsugi's guidance, the Policy Society gave birth to the Greater East Asia Task Force which in turn subdivided into fourteen sections conducting research on policy options for problems of political control, cultural assimilation, labor, trade, technology, communications, population, overseas Chinese, and currency regulation within the purview of the Task Force's scrutiny.

The South Seas Economic Research Center performed for the navy what the Policy Society did for the army. Established in 1937, it was located after 1939 in the Akasaka district of Tokyo. The declared purpose of the center was to study the economic potential of the "South Seas," a term which in wartime parlance embraced everything from Burma to Hawaii and from the Marianas to New Zealand. In fact, the center was the child of the Navy Ministry, preparing studies in accordance with the needs of Admiral Takazumi Oka's Southern Affairs Department *(Nanpō seimubu)*. The center's director, Muneichi Kasuya, was a retired rear admiral with extensive operational and staff experience. Admiral Kasuya's relations with both the Navy Ministry and Navy General Staff are said to have remained close after he went on the inactive list in 1936.

During 1942 and 1943 the center produced hundreds of in-house reports on various parts of the Greater East Asia Co-Prosperity Sphere. These were numbered and put into a series called *Nan'yō shiryō* [South sea sources]. *Nan'yō shiryō* report number 236, dated April 1943, bears the title: "What Should Be Done with Hawaii?" The author's name appears on the report's first page: Kurokawa Naoya. This is none other than Colbert N. Kurokawa, Japan-born member of the Honolulu Lions Club, educational secretary of Honolulu's Nuuanu YMCA, and secretary of the Pan Pacific Union, a Honolulu educational organization.

How did Colbert Kurokawa, the prewar Honolulu community figure, become Kurokawa Naoya of an Imperial Navy–subsidized research center in wartime Japan? Although he returned to Hawaii in 1951 and resumed his community services (this time in journalism, insurance, civic organizations, and religion) until 1958 when he again took up residence in Japan, there is no record that he ever alluded publicly to his connection with the South Seas Economic Research Center, let alone to authoring a paper on Hawaii that set guidelines for restructuring the Islands under Japanese rule.

Kurokawa's wartime activities in Japan remain to this day shrouded by ambiguity and contradictory evidence. His obituary in the Honolulu *Star-Bulletin* (19 July 1978) contains the statement that two days after Pearl Harbor, he was "given the choice of internment or surrendering his passport." The obituary does not indicate which option he selected but reports that after two years (i.e., in 1943) he found work in a "pharmaceutical research bureau in Tokyo." On the other hand, in a biographical sketch printed by the Japan Christian Association and the Kyoto Revival Church on the occasion of Kurokawa's funeral, it is noted that Colbert Kurokawa was put under house arrest for being "pro-American" and then "interned until the end of the war." Kurokawa himself described his experiences between 1941 and 1945 in a speech delivered at Kyoto's Dōshisha University on 27 May 1966:

> The day after the Pearl Harbor Incident [*sic*], my American Passport was taken away, and I became interned; most of my own publications were confiscated and burnt; forced to sign an "affidavit" not to associate with young students nor with any foreign residents in Japan. (Of course we were not able to return to America without having my own passport.)
>
> It is not for me to enumerate the persecution, agony, and difficulties of the following three years. They horrify me even now to recall.

What "horrified" Colbert Kurokawa to recall in 1966 may have been more than he was willing to publicize. The circumstances that led an interned "pro-American" to become the author of *Nan'yō shiryō* number 236 have yet to be explained. What is clear is that "What Should be Done with Hawaii?" offers some of the most insightful suggestions for Hawaii's occupation composed by any analyst of any nationality in wartime Japan.

The third organ preparing studies of Hawaii was informally called the Yoshida Research Center, named after a hill (Yoshida-yama) near the campus of Kyoto Imperial University. Yoshida Research Center was an unofficial appellation for a group of geographers and economists working under the direction of Professor Saneshige Komaki. In 1942 Professor Komaki ranked as one of the best-known geopoliticians in Japan. A torrent of books and articles bearing his name came out during 1941 through 1943. They were characterized by an imaginative flair that must have appalled even the membership of the Japan Geopolitics Society (est. 1941), which can hardly be accused of tepid patriotism. In 1943 Komaki came to the attention of American readers when *Asia* magazine reported a Radio Tokyo broadcast in which he asserted that Columbus was correct in 1492 when he thought that he had reached

Asia. Professor Komaki defined geopolitics as "a scientific weapon for constructing a new world order." He put this definition into practice by providing the military with background studies to the geopolitics of the Greater East Asia Co-Prosperity Sphere.

Tsugio Murakami, one of Professor Komaki's students, developed a keen interest in the geopolitics of the Pacific in general and of Hawaii in particular after his graduation from Kyoto University in 1936. Although he had never been to the islands, Murakami was born in Oshimagun of Yamaguchi Prefecture, located at the southwestern extremity of Honshū—a district that traditionally had sent many emigrants to Hawaii. Under Komaki's encouragement, Murakami set about studying Hawaiian history, economics, and society. In 1943 he came up with some astute recommendations for economic and social reforms.

Scenarios of Hawaii under Japanese rule dealt with one or a combination of three broad areas of policy formulation: political control, economic reconstruction, and social reforms.

Political Control

Creating mechanisms of political control constituted a high priority for analysts writing about the Greater East Asia Co-Prosperity Sphere in general and about Hawaii in particular. In Hawaii's case, there was a consensus that military rule would be necessary for an interim after a successful invasion. In a long-term perspective, a number of options presented themselves: annexation of Hawaii as an integral part of Japan (on the model of Karafuto or southern Sakhalin), nominal political independence under a revived Hawaiian monarchy (on the model of Manchukuo), or some intermediate arrangement combining degrees of local autonomy and Japanese discretionary power.

Kaju Nakamura reflected a widespread conviction when in June 1942 he set forth three principles to guide postwar occupation policies: "utmost discretion should be exercised in the selection of personnel," "strict observance should be kept to pay due respect to the traditions and customs of each race," and "as large a number of native Japanese as possible should be sent to colonize." By his first principle, Nakamura apparently intended to caution against a repeat of what had happened in Manchuria during the 1930s when unscrupulous entrepreneurs, soldiers of fortune, opium dealers, and assorted criminals (types which in Japan were then called *Manshū gorō*) followed in the wake of the Imperial Army and tarnished Japan's self-projected image as a liberator. There were, in other words, measures to be taken so that *Hawaii gorō* would be kept to a minimum. Nakamura's second and third principles contained a contradiction that posed a dilemma to planners: should ethnic pluralism or Japanization *(kōminka)* guide occupation programs?

The presence of a large number of Japanese in Hawaii (160,000 or approximately 40 percent of the population) greatly influenced how planners approached the problem of political control. Ethnic as well as strategic considerations may have underlay the Navy General Staff's categorization of Hawaii as an area to be annexed by Japan (the Staff's 1940 "Draft Outline" of the Co-Prosperity Sphere). Tsugio Murakami also seems to have leaned toward close cooperation with local Japanese in setting up a local political administration. Estimating that about 70 percent of Hawaii Japanese would "immediately" *(sokuza ni)* collaborate with occupation forces, Murakami enumerated the advantages of giving priority to ethnic solidarity:

> . . . believing in Japanese religions, having used Japanese as a daily language, and assuming that they will not have been interned and sent away [by the Americans], about 70% of all the Japanese [in Hawaii] will be useful as ready collaborators. Special attention must be accorded to their leadership in the agrarian sector, which will make an enormous contribution to restructuring production, one of the main tasks in building a new Hawaii. We must also thank these people for having been the pioneers of the all-permeating Imperial Way in Hawaii.

Sōen Yamashita put the matter of ethnic solidarity succinctly in a 1942 book about the islands: "If one speaks of liberation of Hawaii's people, then it is more logical to refer to the Japanese than to the Hawaiians." Yōshi Kanda echoed this sentiment in the assertion that: "For the sake of 150,000 [*sic*] compatriots, Hawaii must belong to Japan."

Not all planners, however, pinned their hopes only on local Japanese. Colbert Kurokawa, for one, shaped his proposals around native Hawaiians. Hawaii, he felt, should be restored to its earlier role as a meeting ground of various Pacific peoples. Achieving multiracial harmony should be Japan's guiding principle in the occupation. Kurokawa asked: "Is not Imperial Japan's great mission really to build a new Hawaii by liberating the natives and making Hawaii a temple of [multiracial] harmony in a new Pacific age?"

Kurokawa's question is not as whimsical as it at first sounds. Japan had ample experience "restoring" areas to "native" inhabitants. In 1932, having occupied large sections of northeastern China, the Imperial Army set up a multiracial puppet state dubbed "Manchukuo," presided over by an ornamental Manchu emperor who had been whisked out of Tientsin and propped up on a throne to "rule" for the next thirteen years under the watchful eyes of Japanese advisors. The Imperial Army also set up puppet regimes in Inner Mongolia and North China during the 1930s, using Mongol princes and pliant Chinese generals and politicians to give them a veneer of legitimacy. Analogous measures were being taken in Burma, the Dutch East Indies, and the Philippines as Japanese forces took over former British, Dutch, and American colonies in 1941 and 1942.

Kurokawa may have had the Manchu-Mongol model in mind when he proposed the restoration of the Hawaiian monarchy: "Reestablishment of the Hawaiian Kingdom would be an appropriate tactic to address the problem of public order and defense." A number of local conditions recommended this tactic to Kurokawa as a practical option. He pointed out that descendants of royal and princely families lived on all of the main Hawaiian islands. Second, Hawaiians were in his estimation skilled at politics and enjoyed the respect of other races. As examples he cited Honolulu's Princess Kawananakoa ("a powerful leader of the anti-Roosevelt Republican Party")* and the Big Island's Samuel Mahuka Spencer ("mayor of Hilo").† Third, Kurokawa detected dissatisfaction with American rule among Hawaiian intellectuals. Fourth, there was a

---

*Princess Abigail Kawananakoa (1882–1945), daughter of wealthy Honolulu businessman James Campbell, in 1902 married Prince David Kawananakoa Piikoi (1868–1908), cousin of King Kalakaua, nephew of Queen Kapiolani, and great-grandson of Kaumualii, the last independent king of Kauai. In 1924 and 1928, she was selected Republican National Committeewoman for Hawaii.

†Samuel Mahuka Spencer (1875–1960) was from 1924 through the 1930s chairman of the Board of Supervisors on the island of Hawaii.

tradition of friendly ties between Hawaiians and Japan, dating back to the 1881 visit of King Kalakaua and still manifested by the education of bright Hawaiian youth in Tokyo's Gakushūin University (Kurokawa cited two employees in the Hawaiian Territorial Government: James Hakuole and Isaac Harbottle).

None of the scenarios directly addressed the question of the future of Hawaii's Caucasians, Portuguese, Chinese, and Filipinos. Indirect evidence suggests that among writers who envisioned a multiracial postwar society, the "Asians" (which included Polynesians) would be accorded an ornamental role in mass organizations whose function was to mobilize support for Japan in general and for specific occupation programs when the occasion demanded. Judging from the experience of the White Russians in Manchukuo, and bearing in mind Hawaii's unique circumstances, local Caucasians (excluding military personnel who would be handled as POWs) would probably have been given three options: they could seek repatriation to the United States, they could continue to live in Hawaii, albeit without prewar socioeconomic perquisites, dedicating their labor to the construction of the Co-Prosperity Sphere; or they could resist. In view of Hawaii's small area and of Japan's "pacification" techniques in China, the last option would have entailed grave risks.

Economic Reconstruction

Projections of Hawaii's economic future under Japanese rule started from the assumption that the Islands had become the victims of the American profit ethic. Hawaii's economy, remarked Colbert Kurokawa, was based upon American capital, native lands, and Oriental labor. Ruthless exploitation had created socioeconomic inequities and structural weaknesses, the rectification of which deserved high priority.

Two characteristics of Hawaii's prewar economy attracted particular attention and became the targets of reformist zeal: the Big Five, and the specialization on sugar and pineapple. The first symbolized a Caucasian monopoly of power with concomitant injustices to "Asians." The second, by occupying a major part of the arable land, had made Hawaii incapable of feeding itself and hence strategically vulnerable.

In the eyes of most analysts, the Big Five and sugar-pineapple overspecialization were related ailments. The Big Five pushed the cultivation of sugar and pineapple, because these were profitable export crops. Hawaii's resultant dependency upon food imports reinforced corporate profits. By monopolizing shipping, the Big Five could sell imported food products to the local population at sizeable mark-ups. Tsugio Murakami acknowledged that firms such as Kress, Sears Roebuck, and the Tokyo department store chain Mitsukoshi had penetrated "crevices" of the Hawaii economy not controlled by the Big Five. Nonetheless, Murakami concluded, such inroads were marginal and did not alter basic ills.

Planners tended to find the solution to Hawaii's economic problems in breaking up the Big Five corporations, sharply reducing sugar and pineapple under cultivation, and making Hawaii self-sufficient in food production. Planners who wanted to dissolve the Big Five did not specify how corporate assets would be distributed. Available evidence suggests that ships, drydocks, and warehouses would be taken over by the navy. Corporate headquarters on Bishop Street could be rented to Japanese firms which, one assumes, would extend operations into Hawaii after the war.

None of the planners mentioned the fate of firms such as Sears, Kress, and Dillingham. Whether this omission derived from an oversight, or whether it foreshadowed some form of discretionary preferential treatment cannot be said with certainty.

Lands owned by the Big Five, which comprised a major part of Hawaii's arable area, formed the basis for proposals to remodel the islands' agriculture. Sugar and pineapple cultivation were to be sharply curtailed. In their place, rice and taro* were to be planted. In addition, hitherto neglected marginal lands were to be utilized. Sweet potatoes were to be grown wherever possible. Hills and mountainous areas were to be planted with trees, laying the basis for a forestry industry that would provide construction materials for housing.

A March 1942 report by Setsuo Nakase of the Policy Society *(Kokusaku kenkyūkai)* gave a general idea of the scale of projected cutbacks in the sugar industry. Nakase noted that in 1940 there were forty-eight mills in Hawaii producing about 8,800,000 tons

---

*A plant commonly found in Polynesia with edible rootstocks of a starchy consistency.

of cane sugar. Only 300,000 to 400,000 tons were consumed locally; the rest was sent to the American mainland. Nakase estimated that two mills should be adequate to satisfy local demand. Over 90 percent of the canefields could then be converted into rice paddies and vegetable farms. Existing irrigation systems would serve handily to provide water for rice fields and taro patches.

While pineapple acreage was also to be reduced, one report suggests that the cutback would not be so drastic as in the case of sugar. Hisaya Kunimatsu, a geographer specializing in South Seas agriculture, noted that pineapple together with coffee already grown in the Big Island's Kona district constituted attractive potential exports to Japan.

Planners did not neglect to think of potential sources of protein in Hawaii's future self-sufficient food economy. Japanese specialists were to enlarge the existing fishing industry. There would also be capital and technical assistance for expanding the scope of livestock-raising. Harvesting of sea kelp *(konbu)* was also envisioned.

When it came to identifying who would carry out the agricultural reforms in postwar Hawaii, writers pointed almost without exception to local Japanese, who were to be assisted by garrison troops, occupation personnel, and additional immigrants from Japan. Hawaii *dōhō* had earned this role by virtue of their past achievements and present qualifications. George Kunitomo wrote in 1943: "The mainstay of Hawaii's economy today—the sugar industry—was built with the blood and sweat of Japanese immigrants. Like agriculture, Hawaii's fishing industry also derives from the tireless toil of Japanese immigrants."

Tsugio Murakami stated that Japanese would be significantly more productive in rice cultivation in Hawaii than were the Chinese, who grew only one crop annually (Murakami estimated that Japanese could grow two). The Kyoto analyst went on to suggest that garrison troops could be enlisted to help with harvests and other seasonal work. Japanese were also seen as best suited, with their tradition of mutual help and group solidarity, to play the leading role in agricultural cooperatives which would replace Big Five management of the rural economy.

Commenting upon the repercussions of economic reforms, Colbert Kurokawa predicted that a food supply based on rice and taro would cause Hawaii to return to an oriental *(tōyōteki)* lifestyle, which "white-skinned people would have difficulty looking forward to." The implication seems to have been adapt or leave.

Social Reforms

In discussing social reforms for Hawaii, planners focused almost exclusively on the local Japanese community, perhaps under the assumption that "our overseas compatriots overwhelm other ethnic groups by their numbers and activities" (*South Seas Yearbook*, 1942). The social future of other Asian groups in Hawaii was referred to in abstract terms, interlaced with phrases such as "awakened ethnic consciousness," "liberation of the Hawaiian natives," and "harmony of all Pacific peoples." Kurokawa wrote of turning Hawaii into the "Switzerland of the Pacific." Sōen Yamashita, on the other hand, referred to non-Japanese in Hawaii as *gaijin* (foreigners). Yoshitarō Hirano struck a harsher chord, writing in 1942 that "a bad habit of Japanese colonists is that they tend to be too soft-hearted to natives, thus spoiling them." In sum, little systematic thought appears to have been given to postwar social policies toward Hawaii's various ethnic groups other than the *dōhō* themselves.

Regarding the future of Hawaii's Japanese, planners thought in terms of both transformation and restoration, of moving toward a new identity and of revitalizing attenuated traditions. Some quotations from Sōen Yamashita, who knew the islands well from nineteen years' residence, sets the tone for the "forward-looking" aspects of envisioned social engineering.

> With a background of some sixty years of struggle, Japanese society in Hawaii, with the defeat of America, is now in a transitional period and rushing toward a new age. [1943]

> In any case, given the fundamental renovation of Pacific history [since 7 December 1941], our compatriots in Hawaii, whether *issei* or *nisei*, will make a new departure in the not distant future. [24 June 1942]

> Our compatriots in Hawaii must be made to understand and to move toward construction of the Greater East Asia Co-Prosperity Sphere. [1942]

In contrast, Yōshi Kanda foresaw a return to tradition in postwar Hawaiian society: "When America loses, Hawaii will naturally be freed from the American yoke, and the nostalgic past shall be revived under the Rising Sun flag."

Whether forward- or backward-looking, social planners realized that occupation authorities would have to deal with different types of local Japanese in Hawaii. Each generation would have its own characteristics and outlooks. Within a single generation some members would have known only life in the islands since birth or early childhood, while others would have spent time in Japan as students, visiting relatives, or even serving in the armed forces. Still others would have spent the war years in Japan and would be returning to the islands after liberation.

The first generation *(issei)*, consisting of thirty-seven thousand or approximately 23 percent of Hawaii *dōhō*, were expected to coop- erate wholeheartedly. Years of residence in the United States had not dimmed *issei* national consciousness. They had been able to withstand American prejudice thanks to their pride and, in the words of Takeshi Haga, because "behind us stands a powerful and righteous Japan."

The 120,000 *dōhō* of the second *(nisei)* and emerging third *(san- sei)* generation, however, posed special problems. They had been born on American soil, had United States citizenship, and most of them had received their education in American schools. How would they react to Japanese rule? How deeply did American values and loyalties penetrate their hearts? Would they be qualified to play leading roles as Japanese in postwar Hawaiian society? What measures could be taken to ascertain their unswerving loy- alty? What educational reforms could be instituted to root out ves- tiges of American-style thinking and to cultivate a world view appropriate to a citizen of Imperial Japan, living in a strategic forepost of the Greater East Asia Co-Prosperity Sphere?

Some commentators approached the *nisei* question simplisti- cally, arguing that Japanese-Americans were already loyal to Ja- pan and would readily embrace their new civic responsibilities after Hawaii's liberation. Journalist Toshio Tomomatsu, writing in a 1942 anthology entitled *Imperial America*, asserted: "Wise *nisei* have probably recognized that the land of their birth is but a false and base foreign country, and that their birth certificate is only a scrap of paper. Therefore, the path which our compatriots in America should take is self-evident." Seattle-born, onetime San Francisco journalist Tamotsu Murayama, who spent the war years in Japan conducting propaganda work among American *nisei*, had no doubts about his generation's feelings or loyalties when he wrote in August of 1942: "*Nisei* are prepared to sweep away past

life-styles and to return to a consciousness of their race, contribut-
ing to the decisive struggle of the Greater East Asia War." One
month later, Murayama wrote: "Henceforth, we *nisei* will live up
to the spirit of the pioneers and will do our utmost to cooperate
fully with the basic policy of the Japanese government for the
establishment of the Greater East Asia Co-Prosperity Sphere."

Other writers were not so sure that the "*nisei* problem" was that
simple and straightforward. During 1942 reports reached Japan
that *nisei* volunteers were serving in the United States Army.*
Yōshi Kanda speculated that the Americans might use *nisei* as sacrificial front-line troops against Imperial forces when the latter
landed on Hawaiian beaches. The question of how a *nisei* in American military uniform would behave if confronted by a soldier in
the Imperial Army evoked considerable comment and speculation.

Most writers doubted that *nisei* would fight for the United States
against their ancestral land. "They may be loyal to the United
States," remarked Kanda, "but they are more loyal to Japan."
Hawaii-born Fred Miike concurred, but for different reasons. In
My Native Hawaii (1942) he wrote: "What person of any color
skin—white, black, yellow, red, brown—would want to fight for a
country that does not grant him equality?"

Other writers foresaw the *nisei* taking desperate steps to avoid
taking up arms on behalf of the United States. Masahei Kawamura
(an official in Yamaguchi Prefecture) and Saneyuki Yoshimori (a
graduate student of Japanese-American relations at Tokyo Imperial University) both wrote that they had talked with individual
nisei who said that they would commit suicide rather than serve
the United States as soldiers.

The combat records of AJA units of the United States Army in
Italy and France was, for obvious reasons, not publicized in Japan
during the war. Repatriated citizens did bring back reports of
these units to the Home Ministry as early as the autumn of 1943.
These reports may have been circulated to certain members of the
government, but the public was kept unaware of them. Within the
Home Ministry the tendency was to dismiss the formation of *nisei*

---

*In early June 1942, during the Battle of Midway, fourteen hundred members
(mostly *nisei*) of the Hawaiian Provisional Infantry Batallion sailed from Honolulu for training at Camp McCoy, Wisconsin, where the unit was renamed the
100th Infantry Battalion.

units as enemy propaganda. There is no evidence that Japanese officials pondered the implications of AJA military units in 1943. By late 1944, when confirmed reports of AJA combat exploits probably reached Japan, the question of Hawaii *dōhō* loyalties had (from Tokyo's perspective) lost any relevance to the war effort.

Were *nisei* in Tokyo's eyes prepared to assume the responsibilities incumbent upon Imperial Japanese citizens as leaders of a new order in Asia and the Pacific? Were they, in the words of Tamotsu Murayama, "ready to carry on the pioneer spirit and passion" of their parents with the "great perseverance and spirit of sacrifice necessary for the construction of Greater East Asia?"

Not everyone thought that they were. Policy Society analyst Setsuo Nakase warned that "Japanese-Americans have become accustomed to American life-styles." Sōen Yamashita lamented the weakening of pro-Japanese sentiment among *nisei* as a result of exposure to American propaganda inculcated in Hawaiian schools. He asserted that young *dōhō* must "sweep away the temptations of the culture of freedom *(jiyūshugi bunka)* and the ideal of individualism" in favor of Japanese values and a Greater East Asia world view. According to the former *Nippu jiji* reporter, such a process was an inevitable part of the Islands' imminent social transformation:

> Consequently, the necessity, nay the inevitability arise of moving our Hawaii compatriots' religion, education, careers, and lives in the direction of constructing the Greater East Asia Co-Prosperity Sphere. Especially insofar as the *nisei* problem is concerned, fundamental changes cannot be avoided. . . . Some of them [*nisei*] may waiver and seek the freedom of choice, but such behavior will not affect the final solution. In the making of a new age, all Hawaii *dōhō* whether *issei* or *nisei* will be required to make a new departure.

Tsugio Murakami of the Yoshida Research Center, however, had reservations about the prospect of all *nisei* being able to achieve spiritual renewal, the prerequisite for political leadership.

> As a whole, the Japanese problem [in Hawaii] will probably be solved under our military rule, but a part of the Japanese youth raised in an American culture, given an American education, and adopting an American character, will not become leaders of Greater East Asia, however much they are made to know about their ances-

tral land's divinity and however much is cultivated in them the spirit of sincerity.

Doubts about *nisei* more explicit than those intimated in Murakami's observations seem to have been held in wartime Japan. This cautious estimation of the *nisei* grieved Tamotsu Murayama, who in a series of articles published during 1942 in *Kaigai no Nippon* [Japan overseas] urged that the children of the "vanguard of the Japanese race" overseas be recognized as loyal citizens and soldiers:

> May I ask why has Japan been so unkind and heartless to the children of the great Japanese pioneers who fought for the cause of Japan for more than 50 years? . . . Whenever I recollect the hardships our parents have undergone in the United States, I spend sleepless nights and simply pray for their safety . . . Our parents went to the United States as vanguards of the Japanese race; therefore, I am sure they are not complaining of anything regardless of the inhuman treatment they are receiving or otherwise losing their various properties of the past half a century. They are undoubtedly sincerely praying for the last and great victory of Japan as well as for the speedy realization of the Greater East Asia Co-Prosperity Sphere.

> But our [*nisei*] real battle has just begun. We are helping each other and joining hands at every happy news of victory of Imperial forces . . .

Despite the doubts and at times outright prejudice against *nisei* in Japan, Tsugio Murakami was not about to write them off as beyond redemption. On the contrary, the young Kyoto researcher devised a carefully considered plan of action based upon a shrewd appreciation of one of the central contradictions of prewar Hawaii society, the contradiction between publicly professed American ideals of democracy and equal opportunity on one hand, and the reality of discrimination, arrogance, and exploitation on the other.

Murakami was not alone in realizing this contradiction. The journalist Takeshi Haga noted it, as did Hawaii-born Fred Miike. Murakami, however, took recognition one step further and turned it into a tactic to further the occupation's sociopolitical goals to break lingering ties to the United States and to cement loyalties to the Japanese Empire. Murakami realized that alienated intellectuals are already to some extent detached from society and receptive to social change, even revolutionary social change. He calculated that among Hawaii *nisei* there would be bright, ambitious individuals who had been well qualified for positions of leadership in American society but who were given no opportunity to achieve their career potentials because white-dominated political and business circles excluded them from power and prestige. Some of these *nisei* had left Hawaii before the war and were in Japan, working in companies or studying at institutions like the Foreign Ministry's *Heishikan.** Others, Murakami calculated, could be recruited locally thanks to expectations nurtured in the Islands' educational system and then frustrated after graduation from college:

> Fortunately, Japanese youth who have the same citizenship as [Caucasian] Americans, who have graduated from the University of Hawaii with academic achievements no less than other Americans, have encountered discrimination in society. They have been told to go back to the sugar plantations. This will make our task all the easier.

Neither Murakami nor other writers specified exactly what functions *nisei* would fulfill in Hawaii's political and social order under Japanese rule. Planning apparently had not reached that degree of detail by the summer of 1943, when the most qualified writers began to suspect that the course of the war after setbacks in Guadacanal and the Aleutians no longer made a Hawaii invasion a likely prospect.

The final studies produced by academics and journalists about Hawaii under Japanese rule were written in mid-1943, over one year after the Battle of Midway precluded an invasion of the Islands. Yet the prospect of Japan's liberation of Hawaii survived in some quarters for years to come.

---

*A special school for *nisei* directed by Sukeyuki Akamatsu, who during 1928–1930 served as consul general in Honolulu.

The Persistence
of Illusion

Apocalyptic visions of Hawaii's liberation, which shimmered in the public eye during the euphoric spring of 1942, and which thanks to censorship survived the Midway disaster, began to pall in 1943 when battlefield losses and a contracting Pacific perimeter intruded upon even the most resolutely sanguinary prognostications. By 1944 Hawaii had lost its topicality as the Greater East Asia War came home to millions of civilians in the form of acute shortages, high conscription quotas, long casualty lists, the evacuation of children from cities, and (in November) the appearance of B-29 bombers in Japanese skies. What had been a torrent of books and articles on Hawaii in 1942 dwindled to a trickle in 1943 and virtually dried up in 1944.

A deteriorating war situation extinguished neither the need for nor the availability of illusions. To compensate for the empire's sagging fortunes, the media wafted readers into ever loftier realms of fantasy. The trend was evident as early as January 1943 when the Imperial Army's withdrawal from Guadacanal was hailed as a "lateral advance" *(tenshin)*. By late 1944, the radio and newspapers were jubilating over chimerical victories, scrupulously tallying the latest score of sunken enemy carriers and obliterated enemy planes. The appearance of "special attack squadrons" *(tokkōtai)*, or in Western parlance *kamikaze* tactics, was accompanied by an escalation of hyperbolic rhetoric. Japanese heard more and more about the "invincibility" of Yamato spirit and were, as the final months of the war approached, told to prepare for the "decisive battle of the homeland" *(hondo kessen)* with bamboo spears.

In this charged psychological atmosphere, there occurred a

modest revival of literary fantasies redolent of the 1910s and 1920s when Yoshikatsu Ōto, Kyōsuke Fukunaga, Kōjirō Satō, and others published scenarios of Hawaii's conquest, California's subjection, and Manhattan's bow to an onslaught of Imperial Army dirigibles backed by American black freedom-fighters.

One of these terminal wartime scenarios did take its cue from recent history. Within a few hours of the Pearl Harbor attack, a Zero pilot whose engine had been damaged by anti-aircraft fire ditched his plane on Niihau, a sleepy island located 150 miles northwest of Honolulu and inhabited by 250 Hawaiians and part Hawaiians, one *issei*, and a *nisei* couple with a two-year-old daughter. From 7 December until 13 December the pilot, helped by the *nisei* husband, imposed his will on the island, whose inhabitants had no communications with the outside world except for a weekly boat from neighboring Kauai. After six days the pilot was killed by a Hawaiian. His *nisei* ally committed suicide.

Using this incident as raw material, the budding writer Sōhachi Yamaoka* spun a remarkable tale which was published as a factual account in August 1944. Refracted through the prism of Yamaoka's imagination, the pilot and *nisei* husband share a glorious death, having held off hordes of enemy attackers and having absorbed "thousands" of machine gun bullets. The reader is left with the arresting image of surviving Niihau *dōhō* defiantly marching off to internment camps while the *sansei* child "waits to grow up and carry on his [sic] father's loyalty."

If the momentary liberation of Niihau (the only Hawaiian island to experience a Japanese "occupation") had a basis in history, the "Bombing of Washington" (1944) by Kiyoshi Ōmori was pure wishful thinking seasoned with borrowings from prewar scenario literature. The plot has the Combined Fleet sailing across the Pacific, rounding Cape Horn, approaching Chesapeake Bay undetected, and linking up with a German squadron. The climax comes when the Axis partners dive-bomb the Washington Monument.

In 1944 such fare may have distracted readers whose daily lives were full of reminders that death was just around the corner. But the idea of assaulting the American mainland was not merely a literary diversion, nor was it confined to writers during the twilight of Imperial Japan.

---

*After the war, Yamaoka won fame for his historical fiction, among them an eighteen-volume novel on the first Tokugawa shogun.

According to the distinguished military historian Ikuhiko Hata, late in 1944 a group of naval officers led by Lieutenant Commander Daiji Yamaoka seriously entertained the prospect of launching a suicide strike in California. Some three-hundred chosen men of the "Yamaoka Parachute Brigade" were to be transported across the Pacific on several mammoth submarines and landed in the vicinity of Santa Barbara. They were then to shoot their way into Los Angeles via Santa Monica, wrecking havoc with the Douglas and Lockheed aircraft factories and taking as many lives as possible before their own annihilation. Training for this operation began in December 1944 but was halted in May 1945 with the selection of a new target, the Mariana Islands.

Except for units in scattered parts of the Pacific and Asia, and for a few die-hards at home, the Greater East Asia War came to an end on or shortly after 15 August 1945 when the emperor broadcast an appeal to "endure the unendurable" because the situation had developed "not necessarily to our advantage." Lingering dreams about Hawaii, such as there were, were soon dispelled by the harsh realities of defeat and occupation.

By the fall of 1945 those individuals who had written about or prepared plans for an invasion and occupation of Hawaii were either dead or adapting to new lives. Military figures fared poorly. Admiral Tamon Yamaguchi had gone down with his flagship at Midway on 5 June 1942. Commander in chief of the Combined Fleet Isoroku Yamamoto had been ambushed and killed in the skies over Bougainville on 18 April 1943. Admiral Matome Ugaki, the architect and champion of "Eastern Operation," took off on a solo *kamikaze* mission from a base outside of Tokyo on the last day of the war and was never seen again. Surviving Combined Fleet and Navy General Staff officers underwent extensive interrogations by the Americans. General Gen Sugiyama and his wife committed suicide shortly after the surrender ceremony on board the *USS Missouri*. General Shin'ichi Tanaka, the opponent-turned-enthusiast for a Hawaii invasion, spent the summer of 1945 in a hospital, recovering from serious injuries sustained in a plane crash outside of Phnom Penh. For all surviving officers, postwar life brought many hardships, not the least of which was being tainted men, "militarists" responsible for leading Japan down the path of overseas aggression and national catastrophe.

On the other hand, civilians involved with Hawaiian affairs made dextrous adjustments to the postwar sociopolitical environment. Identified as an ultranationalist by Occupation authorities, Professor Saneshige Komaki was obliged to resign from Kyoto University in 1945. He found employment, however, in a commuter train company. During the early 1960s, he re-entered academe, emerging as president of Shiga University in 1965. Komaki's student, Tsugio Murakami, spent most of the postwar years in academic life. As of 1979 neither Komaki nor Murakami had visited postwar Hawaii.

Hawaii *issei* and *nisei* who spent the war years in Japan met various fates, some of them painful. Fortune smiled, however, on George Kunitomo and Colbert Kurokawa. Both found employment with SCAP, General Douglas MacArthur's Occupation administration. Kunitomo subsequently taught American literature at Tokyo's Aoyama University. He returned to Hawaii for a brief visit in 1966, one year before his death. Kurokawa came back to Hawaii in 1951 and spent seven years in the islands working in the insurance field. Returning to Japan in 1958, he devoted himself to a religious sect and in 1967 was made a charter member of Lions International. His obituary in the *Honolulu Star Bulletin* (19 July 1978) bore the headline: "Colbert Kurokawa, Fighter for Global Peace, Dies at 87."

Some of the more vociferous wartime jingoists transmogrified like *zeitgeist* litmus paper into pacifists and Marxists after 1945. The floridly chauvinist editor of *Nippon hyōron*, Kōshin Murobuse, surfaced on the podium of Hibiya Hall in 1946 and denounced Emperor Hirohito as a war criminal to an audience that had gathered to welcome the communist leader Sanzō Nosaka back from Mao's Yenan. Yoshitarō Hirano, a wartime publicist of unabashedly hawkish proclivities who in a 1942 book on ethnic politics of the Pacific complained that Japanese were "too softhearted with the natives," bounced back dialectically in the postwar years to a variant of his prewar Marxism. When Hirano passed away at the age of eighty-two in 1980, an *Asahi* obituary wove a seamless fabric over the wartime interlude:

> As one of the editors of *Lectures on the Development History of Japanese Capitalism* published in 1932–1933, Hirano was a leading [Marxist] theorist in the Kōza [symposium] school in a famous controversy with the Rōnō [farmer-labor] school over the definition of Japanese capitalism. After World War II, he devoted himself to the

peace movement and participated in many international meetings. He was internationally known for his activities in support of the Vietnamese people, in the movements for Japan-China friendship and Asian-African solidarity.

The examples of Murobuse, Hirano, and others prompted Kazuo Yatsugi (wartime leader of the National Policy Research Society) to remark wryly that many postwar intellectuals who clamor for "progressive" and "anti-war" causes were among those in the vanguard of propagandists during the Greater East Asia War. To some extent, this can be explained by genuine idealism and a sincere belief in the war as a liberating mechanism. But, remembering the rhetoric of Komaki, Hirano, Murobuse, Noyori, Mochizuke, Kunitomo, Kurokawa, and others, one is reminded of a remark by the late British essayist and World War I veteran Charles Edward Montague: "War hath no fury like a noncombatant."

A significant number of Hawaii *issei* accepted postwar realities far less readily than did Japanese intellectuals. No quantitative data exist tabulating *issei* wartime views, nor would polls have illuminated the complexity of this generation's innermost feelings. Hawaii *issei* were not anti-American and they did nothing overtly against the United States, but to say that they wanted America to win the war would be a grievous misrepresentation. *Issei* were after all Japanese, not American, citizens.

Two postwar Japanese historians (Nobuhiro Adachi and Hidehiko Ushijima) who have written about the subject with insight and sensitivity both affirm that in their innermost hearts most *issei* remained loyal to Japan. According to Adachi, even among those who considered the Pearl Harbor attack a betrayal were many who believed in and hoped for an ultimate Japanese victory. "Great Japan" and the "invincible" Imperial Navy had come to have a special meaning for *issei*. They catalyzed pride and sharpened a sense of self-identity in an alien land. They symbolized the motherland's concern for its overseas children. Indeed, some *issei* viewed the Pearl Harbor operation as an Imperial Navy rescue mission for the benefit of Hawaii *dōhō*. Radio reports of Japanese advances in the Pacific and Southeast Asia (some *issei* had access to short wave sets) during 1941 and the first months of 1942 confirmed for many their motherland's invincibility.

As American reports of Japanese setbacks, including Midway, multiplied during 1942 and 1943, a number of *issei* began to withdraw into a fantasy world. Defeat of the empire in battle was unthinkable. American news reports, therefore, must be false. Some true believers formed underground *kachigumi* (victory groups) which combatted American "rumors" and strove to keep ethnic pride and confidence alive among Hawaii *issei*.

Japan's unconditional surrender came as a traumatic blow to Hawaii's *issei*. Confronted with the emperor's 15 August broadcast, *issei* women wept. The men heard the news, eyes downcast, in stony silence. Amid the celebrations and victory parades, many *issei* stayed indoors, mortified by shame and grief. Some felt awkwardness in facing their children.

A sizeable proportion of the *issei* in Hawaii psychologically refused to accept the events of August 1945 as reality. Rumors gave their delusions sustenance. Japan, it was said, had actually won the war. The Americans were trying desperately to hide this fact. President Truman had sent General MacArthur to Japan to apologize to the emperor for the "indiscriminate" bombing of Hiroshima. In Hilo (on the island of Hawaii), it was whispered that the Combined Fleet lay at anchor off Pearl Harbor, waiting for the Americans to clear the entrance channel of mines.

One *issei* recalled how shortly after the war he heard a rumor that Prince Takamatsu* was about to accept America's capitulation at a ceremony at Pearl Harbor. Eager to catch a glimpse of the momentous event, he climbed Mt. Tantalus and found a ridge overlooking central Oahu. He scanned the sprawling naval base and espied what looked like a huge Rising Sun flag fluttering over Pearl City. Exhilarated, he rushed down the hill for a closer inspection and discovered that he had been looking at a Red Cross flag.

Grasping for any scrap of evidence that would confirm their fantasies, some *issei* latched onto compatriots returning from mainland internment camps. The very appearance of interned *dōhō* gave birth to rumors that the releases had been actuated by America's surrender and the imminent transfer of Hawaii to Japan's jurisdiction. One observer wrote that on the Big Island, where *issei* nationalism was particularly strong, internment camp returnees met with more acclaim than that which was accorded

*The emperor's younger brother.

AJA veterans of the United States Army coming back from European fronts.

Blind faith in their motherland's invincibility cost some *issei* a good part of their life savings. Unscrupulous entrepreneurs, seeing a handy profit to be made from self-delusion, went around to *issei* offering to sell yen for dollars. The prewar exchange rate had been approximately three yen to the dollar. The *issei* were given a chance to get four yen for a dollar. Believing yen to be the currency of the victorious power, some *issei* fell for the deception and willingly gave up their dollars in exchange for what turned out to be a pittance (from 1948 until 1971 one dollar bought 360 yen).

After Japan's surrender, the underground Hawaii *kachigumi* surfaced as *kattagumi* (victory groups, with *katta* in the past tense, implying "we've won"). Among the known island *kattagumi* were the *Karihi hakkōkai* (Kalihi* Eight Corners† Society), the *Parama kōseikai* (Palama* Rebirth Society), the *Tōbu dōshikai* (Eastern Brotherhood Society), and the *Hawaii hisshōkai* (Hawaii Victory Society). The Hawaii Victory Society in 1948 claimed to have four thousand members (out of a total *issei* community of about thirty-five thousand). A 1949 investigation revealed that the actual figure was closer to five hundred.

By 1949 most *issei* had accepted the fact of their ancestral land's defeat. Some began to have doubts on 27 October 1945 (celebrated as Navy Day in prewar Japan) when it was bruited that the Imperial Navy would make a grand entrance into Pearl Harbor. Scores of *issei* flocked to Aiea Heights and waited—in vain. The emperor's radio broadcast on 1 January 1946, in which the now constitutional monarch disavowed his divinity, convinced most Hawaii *issei* that the war was indeed over. Among those who retained their earlier convictions, doubts sprouted in 1948 when someone went around collecting money for the emperor's imminent visit to Hawaii. For others, trips to Japan dispelled vestigial illusions.

A small core of Hawaii *issei* clung to their fantasies for years, much as did isolated Imperial Army soldiers hiding in remote cor-

---

*Kalihi and Palama are districts of Honolulu where many *dōhō* residences were formerly concentrated.

†The first two ideographs of the slogan "Eight Corners of the World Under One Roof."

ners of the Philippines and in the hills of Guam. Only on 17 November 1977, thirty-two years, three months, and two days after the end of the Greater East Asia War did the Hawaii Victory Society formally disband. In an announcement published in the *Hawaii hōchi*, Victory Society secretary Seiichi Masuda related the course of events that led to Japan's Occupation. He discussed the postwar growth of the motherland and praised the *nisei* for their loyal and heroic service in the United States Army. He concluded: "From now on, as a resident of a Hawaii that has passed into another world, I join my hands together and go to seek that paradisaical Hawaii."

If World War II offered some Hawaii *nisei* opportunities to demonstrate their loyalty to the United States, it evoked in others an awareness of their roots. Although only a tiny percentage of Hawaii *nisei* experienced internment (about 480 out of 120,000), there were those for whom the war catalyzed a fateful decision. As one Hawaii-born youth wrote his draft board in September 1944: "This war has made me clearly realize that my love and attachment to Japan have been deeper and stronger than I imagined." That young man spent a year in prison. Upon release, he renounced his American citizenship.

There are no statistics in the public domain telling how many Hawaii *nisei* gave up life in the United States and moved to Japan. It is certain, however, that those who took this step felt strongly enough to face formidable economic, linguistic, and cultural hurdles. For them, the "melting pot" and "Americanization" had become illusions from which they weaned themselves only gradually and not without pain, much as their parents were doing with their own illusions about Japan's invincibility.

Some twenty years after the war, Seattle-born Tamotsu Murayama wistfully wrote that if Emperor Meiji had only taken up King Kalakaua's 1881 proposals, Hawaii might have become Japanese territory. Murayama's wishful thinking had in the 1960s already become an anachronism, a nostalgic relic of a bygone age.

Nearly twenty years after Murayama's remark and over forty years since Pearl Harbor, time has pulled a curtain of amnesia across society's memories of the Greater East Asia War. In December 1981, in conjunction with the fortieth anniversary of Pearl Harbor, a *Yomiuri* newspaper poll revealed that 80 percent of Japanese men and women in their twenties were unable to associate "Pearl Harbor" with "7 December 1941." Asked what the words Pearl Harbor evoked, many answered: honeymoon trips to Hawaii.

And yet, time has a curious way of shading old ideas with new hues, of neutralizing their former toxicity so that they reappear as mellifluous, even salutary, innovations. The early 1980s have reverberated with talk about a "Pacific Community," about "Pacific Basin cooperation," and about "Pacific solidarity." Japanese statesmen, notably the late Prime Minister Masayoshi Ōhira, have been actively involved in such talk, perhaps more actively than their counterparts in any other Pacific rim country.

While making a stopover in Honolulu in July 1980, Japan's ambassador to the United States, Yoshio Okawara, delivered an address to a local dinner audience in which he said: "If it is indeed true that this vast Pacific Ocean has become an inland sea—perhaps the Mediterranean of the twenty-first century—then I would dare to predict that Hawaii, where all the roads of the Pacific intersect and the East meets West, will be the Rome of the twenty-first century.

A "Rome of the twenty-first century" is a far cry from Admiral Kanji Katō's "cancer in the Pacific," but not quite so far from Colbert Kurokawa's "Switzerland of the Pacific." Moreover, Prime Minister Zenkō Suzuki's remark at Honolulu's East-West Center on 16 June 1982 that Hawaiian society was "symbolic of Pacific solidarity" seems like a fulfillment of Kurokawa's 1943 suggestion that Hawaii be turned into a "temple of *ho'omalemale*."*

It would be both uncharitable and misleading to equate current Japanese pronouncements about a Pacific Community with wartime rhetoric about the Greater East Asia Co-Prosperity Sphere. One writer in the prestigious *Chūō kōron* [Central review] has observed that the association has occurred to a number of politicians. Current talk about the Pacific would appear to be a new departure in regional consciousness, but there are elements that can be traced to wartime antecedents.

One element with an unmistakable pedigree is Pacific geopolitics, a "science" practiced by Saneshige Komaki and others during the Greater East Asia War, which has arisen Phoenix-like from the

---

*As used by Kurokawa, the term meant the achievement of harmony through the reconciliation of differences.

ashes of Japanese chauvinism. In the early 1980s, works by Masaomi Ōmae, Tetsuo Maeda, and Morimochi Kuramae issued blunt
manifestoes urging Japan to take bold political initiatives in the
Pacific Basin. According to Kuramae, the twenty-first century will
be dominated by Pacific maritime countries among which Japan
has the oldest maritime culture. He then says: "Although Japan's
area is narrow and it cannot be self-supporting in resources and
foodstuffs, it has the highest civilization in terms of the level of
intellectual ability and as such can be a country which leads a
Pan-Pacific age."

Maeda identifies Japan's task for the twenty-first century as that
of creating a unified sphere in the Pacific that would give Japan
self-suffiency in resources, energy, and foodstuffs. Such words
might well have come from the wartime South Seas Economic
Research Center.

The above opinions are by no means representative of "mainstream" thinking about international politics and economics in
contemporary Japan. Moreover, the geopoliticians of the 1980s,
unlike their colleagues of the 1940s, stress cooperation with the
United States as a fundamental principle of Japanese foreign policy. Whatever the rhetorical antecedents, current talk about the
Pacific in Tokyo strongly suggests that Hawaii can expect to have
closer ties with Japan in the future.

Could Hawaii have been successfully invaded during the Greater East Asia War? Yes, and it nearly was. Only the unexpected
reverse at Midway aborted "Eastern Operation."

Both Japanese and Americans have reason to be thankful that
the islands were not seized in 1942 or 1943. However humanely
occupation authorities may have acted, Hawaii would have become a battleground like Okinawa and Saipan in the course of the
inevitable American counterinvasion. The scars left by combat
and collaboration in Hawaii would have affected not only postwar
Japanese-American relations but would have postponed and possibly precluded Hawaii's candidacy for statehood.

What lessons can be gleaned from an inquiry into Japan's wartime writing and planning about Hawaii? Perhaps the most important lesson is that we are reminded of the power and tenacity of
illusions. The more enduring illusions, however, have not been
those of wartime writers in Japan or of the Hawaii *issei* but our
own. Popular stereotypes still portray the Pacific War as a collision

of American democracy and Japanese militarism, when the war may have been closer to what Akira Iriye describes as an ongoing search for an international order in which both sides exhibit parallel rather than conflicting concepts of an Asia-Pacific "community."

Another contemporary illusion has been the habit of pointing to the Imperial Army and Navy when explaining Japanese overseas expansion. This stereotype has been shown to be oversimplified in the case of planning for Hawaii. The military planners (Yamamoto, Ugaki, Tanaka, and their staffs) had more restricted and clearly defined purposes for seizing the Hawaiian Islands. There is evidence that Yamamoto envisioned their retrocession to the United States after the war. Civilian planners (Komaki, Murakami, Kurokawa, Kanda, and others), however, exhibited acquisitive instincts and designs that in some cases went well beyond the pronouncements of Japan's military leaders.

Finally, it has been common to write about Hawaii's Japanese before and during the Second World War as if their "loyalty" were a self-evident, quantifiable phenomenon. In the justifiable impulse to indict the relocation of West Coast Japanese and Japanese-Americans and to highlight the heroic achievements of *nisei* in American military uniforms, writers have in many cases dealt simplistically with what is full of complex nuances and ambiguities. The experience of Hawaii *nisei* in the Imperial Japanese Army and Navy and of Hawaii *dōhō* in wartime Japanese educational and research institutions has been, with the exception of a handful of autobiographical accounts, a neglected subject.

If these illusions can be recognized and examined, then perhaps the "Pearl Harbor encore " (as the late Prime Minister Shigeru Yoshida dubbed the Hawaii invasion idea), will have made an unintended contribution to Japanese-American understanding.

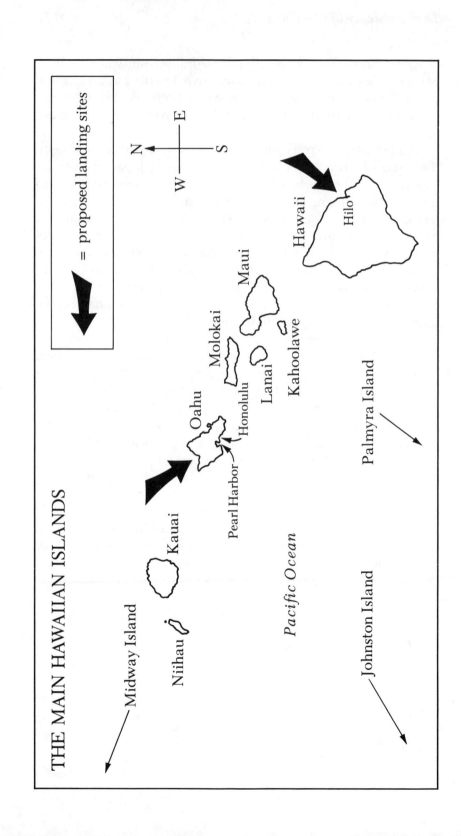

THE MAIN HAWAIIAN ISLANDS

Midway Island

Niihau

Kauai

Oahu

Pearl Harbor

Honolulu

Molokai

Lanai

Maui

Kahoolawe

Hawaii

Hilo

Pacific Ocean

Johnston Island

Palmyra Island

N
W — E
S

◼ = proposed landing sites

Notes

Sources cited in the notes are given in abbreviated form. For full bibliographical information on each source, see the Select Bibliography.

PREFACE

pages

x   sensitive naval documents had been filed separately: Professor Hisao Iwashima, interview, 7 January 1980.

x–xi   Destruction of Hawaii-related material at end of war: Professor Tsugio Murakami, interview, 18 August 1979.

xi   The staff officer to whom historians were owe a debt: officer who took the documents was Captain Noriyoshi Shiina. The material was hidden during the Occupation in the home of Lieutenant General Shūichi Miyazaki. Preface to volume 6 of Japan, Army General Staff, "Dai riku shi."

INTRODUCTION

3–4   "Actually, Japanese documents . . .": Allen, *Hawaii's War Years*, p. 63.

4   "As we now know, the Japanese did not . . .": Porteus, *And Blow Not the Trumpet*, pp. 42, 198.

     martial law in Hawaii: For a critical analysis see J. Garner Anthony, *Hawaii Under Army Rule* (Stanford: Stanford University Press, 1955). Reprinted by the University Press of Hawaii, 1975.

5–6   two genres of stereotypes: For changing stereotypes of Japanese-Americans, see Ogawa, *From Japs to Japanese*.

7–8   hardships of *nisei* veterans: On the postwar fate of Hawaii *nisei* who served in the Imperial Japanese Army, see Murayama, *Hawaii nisei*, p. 99.

8   "If the Japanese fleet arrived . . .": Quoted in Allen, *Hawaii's War Years*, p. 83.

9   Jun Etō remarked: Etō, Jun, ed., *Shūsen shiroku: bekkan* [Historical materials about the end of the war: supplementary volume] (Tokyo: Hokuyōsha, 1980), p. 9.

CHAPTER I: A Mid-Pacific Frontier

11   traditions were more faithfully preserved: Murayama, "Dai Nisei to kyōiku," p. 15.

12   Japanese were transported to Honolulu: For the history of Japanese immigration to Hawaii, see Conroy, *Japanese Frontier in Hawaii;* Wakukawa, *History of the Japanese People in Hawaii;* Ogawa, *Kodomo no tame ni;* Masaji Marumoto, " 'First Year' Immigrants to Hawaii and Eugene Von Reed," in Hilary Conroy and T. Scott Miyakawa, eds., *East Across the Pacific* (Santa Barbara, California: ABC Clio Press, 1972), pp. 5–39.

         more than double that of any other ethnic group: Conroy, *Japanese Frontier in Hawaii*, p. 136.

15   *issei* pride at victories in Sino-Japanese and Russo-Japanese wars. Ibid., p. 94. Wakukawa, *History of the Japanese People in Hawaii*, pp. 167–168.

15–16   dispatching the warship *Naniwa:* Bailey, "Japan's Protest," p. 48.

16   *Banzais* greeted the ship: Yamashita, *Nihonjin no Hawaii*, pp. 244–245.

         some local Japanese families named their children "Tōgō" or "Naniwa": Yamashita, *Nippon-Hawaii kōryūshi*, p. 233.

         Tōgō Masamune sake: advertisements in *Jitsugyō no Hawaii* during 1930s.

17   "men of means" leasing Hawaiian land: Conroy, *Japanese Frontier in Hawaii*, p. 48.

         King Kalakaua proposal: Ibid., pp. 50–53; Marumoto, "Vignette of Early Hawaii-Japan Relations," pp. 52–63.

         Hawaii was a household word: Mizuno, *Dakai ka*, p. 157.

         called the Islands a springboard: Iriye, *Pacific Estrangement*, pp. 42–43.

18   activists such as: In addition to Keishirō Inoue, there were Keisuke Kamio, Shinobu Inoue, Kōjirō Sakurada, and Den Sugawara. Sawada, *Kaigai hatten*, p. 173.

         Hiroharu (Kanji) Katō . . . felt deep regret: Hirano, *Minzoku seijigaku no riron*, p. 371.

         Soejima is reported to have considered taking over: Yamashita, *Nippon-Hawaii kōryūshi*, p. 13.

         Emperor Meiji's answer: Conroy, *Japanese Frontier in Hawaii*, pp. 52–53.

         an outcry in nationalist circles: Iriye, *Pacific Estrangement*, p. 53.

         Hoshi to Sherman: Bailey, "Japan's Protest," p. 52.

18-19   Hoshi to Ōkuma: *Nihon gaikō bunsho* [Documents of Japanese foreign policy], vol. 30 (Tokyo, 1954), 978.

19   One Japanese diplomat (Masanosuke Akiyama) . . . attempted suicide: Iriye, *Pacific Estrangement*, p. 53.

Suzuki address in Honolulu was attended by author. See also *Honolulu Advertiser*, 17 June 1982.

Reception at Honolulu Japanese Chamber of Commerce (23 June 1982) attended by author.

20   Japanese tourists came to Hawaii: Hawaii Visitors' Bureau, Research Department, "Revised Estimates of Overnight and Longer Visitors to Hawaii by National Origin for 1978, 1979, 1980, and 1981," Honolulu, March 1982.

Mitsukoshi Department Store opened: Murakami, "Hawaii no sugata," p. 201.

Japanese nationals have taken up residence: According to a telephone conversation on 2 August 1979 with a staff member of the Hawaii State Department of Health, Bureau of Statistics, the figure for 1978 was 13,525.

yakuza (gangsters): James Dooley, "Japanese Gangs Investing Heavily Here," *Honolulu Advertiser*, 10 January 1982.

21   43 percent of the total population: Wakukawa, *History of the Japanese People in Hawaii*, p. 353.

population . . . in 1980: Robert Hollis, "Melting-pot Mixture Grows More Diverse," *Honolulu Advertiser*, 9 May 1982.

nisei have transformed . . . political landscape: "Hawaii: The A.J.A.s: Fast-Rising Sons," *Time*, 20 October 1975. Wallace Turner, "Hawaii's Japanese Gain Power," *New York Times*, 24 October 1970.

CHAPTER II: The Prewar Japanese Community

23   "a second Japan": Uehara, *Nichi-Bei no setten Hawaii*, p. 1.

Territory's population: Matsumoto, *Ajia minzoku*, p. 227. Clark, "Some Japanese in Hawaii," p. 723. *Jitsugyō no Hawaii*, 19 September 1941, p. 2. Schmitt, *Historical Statistics of Hawaii*, pp. 10, 25. Mehnert, "Die Japaner auf Hawaii," pp. 596–598.

23-24   In 1940 a majority of Hawaii *nisei*: Lieutenant Commander M. C. Portello, "Nisei in Hawaii," 4 April 1940, in U.S. Army, G-2 Hawaiian Region, RF 165, Box 1917, National Archives.

24   liable to serve . . . in the Imperial Army: Wakukawa, *History of the Japanese People in Hawaii*, pp. 319–320. Murayama, *Hawaii nisei*, pp. 78–79.

1924 law: Yamashita, *Nihonjin no Hawaii*, p. 406.

accompanied by appropriate documentation: The process could nonetheless be complicated and time consuming. Murphy, *Ambassadors in Arms*, pp. 20–21.

renounced their Japanese citizenship: Barber, *Restless Rampart*, p. 140.

sansei . . . were eligible for registration: *Paradise of the Pacific*, vol. 50 (March 1938), p. 4.

26   "as long as you treat . . .": Blakeslee, "Hawaii: Racial Problem and Naval Base," p. 97.

"If we Japanese in Hawaii . . .": Clark, "Some Japanese in Hawaii," p. 725. See also Romanzo Adams interview in *Nippu jiji*, 26 October 1937.

Public Law 853: *Nippu jiji*, 6 January 1941, 25 July 1941.

Hawaii *nisei* . . . decided . . . not to return: Minoru Shinoda, interview, 31 January 1983.

issei attributed . . . superior status: Shibutani, *Derelicts*, p. 32.

27   Hitler and Saigō: *Jitsugyō no Hawaii* (March 1938), p. 2.

"Adolf Hitler has stark courage . . .": Ibid., 12 October 1938.

criticism of the Imperial Army was "unthinkable": Tamaru, *Hawaii*, pp. 21–22.

28   "Fellow compatriots . . .": *Jitsugyō no Hawaii* (February 1938), p. 5.

"holy war": The term appeared regularly in the vernacular press until 1941. See headlines of *Nippu jiji*, 1 January, 6 October 1941.

29   "The first generation . . .": Embree, *Acculturation*, p. 138.

"Japanese press reports . . .": *Jitsugyō no Hawaii* (January 1938), p. 49.

hailed the fall of China's capital: One headline read "Kagayakashii rekishiteki Nankin kanraku" [Brilliant historic fall of Nanking], *Jitsugyō no Hawaii* (January 1938), p. 39.

Allison . . . "slandering" Imperial Army: *Jitsugyō no Hawaii* (March 1938), p. 7. See also issue of February 1938, pp. 4, 5, 18.

29–30   Honolulu-za . . . and *Dōmei* newsreels: *Nippu jiji*, 1 October 1937.

30   Tokyo broadcasts to Hawaii: Barber, *Restless Rampart*, p. 153.

"Hear Japan": *Nippu jiji*, 3 October 1937.

prominent visitors: *Nippu jiji*, 11, 13, 23 October 1937; 22 February 1938.

Seigō Nakano: Ibid., 22 February 1938.

Nakano article attacking *"gomenasai gaikō"* [apologetic foreign policy]: *Jitsugyō no Hawaii*, 26 August 1938.

30–31   [Navy ships] calls in the Islands: Yamashita, *Nippon-Hawaii kōryūshi*, p. 27. Yamashita, *Nihonjin no Hawaii*, p. 259.

31   *issei* saw . . . as gratifying reassurance: Captain Takaji Terasaki, interview, 19 January 1980.

"A naval ship . . .": Miyamoto, *A Nisei Discovers Japan*, p. 23.

Vernacular press on careers of naval officers who had visited Hawaii: See articles on Rear Admiral Seo Tomoyuki in *Nippu jiji*, 5 January 1940; on Lieutenant Commander Terasaki Takaji in *Jitsugyō no Hawaii* (February 1938), pp. 11–13.

Admiral Ōkōchi letter: *Nippu jiji*, 18 October 1937.

Commander Kawasaki letter: *Jitsugyō no Hawaii*, 8 June 1937.

Captain Terasaki in Hawaii: *Jitsugyō no Hawaii*, 29 September 1938. Captain Takaji Terasaki, interview, 7 January 1980.

"Shining War Deeds . . .": *Jitsugyō no Hawaii* (April 1938), p. 13.

31–32   Kona hospitality to sailors from same prefecture: Embree, *Acculturation*, p. 133.

32   *Ondo* & *Erimo* called at Hilo: *Nippu jiji*, 16, 23 June 1937. *Jitsugyō no Hawaii*, 8 June 1937.

Hawaii *nisei* maiden and an "angry eagle": *Nippu jiji*, 19 April 1941.

Captain Takeda lectures: *Jitsugyō no Hawaii*, 25 November, 16 December 1938. "Propaganda of Foreign Origin," no. 2930 (30 August 1939), in U.S. Army, G–2 Regional Files, Hawaii, RG 165, Box 1921, National Archives. Burrows, *Chinese and Japanese in Hawaii*, p. 27.

32–33   mail from Hawaii *dōhō:* Admiral Suguru Suzuki, interview, 20 August 1979.

33   "Anyone who acts . . .": Embree, *Acculturation*, p. 134.

dōhō contributions to defense fund: Yamashita, *Nippon-Hawaii kōryūshi*, p. 376. Burrows, *Chinese and Japanese in Hawaii*, p. 32. Adachi, *Hawaii*, p. 74. Figures on Hawaii defense contributions after 1939 are not available. According to an Imperial Navy announcement of 8 July 1941, overseas *dōhō* contributions from all regions rose from 12,730,000 yen in 1939–1940 to 22,770,000 yen in 1940–1941. *Nippu jiji*, 8 July 1941. Some defense fund contributions went unreported to the United States Securites and Exchange Commission. In October 1938, a local group on the island of Hawaii raised 1,000,000 yen for war bonds by having subscriptions purchased in Japan through the Yokohama Specie Bank. Sōga, *Gojūnen no Hawaii kaikō*, p. 569.

Hawaii dōhō donated more per capita: Memo of George Roberts, Inspector of Customs, to Honolulu Collector of Customs, 21 August 1939. U.S. Army G–2 Regional File, Hawaii, RG 165, Box 1918, National Archives. *Nippu jiji*, 26 July 1939.

imonbukuro: Tahara, "For Sake of Fatherland," pp. 105–108. *Jitsugyō no Hawaii* (January 1938), p. 65.

34   Yonai letter: *Nippu jiji*, 2 October 1937.

Sugiyama letter: *Hawaii hōchi*, 15 October 1937. *Jitsugyō no Hawaii* (February 1938), pp. 30–31.

"Dedicated to serve . . .": *Jitsugyō no Hawaii* (February 1938), pp. 11–13.

message of encouragement: *Nippu jiji*, 1 January 1940, 1 January 1941; *Hawaii hōchi*, 1 January 1940, 1 January 1941.

"Japanese of Hawaii!": *Jitsugyō no Hawaii* (February 1938), p. 31.

35   half of their [*dōhō*] total assets: Tahara, "For Sake of Fatherland," p. 109.

"comfort visits": *Jitsugyō no Hawaii* 16 December 1938. Tahara, "For Sake of Fatherland," p. 107.

Nōnin in China: *Jitsugyō no Hawaii* (February 1938), pp. 26–27, 26 August 1938, p. 1.

vernacular press carried several articles [on Hawaii *nisei* in Imperial Japanese Army]: *Hawaii hōchi*, 20 September 1937, 6 October 1937; *Nippu jiji*, 4 January 1940.

36   One memory remained vivid: Hanama Tasaki, interview, 6 June 1980. For biographical information see also George Yamamoto review of *Long the Imperial Way* in *Paradise in the Pacific*, vol. 62, no. 9 (September 1950), 20–21.

Kona recruits: *Nippu jiji*, 23 October 1937.

praised a Honolulu family for sending . . . sons: *Hawaii hōchi*, 20 September 1937.

37   Kan Matsumura: *Nippu jiji*, 18 September 1941.

nisei and *sansei* should emigrate: Kiyokura Ibuka, ed., *Nippon minzoku no sekaiteki bōchō* [World expansion of the Japanese people] (Tokyo: Keigansha, 1933), p. 101.

nisei . . . should spearhead a propaganda drive: Yamashita, "Tai-Bei senden kōsaku," pp. 20–29.

nisei . . . to convince Americans of the justice of Japan's actions in East Asia: Azumi, "Kokumin gaikō," pp. 8–9.

38   "advance guard" of Japan's "holy war": Kiyohiro (Seikō) Ebizaka in Yamashita, *Hōshuku kigen*, pp. 203–205.

"*shishi* of a Showa Restoration": Azumi, "Tōa kyōeiken kakuritsu," pp. 12–13. Japan's consul-general in Honolulu in 1940, Kiichi Gunji, was recalled after making a remark about Hawaii Japanese being "all determined to undergo great sacrifices for Japan during the present uneasy condition of relations" between Japan and the United States. *Honolulu Advertiser*, 8 September 1978.

U.S. would do nothing: *Jitsugyō no Hawaii*, 9 December 1938.

"American Capital Welcome": Ibid., 4 November 1938.

38–39   "The United States has friendly relations . . .": Ibid., (January 1938), p. 1.

39   no contradiction between being pro-Japanese and pro-American: *Nippu jiji*, 30 June 1939. One nisei recalled: ". . . it never entered our minds that war between the two countries [Japan and USA] was imminent." Yoshida, *The Two Worlds*, p. 33.

downplayed . . . action against Singapore: *Nippu jiji*, 15 April 1941.

gave prominent coverage to Konoe's statement: Ibid., 11 April 1941.

Roosevelt had frozen Japanese assets: Ibid., 26 July 1941.

issei . . . putting their property in the name of *nisei:* Ibid., 3 January 1941.

changed their dollar savings into yen: Murayama, *Hawaii nisei*, p. 39. Yamashita, *Hōshuku kigen*, p. 217.

Hundreds returned to Japan: Ueda, "Hawaii no jitsujō," p. 160, mentions 440 applicants to board the *Taiyomaru* on 17 November 1941.

40   Tōgō Masamune brand was renamed Hilo Masamune: Advertisements
          in *Jitsugyō no Hawaii*, April 1938 and September 1941 (magazine for-
          mat) issues. Unfortunately, issues between these two dates could not be
          located.

CHAPTER III: Hawaii Japanese in Japan

41   forty-thousand *nikkeijin* in Japan: Yamashita, "Zai-Nichi daini-
          sei," p. 26.

          fourteen thousand were Hawaii-born: Blakeslee, "Hawaii," p. 93. Bar-
          ber, *Restless Rampart*, p. 142. One American source gives the figure of
          20,000 Japanese-Americans in Japan in 1938 (including those from
          Hawaii and the West Coast). U.S. War Office, *Final Report*, p. 14.

          Sino-Japanese hostilities in 1937 [boosts number of *nisei* going to Ja-
          pan]: Adachi, *Hawaii*, p. 74.

          Nisei educated in Japan: Embree, *Acculturation*, p. 132. Shirota, *Lucky
          Come Hawaii*, p. 2.

42   youth who went to Japan . . . came from better educated elements: Bar-
          ber, *Restless Rampart*, p. 145.

          prospects for better employment: Hanama Tasaki, interview, 6 June
          1980. Nisei Survey Committee, *The Nisei*.

          Exchange rates of . . . currencies: Yamashita, *Nihonjin no Hawaii*, pp.
          362–363.

          Patriotism . . . contributed: Hanama Tasaki, interview, 6 June 1980.
          Yamashita, *Nihonjin no Hawaii*, p. 363.

          ". . . all the while I grew up . . .": Knaefler, "House Divided," *Honolulu
          Advertiser*, 5 December 1966.

43   "more fanatically Japanese . . .": Lind, *Japanese in Hawaii Under War
          Conditions*, p. 25.

          1939 survey of *nisei*: Nisei Survey Committee, *The Nisei*.

          only 40 percent returned to the United States: Yamashita, *Nihonjin no
          Hawaii*, p. 363. This figure may be suspect. According to the recollec-
          tion of Akira Fukuoka, counsellor in the Treaty Section of the Foreign
          Ministry on 10 January 1948, there were 3,000 *nisei* in Japan during
          the war. Taking 14,000 (1938) as a base figure, it would seem that a
          large majority returned before 7 December 1941. For Fukuoka inter-
          view, see Supreme Commander for the Allied Powers, Education Re-
          search Branch, Civil Information and Education Section, General
          Headquarters, Far East Command, *Foreign Students in Japan, 1896–
          1947* (Washington, 1948).

          prejudice against *nisei* in Japan: Murayama, *Hawaii nisei*, p. 98. Miya-
          moto, *A Nisei Discovers Japan*, ii.

          Tokyo *Hōchi* . . . call[ed] for return of American *nisei*: *Nippu jiji*, 8
          August 1941.

44   intensive study . . . to compensate: Murayama, *Hawaii nisei*, p. 39.
          Yoshida, *The Two Worlds of Jim Yoshida*, passim.

Hawaii *nisei* private serving . . . in China: Yoshida, *The Two Worlds of Jim Yoshida*, pp. 160–163.

dōhō formed a number of organizations: Yamashita, *Nikkei shimin no Nihon ryūgaku jijō*, passim. *Nihon bunka dantai nenkan* [Yearbook of Japanese cultural organizations](Tokyo, 1943), p. 667.

Kaju Nakamura: Akita, "Taezaru happun kentō no chikara," p. 7. Nakamura, "Hoku-Bei zendo," pp. 26–33.

44–45   George Kunitomo: Kunitomo, *Chi no shio*, passim. Hanama Tasaki, interview, 6 June 1980.

45–46   Colbert Kurokawa: Kurokawa, "Raionizmu igai no shakai hōshi" [Social service outside of the Lions], 1966, autiobiographical manuscript in Kurokawa Papers, Honolulu. Kurokawa, "Hawaii ryō no yūrai to 30 nen no ayumi" [Genesis of the Hawaii ryō and its 30-year path], manuscript in Kurokawa Papers, Honolulu. Kurokawa, "Dōshisha Hawaii ryō: the Friend Peace House," address delivered at Dōshisha University, 27 May 1966, manuscript in Kurokawa Papers, Honolulu. *Honolulu Star-Bulletin*, 19 July 1978.

46   Kichisaburo Nomura and Ryozo Nakamura: Nihon Kindoi shiryō kenkyūkai, ed., *Nihon rikukaigun no seidō, soshiki, jinji*, p. 246.

in-house report on Hawaii: Kurokawa, "Hawaii o ika ni subeki ya."

Sōen Yamashita: Yamashita, *Hawaii shotō*, p. 173. Ritsuka Fujioka, interview, 19 September 1979.

47   Koiso view of *dōhō*: *Kigen nisenroppyakunen*, p. 33. Yano, *"Nanshin" no keifu*, p. 154.

Admiral Kanna on *nisei*: *Okinawa kindai shi jiten* [Dictionary of modern history of Okinawa] (Tokyo, 1977), p. 183.

48–52   Grand Congress of Overseas Compatriots: Yamashita, *Hōshuku kigen*.

49   Hawaii delegation: Ibid., pp. 69, 74, 96, 98, 100–104. According to the *Nippu jiji* (5 November 1940), the Hawaii delegation consisted of 300 individuals.

scene reminded him of troops being sent off to front: Yamashita, *Hōshuku kigen*, p. 190.

"Because the Japanese in Hawaii . . .": Ibid., p. 182.

49–50   "The greater the past afflictions . . .": *Kigen nisenroppyakunen*, p. 1.

50   deep impression upon the Hawaii delegation: Yamashita, *Hōshuku kigen*, pp. 213–214.

50n   "Overseas *Dōhō* Hymn": Ibid., p. 3.

50–51   Matsuoka address: Ibid., p. 55.

51   "On the occasion . . .": Ibid., p. 54.

lectures by officers of the armed forces: Ibid., p. 67.

tour of Army Air Base at Tachikawa: Ibid., p. 68.

52   "An unseverable relationship . . .": Ibid., p. 71.

"Linked by the Pacific . . .": Ibid.

tour of Manchuria and North China: Ibid., p. 93.

"The economic strength of our ancestral land . . .": Ibid., p. 69.

52n   referred to as *gaijin:* Ibid., pp. 178f, 183.

53   "Japan is going to win": Ibid., p. 212.

Kaigai dōhō chūō kai: Yamashita, *Hōshuku kigen,* p. 81.

Toshio Shiratori views: Robert W. Barnett (Research Secretary, American Council, Institute of Pacific Relations) interview, *Honolulu Advertiser,* 4 March 1942.

CHAPTER IV: Invasion Scenarios, 1909–1941

56   Mahan wrote . . ."take the islands first": Captain W. D. Puleston, *Mahan: The Life and Work of Alfred Thayer Mahan, USN* (New Haven: Yale University Press, 1939), p. 182.

Tokyo . . . infiltrating war veterans into Hawaii: Iriye, *Pacific Estrangement,* p. 160.

Lodge expressed misgivings: Lodge to William Sturgis Bigelow, 12 June 1907, quoted in Ibid., p. 164.

56n   Mahan . . . identified China as a threat: Mahan, "Hawaii and Our Future Sea Power," *The Forum* (March 1893), reproduced in Mahan, *The Interest of America in Sea Power.*

56–57   Homer Lea: Clare Boothe, "The Valor of Homer Lea," preface to 1942 edition of *The Valor of Ignorance.*

58–59   uprising among [Hawaii] Japanese: Bywater, *The Great Pacific War,* pp. 232–239.

59   Hawaii occupation of 1913 scenario: Kokumin gunji kyōkai, *Nichi-Bei kaisen yume monogatari,* pp. 212–216.

60   1914 . . . similar fantasy: Ōto, *Nichi-Bei,* pp. 50–53, 64–65.

1921 scenario: Satō, *Nichi-Bei sensō,* pp. 192, 199, 200, 204, 206, 214, 222.

61   Navy officers' . . . conversation about . . . *dōhō:* Fukunaga, *Nichi-Bei sen miraiki,* p. 80.

"Let's hurry up and take this island!" Ibid., p. 79

Admiral Suetsugu recommended the novel: translation by Mark Peattie. Peattie, "Forecasting," p. 62.

"Books like these . . .": Ibid., p. 8.

62   Admiral Kawashima lecture: Kawashima, "Kaigun yori mitaru Nichi-Bei mondai," pp. 187–224.

62–63   more refined public scenarios: Whimsicality did not disappear from Japanese scenarios during the 1930s. One author asked the U.S. to give Alaska to Japan in order to "bring world peace." Kiyosawa, *Amerika wa Nihon to arasowazu,* p. 364.

63   "Hawaii is the Tennōzan . . .": partial quote in Peattie, "Forecasting," p. 51. Full quote in Mizuno, *Dakai ka,* p. 163.

"If America loses Guam . . .": Mizuno, *Dakai ka,* p. 165.

"If Japan can seize Hawaii . . .": Ibid., p. 161.

64   *dōhō* insurrection . . . no more utility than a "children's movie": Ibid.,
          p. 166.

64-65   Chūkō Ikezaki: Peattie, "Forecasting," pp. 45-47. Ikezaki, *Taiheiyō
          senryaku ron*, p. 141. Ikezaki, *Nichi-Bei arasowaba*, p. 271.

65   Kanji Katō to Ikezaki on Hawaii a "cancer of the Pacific": Peattie,
          "Forecasting," p. 46.

65-66   1940 scenario: Matsuo, *Sangoku dōmei*, pp. 319-329.

67   Saitō on Hawaii: Saitō, *Taiheiyō senryaku joron*, p. 180-182.

CHAPTER V: Hawaii in Imperial Naval Strategy

70-71   internal tensions plagued the navy: Asada, "The Japanese Navy," pp.
          225-259. Dull, *A Battle History*, p. 7. Pelz, *Race to Pearl Harbor*, p. 28.

72   U.S. . . . named a hypothetical enemy: Iriye, *Pacific Estrangement*,
          p. 148.

          British and German military circles: Raymond A. Esthus, *Theodore
          Roosevelt and Japan* (Seattle: University of Washington Press, 1966),
          p. 188.

          Tokyo rated American capabilities very highly: Fukudome, *Shikan:
          Shinjuwan kōgeki*, p. 115.

          yōgeki sakusen: Ibid., pp. 135-136. Peattie, "Forecasting," p. 43.

72-73   Japan's "mainstream" naval strategy: U.S. Strategic Bombing Survey,
          Naval Analysis Division, *Campaigns in the Pacific War*, p. 2. Agawa,
          Reluctant Admiral, p. 194.

73   Guam and the Philippines were marked for landings: Peattie, "Fore-
          casting," p. 28.

          Hawaii . . . not mentioned as a target: Japan, Bōei-chō, *Daihon'ei, kai-
          gunbu*, 2:299. *Chūbu Taiheiyō*, 1:303.

73-74   Yamamoto's background: Agawa, *Yamamoto Isoroku.* Nihon kindai
          shiryō kenkyūkai, *Nihon rikukaigun*, p. 119.

74   Yamamoto . . . lost two fingers: Toland, *Rising Sun*, p. 150.

          "In operations against America . . .": Japan, Bōei-chō, *Daihon'ei, kai-
          gunbu*, 2:300.

75   1935 maneuvers: Pelz, *Race to Pearl Harbor*, p. 198. Admiral Akira
          Yamaki, interview, 19 January 1980.

          unsettled the Navy General Staff: Zacharias, *Secret Missions*, pp. 191ff.

          1936 Navy War College study: Asada, "The Japanese Navy and the
          United States," pp. 237-238.

75-76   1938 American Fleet maneuvers: Mehnert, "Problem XIX," pp. 559-
          569.

76   Hawaii dependence upon food imports: Mehnert estimated that 85 per-
          cent of "supplies" were imported from the mainland, that the military
          population (25,000) had adequate long-term stores, but that the civilian
          population (210,000) had foodstuffs for only sixty days. Mehnert, Ibid.,
          p. 568.

76-77   backgrounds of Yamamoto staff: Nihon kindai shiryō kenkyūkai, *Nihon
          rikukaigun.* Toland, *Rising Sun*, p. 151.

77   Yamamoto and Watanabe played *shōgi:* Agawa, *Reluctant Admiral,* p. 257.

78   4 July 1940 leading officers . . . reached a consensus: Crowley, "Japan's Military," p. 85.

Matsuoka as first to air Greater East Asia Co-Prosperity Sphere on 1 August 1940: *Nihon gaikōshi jiten* [Dictionary of Japanese diplomatic history] (Tokyo: Gaimushō, 1979), p. 475. Yano, *"Nanshin" no keifu,* p. 156.

78–79   concept . . . broached by Hachirō Arita: Horiuchi, "Chiseigaku," p. 22.

79   Sphere a fundamental objective of Imperial foreign policy: Crowley, "Japan's Military," p. 83.

Konoe address to the Diet on 21 January 1941: Sakurai, "Ajia no saiken," p. 2.

Sphere "overlapped" with American interests: Rōyama, "Dai Tōa kōiki-kenron," p. 33.

Konoe hoped Sphere could be established without war: Crowley, "Japan's Military," p. 81.

79–80   "Draft Outline . . .": Japan, Kaigun, Gunreibu, "Dai Tōa kyōeiken kensetsu taikō (shian)."

80   Yamamoto certain Japan could not win war of attrition: Japan, Bōei-chō, *Daihon'ei, kaigunbu,* 1:552. Fukudome, *Shikan: Shinjuwan kōgeki,* pp. 124–125.

"If I am told to fight . . .": Morison, *Rising Sun in the Pacific,* p. 46.

81   Yamamoto began seriously considering a Pearl Harbor attack: Japan, Bōei-chō, *Hawaii sakusen,* pp. 80–81.

1928 paper outlining ingredients of a Pearl Harbor strike: Agawa, *Reluctant Admiral,* p. 193.

Yamamoto letter to Oikawa: Japan, Bōei-chō, *Daihon'ei, kaigunbu,* 1:552.

General Staff reacted negatively: Ibid., 2:116–117.

81–82   Kuroshima and Watanabe plans: Holmes, *Double-edged Secrets,* pp. 78ff.

82   7 August exchange between Kuroshima and Tomioka: Agawa, *Reluctant Admiral,* p. 223.

task force would suffer heavy losses: Agawa, *Reluctant Admiral,* p. 228.

Kuroshima and Itō argued the pros and cons: Potter, *Yamamoto,* p. 63. Zacharias, *Secret Missions,* p. 245.

83   recruit Japanese bank officials for espionage: U.S. Department of Defense, *"Magic" Background,* 1:29.

83–84   Matsuoka advised "utmost caution": Ibid., 1:A–76–77.

84   *kibei* were approached in Japan: Admiral Suguru Suzuki, interview, 19 January 1980.

Yoshikawa did not trust local Japanese: Interview of Takeo Yoshikawa by Ron Laytner, *Washington Post,* 10 December 1978.

Fukudome echoed . . . doubts: Fukudome, *Shikan: Shinjuwan kōgeki*, pp. 186–187.

Suzuki not permitted to go ashore: Toland, *Rising Sun*, pp. 166–167. Admiral Suguru Suzuki, interview, 20 August 1979.

84n Suzuki family background: Nihon kindai shiryō kenkyūkai, *Nihon riku-kaigun*, p. 101.

84–85 learned no ships were at Lahaina: Admiral Suguru Suzuki, interview, 20 August 1979. Fukudome, *Shikan: Shinjuwan kōgeki*, p. 189.

85 Suzuki met with Ugaki: Admiral Suguru Suzuki, interview, 20 August 1979.

85–86 two projected stages [of strategic war aims]: Japan, Bōei-chō, *Daihon'ei, kaigunbu*, 2:5, 298.

86 Nagano statement: Fukudome, *Shikan: Shinjuwan kōgeki*, p. 125.

Inoue assertion: Niina, *Kaigun sensō*, pp. 166, 174.

86–87 comparisons of U.S. and Japan's power: U.S. Navy Department, Office of Naval Intelligence, "Japanese Estimates and Comparisons of Resources as of the Beginning and End of the War," no. 7 (26 June 1946). Michel, *Second World War*, 1:333; 2:809. Zacharias, *Secret Missions*, p. 240. Toland, *Rising Sun*, p. 94.

87 special circumstances compensated for Japan's disadvantages: For psychology underlying Japan's decision for war, see Ike, *Japan's Decision for War*. Butow, *Tojo and the Coming of the War*.

88 Yamamoto . . . reconciled himself to war: Pelz, *Race to Pearl Harbor*, p. 225.

CHAPTER VI: The Birth Pangs of "Eastern Operation"

89–90 Scene in *Nagato* operations room; Yamamoto remark: Japan, Bōei-chō, *Daihon'ei, kaigunbu*, 2:78.

90 no aircraft carriers in Pearl Harbor disturbed the commander in chief: Japan, Bōei-chō, *Middowei kaisen*, p. 28.

ease of Pearl Harbor attack: Ibid., p. 18.

91 "If we had known . . .": Quoted in Watanabe, *Shiden Yamamoto gensui*, p. 277.

twin disappointments heightened Yamamoto's appreciation: Japan, Bōei-chō, *Daihon'ei, kaigunbu*, 2:300.

by actions more than by words: Ibid., 2:1, 241–244.

Yamamoto talked with Kuroshima: Kuroshima recollections, Ibid., 2:242.

Yamamoto asked Watanabe whether . . . Hawaii could be seized: Ibid., 2:242.

"From point L . . .": Ibid., 2:242–243.

92 [Yamamoto] talking "repeatedly" about invading Hawaii: Ibid., 2:309.

9 December instructions to Ugaki: Ibid., 2:243. Japan, Bōei-chō, *Hawaii sakusen*, p. 480.

Yamamoto believed that Washington: Japan, Bōei-chō, *Daihon'ei, kaigunbu,* 2:243.

happō yabure: Ibid., 2:300. This strategy later was expressed in the Navy General Staff's operations diary *(Gunreibu sakusen nisshi)* on 29 April 1942.

93   Americans living under Japanese rule . . . a "spiritual blow": Japan, Bōei-chō, *Daihon'ei, kaigunbu,* 2:243.

Yamamoto did not envision a Japanese annexation of Hawaii: Ibid., 2:317.

93–94   55 percent of the respondents wanted U.S. to come to its rescue: Poll inserted in *Fortune* magazine, August 1940. During the course of the war, repatriated Japanese reinforced the impression in some quarters that Americans would be reconciled to the loss of Hawaii. See "Zai Beishū dōhō no dai issen o mukaeta" [Meeting the first boat of dōhō being repatriated from America], *Kaigai no Nippon,* vol. 16, no. 8 (September 1942), p. 4.

94   *miryoku:* Admiral Buguru Suzuki, interview, 20 August 1979. Suzuki used the words *"hitotsu no miryoku"* [one of the attractions].

Ugaki assumed personal control: Japan, Bōei-chō, *Daihon'ei, kaigunbu,* 2:318.

lack of up-to-date intelligence: Japan, Imperial Navy, Yokosuka Naval Air Base, "Dai Tōa sensō senkun," p. 5.

vessels operating in Hawaiian waters: Japan, Bōei-chō, *Chūbu Taiheiyō,* 1:305.

reconnaissance flights over Pearl Harbor: Japan, Navy General Staff, "Sanagi nisshi," 5 January 1942. *Honolulu Star-Bulletin,* 16 July 1957.

95   Nagano pointedly fell asleep: Nukada, *Rikugunshō,* p. 111.

Vague accommodation both . . . viewpoints in language: Japan, Bōei-chō, *Middowei kaisen,* p. 32.

95–96   General war plan: Japan, Bōei-chō, *Daihon'ei, kaigunbu,* 2:294–295. Ugaki, *Sensōroku,* p. 101. Takagi, *Taiheiyō kaisenshi,* p. 47.

96   Army General Staff priorities: Japan, Bōei-chō, *Daihon'ei rikugunbu,* 3:337. Japan, Bōei-chō, *Daihon'ei, kaigunbu,* 2:301–302, 311.

Navy General Staff priorities: Japan, Bōei-chō, *Daihon'ei, kaigunbu,* 2:296. 312–315.

Combined Fleet priorities: Ibid., 2:312–315, 322.

97   Tomioka-Kuroshima meeting: Japan, Bōei-chō, *Middowei kaisen,* p. 43. Japan, Bōei-chō, *Daihon'ei, kaigunbu,* 2:310.

98   ". . . problem of Hawaii assault . . .": Tanaka, "Gyōmu nisshi," 12 December 1941, in Japan, Bōei-chō, *Daihon'ei, kaigunbu,* 2:248.

Tanaka conveyed views to Tomioka: Japan, Bōei-chō, *Daihon'ei, kaigunbu,* 2:312.

98n   accorded strategic significance to Hawaii: General Ishiwara favored an occupation of Hawaii "if possible" during 1926–1928 as lecturer in military history at Army Staff College. Peattie, "Forecasting," p. 33.

Peattie, *Ishiwara Kanji*, p. 69. Kenryō Satō regarded Hawaii as part of the "encirclement" of Japan. Satō, *Dai Tōa sensō kaisōroku*, p. 220.

98–99   Miwa to Tokyo: Japan, Bōei-cho, *Daihon'ei, kaigunbu*, 2:318.

99   Tomioka to Tanaka, 4 January 1942: Ibid., 2:314.

Captain Kami's study: Ibid., 2:244.

100   10 January 1942 liaison conference: Japan, Bōei-chō, *Daihon'ei riku-gunbu*, 3:333.

Sasaki in Tokyo to report: Japan, Bōei-chō, *Daihon'ei, kaigunbu*, 2:318. *Middowei kaisen*, p. 29.

Ugaki wrote in his diary: Ugaki, *Sensōroku*, p. 68. Japan, Bōei-chō, *Daihon'ei, kaigunbu*, 2:320.

additional options [to "Eastern Operation"]: Ugaki, *Sensōroku*, pp. 101–102. Japan, Bōei-chō, *Middowei kaisen*, pp. 26–27, 29.

Fiji-Samoa operation evoked the least enthusiasm: Japan, Bōei-chō, *Chūbu Taiheiyō*, 1:515.

101   Yūji Yamamoto on Hawaii invasion: Japan, Bōei-chō, *Daihon'ei riku-gunbu*, 3:567.

Navy General Staff infected by Combined Fleet adventurism: Colonel Kumao Iimoto of Second Section, Army General Staff. Japan, Bōei-chō, *Daihon'ei, kaigunbu*, 2:315.

General Tanaka noted in his diary: Japan, Bōei-chō, *Daihon'ei riku-gunbu*, 3:344.

26 January meeting: Japan, Bōei-chō, *Daihon'ei, kaigunbu*, 2, insert.

Yūji Yamamoto . . . to convey bad news: Ibid., 2:323–324.

Ugaki and his men still had their sights on Hawaii: When Commander Yūji Yamamoto returned to Tokyo and reported to Captain Tomioka, another member of the Planning Section, Commander Tsuyoshi Sanagi wrote in his diary (30 January 1942) that the Combined Fleet staff still wanted to take Hawaii *(dekiru dake toritai)*, adding that especially Ugaki was enthusiastic *(toku ni sanbōchō nesshin)*. Ibid., 2:324.

air raids on the Marshall Islands: Ugaki, *Sensōroku*, entry for 2 February 1942. pp. 74–75.

Fujii to Tokyo: Japan, Bōei-chō, *Middowei kaisen*, p. 29. Japan, Bōei-chō, *Daihon'ei, kaigunbu*, 2:335.

Differences between Navy General Staff and Combined Fleet: Takagi, *Taiheiyō sensō to rikukaigun no kōsō*, p. 54.

army-navy disagreements over perimeter expansion: Tanemura, *Daihon'ei kimitsu nisshi*, p. 117.

102   "How is the war . . .": Japan, Bōei-chō, *Daihon'ei, kaigunbu*, 2:252.

army and navy views of Ceylon operation: Japan, Bōei-chō, *Chūbu Taiheiyō*, 1:515.

Yamamoto on Ceylon and Hawaii: Japan, Bōei-chō, *Daihon'ei, kaigunbu*, 2:246, 309, 351. Yamamoto's view on this matter was represented by the postwar reminiscences of his planning officer, Commander Yasuji Watanabe. Japan, Bōei-chō, *Daihon'ei, kaigunbu*, 2:351.

103   Tamon Yamaguchi background: Admiral Akira Yamaki, interview, 19 January 1980. Nihon kindai shiryō kenkyūkai, *Nihon rikukaigun no seidō*, p. 119. Zacharias, *Secret Missions*, pp. 30, 160.

             [Yamaguchi] assumed . . . another strike on Pearl Harbor: Agawa, *Reluctant Admiral*, p. 264.

104–   "Yamaguchi plan": Japan, Bōei-chō, *Daihon'ei, kaigunbu*, 2:304–307.
105   Draft in War History Office, Tokyo, gives list of officers to whom the plan was circulated. The Draft notes that the plan was prepared by a "Commander Suzuki." The officer is neither Suguru Suzuki of Naval Intelligence nor Eijirō Suzuki who, although an air warfare specialist, wrote to me (17 September 1979) that he had no recollection of such a plan.

105   Tanaka came out against a Hawaii invasion: Japan, Bōei-chō, *Daihon'ei, kaigunbu*, 2:336–337.

106   4 March conference: Ibid., 2:287.

106–   7 March liaison conference: Japan, Rikugun, Sanbō honbu, *Sugiyama*
107   *memo*, 2:52. Japan, Bōei-chō, *Daihon'ei, kaigunbu*, 2:287–289. Japan, Bōei-chō, *Middowei kaisen*, p. 33. Tanemura, *Daihon'ei kimitsu nisshi*, p. 118.

107   "Fundamental Outline" presented to the emperor on 13 March: Japan, Bōei-chō, *Daihon'ei, kaigunbu*, 2:290–292. Hawaii was not explicitly mentioned in this document. The phrase "more positive war leadership" was explained as referring to India and Australia.

             Miwa-Kami misunderstanding: Japan, Bōei-chō, *Daihon'ei, kaigunbu*, 2:332–335.

CHAPTER VII: Stillborn Invasion

109   "the sentry for Hawaii": Nagumo quoted in Morison, *Coral Sea, Midway, and Submarine Actions*, p. 70.

110   when research on a Midway operation began: Japan, Bōei-chō, *Middowei kaisen*, pp. 38–39.

             Pacific target consistent with a Hawaii invasion: Japan, Bōei-chō, *Daihon'ei, kaigunbu*, 2:340.

             "ninth inhabited Hawaiian Island": Murakami, "Hawaii no sugata," p. 188.

             Yamamoto intended to urge . . . peace negotiations: Yamamoto, *Chichi Yamamoto Isoroku*, p. 185. Potter, *Yamamoto*, p. 179.

111   "If we could, we wanted to go to Pearl Harbor . . .": Yasuji Watanabe quoted in U.S. Strategic Bombing Survey, *Interrogations of Japanese Officials*, 1:66. The late Gordon Prange recalled that Watanabe had expressed himself strongly in favor of a Hawaii invasion (interview with author, 15 June 1979). Another source qualifies such an impression, saying that Watanabe favored an assault on Hawaii but unlike his superior, Admiral Ugaki, he had reservations about the Combined Fleet's air power being adequate to cope simultaneously with carrier-based and Oahu-based enemy planes. Japan, Bōei-chō, *Daihon'ei, kaigunbu*, 2:322.

Tomioka to Tanaka about Midway: Ibid., 2:341.

Sugiyama to emperor: Ibid., 2:338.

Completed Midway plan: Japan, Bōei-chō, *Middowei kaisen*, p. 41.

111–   Watanabe-Tomioka argument: Japan, Bōei-chō, *Daihon'ei, kaigunbu*,
112   2:343. Japan, Bōei-chō, *Middowei kaisen*, p. 44.

112   Nagano decided to . . . approve the Midway operation: Japan, Bōei-chō,
         Middowei kaisen, pp. 46–48. Japan, Bōei-chō, *Daihon'ei rikugunbu*,
         3:578. Japan, Bōei-chō, *Daihon'ei, kaigunbu*, 2:347.

113   invasion of Hawaii would take place in stage four: Japan, Bōei-chō,
         Middowei kaisen, p. 64.

         Nagano submitted [Midway] plan to the emperor: Japan, Bōei-chō, *Mid-
         dowei kaisen*, p. 52. Japan, Bōei-chō, *Daihon'ei, kaigunbu*, 2:350. Ja-
         pan, Bōei-chō, *Daihon'ei rikugunbu*, 3:582.

         psychological effects of the Doolittle raid: Tanemura, *Daihon'ei kimitsu
         nisshi*, pp. 120–121.

114   Nagano statement after Doolittle raids: Sorimachi, *Ningen Yamamoto
         Isoroku*, 2:239.

         Ugaki's worst fears: Japan, Bōei-chō, *Middowei kaisen*, pp. 34–35.
         Japan, Bōei-chō, *Daihon'ei, kaigunbu*, 2:172. Ugaki, *Sensōroku*, pp.
         74–75.

         Tanaka made an about-face: Japan, Bōei-chō, *Daihon'ei, kaigunbu*,
         2:366, 403.

115   Shin'ichi Tanaka background: Nihon kindai shiryō kenkyūkai, *Nihon
         rikukaigun no seidō*, p. 43. Tanaka, *Tanaka sakusen buchō no shōgen*.

         netsui: Japan, Bōei-chō, *Daihon'ei, kaigunbu*, 2:403.

115–   order . . . for the training of certain units: Japan, Army General Staff,
117   "Dai riku shi," vol. 6, no. 1159. "Haruki Makoto shuki," May 1942.
         "Iimoto nikki," May 1942. Japan, Bōei-chō, *Daihon'ei rikugunbu*,
         4:216– 218. Japan, Bōei-chō, *Daihon'ei, kaigunbu*, 2:403.

118   assignments for the Hawaii invasion: Ikuhiko Hata, interview, 14
         August 1979.

         Army estimate of American forces on Oahu: Japan, Bōei-chō, *Daihon'ei
         rikugunbu*, 3:586.

119   low regard of army officers for American infantryman: Fukudome, *Shi-
         kan: Shinjuwan kōgeki*, p. 112.

         Tanaka ordered feasibility study: "Iimoto nikki," in *Daihon'ei, kaigun-
         bu*, 2:403.

120   Yamaguchi, had he lived, would have succeeded Yamamoto: Testimony
         of Yasuji Watanabe in U.S. Strategic Bombing Survey, *Interrogations of
         Japanese Officials*, 1:66.

         Hawaii assignments were terminated: Japan, Bōei-chō, *Daihon'ei riku-
         gunbu*, 4:218.

CHAPTER VIII: Victory Disease

124   *senshōbyō* . . . expression   coined   by   Ikezaki: Peattie,   "Forecast-
         ing," p. 36.

Tōjō felt compelled to caution elected officials: Butow, *Tojo and the Coming of the War*, p. 416.

[Yamamoto] predicted war could last . . . ten years: Letter to his sister, Kayoko Takahashi, 18 December 1941. Watanabe, *Shiden Yamamoto gensui*, p. 277.

inflated public expectations: Shin'ichi Tanaka recollections, Japan, Bōei-chō, *Daihon'ei rikugunbu*, 3:337.

88 percent of army and navy personnel . . . killed or wounded: Radio Tokyo, 2 February 1942. U.S. Navy, "Japanese Broadcasts."

Enterprise and *Lexington* sunk: Ibid., 14 January 1942.

125   255 [warships] were in Pearl Harbor: Miyashiro, *Hawaii*, p. 369.

"ruled out" an enemy counteroffensive: Taniguchi, *Dai Tōa keizai no riron*, p. 479.

24 December and 24 January Radio Tokyo broadcasts: U.S. Navy, "Japanese Broadcasts."

Roads along West Coast deserted: Miyashiro, "Hawaii no gunbi," p. 90.

Roosevelt ordered evacuation of West Coast factories: Nakamura, "Building Greater East Asia," p. 3.

"Sensible Americans know . . .": U.S. Navy, "Japanese Broadcasts."

126   Pearl Harbor electrified black communities: Masayoshi Murakami, *Amerika no genjō bunseki* [An on-the-spot analysis of America] (Tokyo: Kōa shobō, 1942), pp. 284–286.

"They . . . never felt so high an elation . . .": Nakamura, "Grandiose Policy Needed," p. 2.

"farms in California . . .": U.S. Navy, "Japanese Broadcasts."

"The western Pacific is in our hands . . .": Murobuse, *Nihon no risō*, p. 9.

eastern Pacific was already under Japanese control: Nakamura, "Building Greater East Asia," p. 2.

"expense of water between Hawaii . . .": U.S. Navy, "Japanese Broadcasts."

126n   Murobuse background: *Gendai jinbutsu jiten* [Biographical dictionary of contemporary figures] (Tokyo: Asahi shinbunsha, 1977), p. 1396.

127   "As the Imperial Navy now controls . . .": Hiraide, "Sekai ni tatsu teikoku kaigun," p. 21.

Pacific to be "restored" to "natural unity" with Asia: Shibuya, *Minami Taiheiyō shotō*, passim.

"Pacific Ocean is the *furusato* . . .": Yamashita, *Nippon-Hawaii kōryūshi*, p. 93.

Pacific islands "extensions" of Japanese archipelago: Kada, *Sensō honshitsu ron*, p. 431.

"Pacific must become an Asian ocean": Komaki, "Dai Tōa no chiseigaku," p. 26. Komaki, *Chiseigaku yori mitaru Dai Tōa*, p. 101.

international dateline: Komaki, "Dai Tōa no chiseigakuteki gaikan," p. 479.

128 Komaki suggested . . . *Shin Nipponkai*: Komaki, "Dai Tōa no chiseigaku," p. 26.

Komaki on renaming the continents: Komaki, "Dai Tōa no chiseigakuteki gaikan," pp. 473–480.

Washington . . . within range of Imperial bombers: Nakamura, "Building Greater East Asia," p. 3.

129 "The Rising Sun flag flutters proudly over Rocky Mountain peaks . . .": Mochizuki, *Amerika dō deru ka*, p. 194.

130 "The time has come when it is feasible . . .": Noyori, *Bei-Ei gekimetsu*, p. 112.

Tago article: *Jitsugyō no Hawaii*, 12 August 1938. p 5.

Shinmura understatement: Ienaka, *Hawaii no rekishi to fūdo*, p. 1.

"Hawaii's strategic significance for Japan . . .": Motogawa, "Hawaii no chiseigakuteki kōsatsu," p. 70.

"If America loses Hawaii . . .": Miyashiro, *Hawaii*, p. 369.

131 Hawaii must be captured: Hirano, "Taiheiyō seikensen ni okeru Hawaii," p. 39.

"If only we could take Hawaii . . .": Miyashiro, "Hawaii no gunbi," p. 91.

problem of the Pacific could be solved . . . by taking Hawaii: Kanda, *Dai Tōa jōshiki tokuhon*, p. 267.

"Hawaii's fate is like a lantern . . .": Mochizuki, *Amerika dō deru ka*, p. 169.

"Hawaii is a part of Japan": Komaki, *Nippon chiseigaku*, p. 96.

Japan's duty to restore Hawaii to Asia: Murakami, "Hawaii no sugata," pp. 189–190, 192, 203, 207.

"cleanse" Hawaii of [American] "pollution": Miyashiro, "Hawaii no gunbi," p. 94.

"Hawaii is yet to be brought under complete suzerainty . . .": Nakamura, "Building Greater East Asia," pp. 2–3.

132 "Panicked at the surprise attack . . .": Asai, "Hawaii no omoide," p. 445.

dōhō joke about salvo: Miyashiro, *Hawaii*, p. 344.

"Only after we've occupied it": Inoue, "Hawaii no koto," pp. 44–45.

"We should not lose a moment . . .": Murakami, "Hawaii no sugata," p. 203.

Hawaii was no easy target: Ibid., pp. 203–205.

133 Murakami's prescription: Ibid., p. 205–207.

Americans were going to have great difficulty defending their Pacific island territories: Nakamura, "Dai Tōa sen no tenbō," p. 15.

24 December and 4 January broadcasts: U.S. Navy, "Japanese Broadcasts."

134　　Emmons "the laughing stock": Ibid.

　　　Honolulu residents were thrown into "great confusion": *Dōmei junpō*, vol. 6, no. 2 (30 January 1942), p. 4017.

　　　Evacuating women and children to the West Coast: U.S. Navy, "Japanese Broadcasts."

　　　23 June broadcast: Ibid.

　　　"It is only a matter of time . . .": Moriyasu, *Dai nan'yō no genjitsu*, p. 293.

CHAPTER IX:　Hawaii in Greater East Asia

135　　Greater East Asia War: Tanemura, *Daihon'ei kimitsu nisshi*, p. 263.

　　　"holy war" to cleanse . . . Asia of . . . Anglo-Saxons: Among the 1942 patriots who intoned these phrases was the prewar Marxist (and postwar Marxist reborn) Yoshitarō Hirano. See Hirano, *Taiheiyō no minzoku seijigaku*, p. 224.

136　　extent of Greater East Asia: Kyoto University's Professor Saneshige Komaki wrote in 1942 that "Greater East Asia is not a geographical region but something like 'Europe' in modern world history, nay, it goes beyond and means the great ideal of *hakkō ichiū* [eight corners of the world under one roof]." Komaki, "Dai Tōa kensetsu no chiseiteki kōsatsu," p. 59.

　　　scope of *Nan'yō* before 7 December 1941: One author included Hawaii (Hisaya Kunimatsu, *Shin Nan'yō chishi*, pp. 2, 6, 235) but most did not (see works in bibliography by Ken'ichirō Kamei and Tetsuji Kada).

　　　"New Japan Sphere Series": In Japanese, the title *(Hawaii no genjitsu)* can be translated as "the reality of Hawaii." The author's name is given as "Paakaa" [Parker]. The closest approximation seems to be Elizabeth Parker's *The Sandwich Islands as They Are Not as They Should Be* (San Francisco, 1852).

　　　September 1941 booklet . . . included Hawaii in . . . Sphere: Hashimoto, *Dai Tōa kōkaken kensetsu taikō*, p. 15.

　　　"Draft Outline": Japan, Imperial Navy, Navy General Staff, Research Section, "Dai Tōa kyōeiken kensetsu taikō (shian)."

137　　task of the Sphere would be the unification of the Pacific area: Hanme, "Taiheiyō no shinchitsujō o ronzu," p. 89.

　　　Shinji Nishimura on "Greater South Seas Co-Prosperity Sphere": *Dai Nan'yō nenkan, 1942*, p. 218.

　　　Japanese themselves are islanders: Komaki, *Chiseigakujō yori mitaru Dai Tōa*, p. 109.

137–　Let the war take its course: Kada, *Sensō honshitsu ron*. Professor Kada
138　　led forty-nine Keio University students through Hawaii on the *Asamamaru*. *Nippu jiji*, 24 June 1937, p. 2.

138　　Admiral Shimada on Sphere: Japan, Rikugun, Sanbō honbu, *Sugiyama memo*, 2:43–44. Japan, Bōei-chō, *Daihon'ei, kaigunbu*, 2:265–266.

Teiichi Suzuki on Sphere: Japan, Rikugun, Sanbō honbu, *Sugiyama memo*, 2:107.

"Hawaii is geographically . . . part of . . .": Haga, *Hawaii*, p. 2.

"It is only a matter of time . . .": Kunitomo, *Hawaii shi*, p. 1.

<table>
<tr><td>138–
139</td><td>"The Philippines, Thailand, and Burma . . .": Kidō, *Hawaii shi monogatari*, p. 233.</td></tr>
<tr><td>139</td><td>"the first line of defense": Naokichi Tanaka, "Toa renmei no chiseigaku-teki kōzō," *Chiseigaku zasshi* (April 1942), p. 193 as cited by Horiuchi, *Chiseigaku*, p. 81.</td></tr>
</table>

"the eastern anchor" of the Sphere: Yamashita, *Hawaii shotō*, p. 14.

"second stage" of the Sphere's construction: Sakurai, "Ajia no saiken o kataru," pp. 2–3.

"in the west Singapore, in the east Hawaii": Yamashita, *Hawaii shotō*, p. 14.

"In the not so distant future . . .": Kunitomo, *Hawaii shi*, p. 7.

140   "As Hawaiians are of the Asian race . . .": Ibid., p. 3.

Hawaii was part of Greater East Asia: Tsurumi, "Shin Taiheiyō mondai," p. 50.

Hawaiians are "an extension of the Japanese race": Haga, *Hawaii*, p. 2.

"Japan's relationship with Hawaii . . .": Ibid., p. 260.

ancient Hawaiians felt a sense of kinship . . . [with] Japanese: Watanabe, *Sekai ni okeru Nihonjin*, p. 225.

1914 Shiga lecture in Honolulu: Takei, *Hawaii ōchōshi*.

141   guidebook to Hawaii cautioned: *Hawaii annai* (Tokyo 1938), p. 49.

"suntanned" Japanese fishermen: Kunitomo, *Hawaii shi*, pp. 1–2.

[Japanese] fishermen came ashore at Wailuku: Ienaka, *Hawaii no rekishi to fūdo*, pp. 18ff, 260.

Japanese . . . landed at Kahului: Yamashita, *Nihonjin no Hawaii*, p. 129.

[Japanese] fisherman first set foot . . . at Makapuu: Yamashita, *Nippon-Hawaii kōryūshi*, pp. 1–2.

"You have been taught . . .": Quoted in confidential report by Colonel Kendall J. Fiedler, 1 August 1942. G–2, Hawaiian Department, Fort Shafter. G–2 Regional File, RG 165, Box 1917, National Archives.

Kalakaua's intention that a Japanese succeed him: Komaki, *Nippon chiseigaku*, p. 96.

<table>
<tr><td>141–
142</td><td>King's hope that Japanese immigrants would intermarry with . . . Hawaiian population: Komaki, "Taiheiyō no chiseigaku," p. 104.</td></tr>
<tr><td>142</td><td>Kalakaua's Asian federation proposal a forerunner of Sphere: Hirano, *Minzoku seijigaku no riron*, pp. 66–67.</td></tr>
</table>

Hawaii's development the result of "blood and sweat" of *dōhō*: Kidō, *Hawaii shi monogatari*, p. 233.

Hawaii was first base of Japanese overseas expansion: Yamashita, *Hawaii shotō*, p. 14.

It would not have been unnatural for Hawaii to be Japanese: Yamashita, *Nippon-Hawaii kōryūshi*, p. 3.

writers blamed the Tokugawa shogunate's seclusion policy: Kanji Katō, cited by Yoshitarō Hirano, "Taiheiyō seikensen ni okeru Hawaii," p. 39.

caution of Meiji leaders: Watanabe, *Sekai ni okeru Nihonjin*, p. 226.

U.S. violated the "historic unity" of Asia and Pacific: Matsumoto, *Ajia minzoku to Taiheiyō*, p. 259.

"until the American takeover, Hawaii was very pro-Japanese": Kawamura, *Amerika no shimeisen*, p. 91.

from "Mark Twain's Pacific paradise" into a "Pacific Gibralter": Yamashita, *Hawaii shotō*, p. 1.

"a cancer to international peace": Kurokawa, "Hawaii o ika ni subeki ya," p. 4.

"shame of American history": Ibid., p. 6.

"This is an Asian country...": Kidō, *Hawaii shi monogatari*, pp. 232–233.

143   depth of racial prejudice [in Hawaii]: Shōzō Kawakami remarks in Yamashita, *Hōshuku kigen*, p. 179. Yamashita, *Nihonjin no Hawaii*, p. 4. Ichihara, *Nanpōken tōchi gaisetsu*, p. 17. Miyashiro, *Hawaii*, p. 178. *Nanpōken yōran*, p. 362. *Shūkan Asahi*, 1 February 1942, p. 14.

"With neither right nor reason...": Miike, *Watakushi no umareta Hawaii*, pp. 268–269.

144   "fierce excitement": Ibid., p. 2.

how excited and moved "almost all" *dōhō* were as they saw ... bombs: Miyashiro, *Hawaii*, pp. 343–344.

"Remember Pearl Harbor": Kidō, *Hawaii shi monogatari*, p. 233.

Pearl Harbor a turning point in Hawaiian history: Yamashita, *Hawaii shotō*, pp. 1–2

"waiting for release from American domination": Nakamura, "Building Greater East Asia," p. 3.

"Hawaii *dōhō* saw with their own eyes...": *Nanpō nenkan, 1943*, p. 1235.

figures on overseas *dōhō*: *Nihon gaikō nenkan*, 1943, pp. 141–142.

Foreign Ministry set up an Emigrant's Office: this was called the *Zai tekikoku iryūmin kankei jimushitsu*. Japan, Foreign Ministry Archives, A. 7.0.0.9–11–3–2.

144–
145   Interviews with *issei* and *nisei* who opted for repatriation: Miyashiro, *Hawaii*, p. 367. Ueda, "Hawaii no jitsujō," p. 161.

145   violence against Japanese nationals on Mindanao: Radio Tokyo, 28 December 1941. U.S. Navy, "Japanese Broadcasts."

"It is certain that Army authorities...": Miike, *Watakushi no umareta Hawaii*, p. 265.

Hawaii Japanese ... rounded up: Ebina, *Karifuorunia to Nipponjin*, pp. 241, 244.

"many" *dōhō* ... sent to mainland camps: Murakami, "Hawaii no sugata," p. 206.

"the most inhuman treatment": Nakamura, "First American-detained Japanese Exchange Vessel," p. 3.

threats by edgy guards: Nakamura, "Dai Tōa sensō to zai-Bei yokuryū dōhō," *Kaigai no Nippon*, vol. 16, no. 8 (September 1942), p. 19.

248 . . . opted for repatriation: Allen, *Hawaii's War Years*, p. 141.

145n   FBI took into custody 1,450 *dōhō:* Allen, *Hawaii's War Years*, p. 134.

694 male and 8 female *dōhō* sent to mainland: Adachi, *Hawaii nikkei-jin shi*, p. 87. 1,875 Hawaii *dōhō* sent to mainland: United States, Congress, Commission on Wartime Relocation and Internment of Civilians. *Personal Justice Denied*, p. 277.

146   Swedish diplomat visited a Honolulu internment center: Kanda to Shigenori Tōgō, 3 February 1942. Japan, Foreign Ministry Archives, A.7.0.0.9–11–3–2.

Japan's foreign minister was permitted to send New Year's greetings: Ibid.

Protests were filed: Ibid. "Statement of the Spokesman of the Board of Information Concerning the American Treatment of the Japanese Evacuees and Residents," in Japan, Gaimushō, Jōhōkyoku, pp. 37–41.

internees being subjected to forced labor: "Teiamaru kichōsha Bei-Ka jōkyō chōshūkai" [Interviews with returnees on the Teia-maru about conditions in the United States and Canada]. 24–27 November 1943. Japan, Foreign Ministry Archives, A.7.0.0.9–11–3.

Foreign Minister Tani address to Diet: *Nihon gaikō nenkan*, 1943, pp. 140–141.

postwar reparations claims: Ibid., p. 141.

Committee for *Dōhō* in Enemy Countries [*Tekikoku zairyū dōhō taisaku iinkai*]: Japan, Naimushō, *Gaiji geppō* (February 1943), pp. 82–84.

147   "Over 150,000 compatriots are now scattered . . .": Kunitomo, *Hawaii shi*, p. 7.

Greater East Asia War would end . . . in Hawaii: Yamashita, *Nihonjin no Hawaii*, p. 35. Kurokawa, "Hawaii o ika ni subeki ya," p. 14.

CHAPTER X: Hawaii Under Japanese Rule

148   no systematic planning for postwar: Iriye, "Wartime Japanese Planning for Post-War Asia," pp. 177–178.

Greater East Asia Ministry: Iriye, *Nichi-Bei sensō*, p. 100.

149   Professor Komaki warned assistants not to share information Tsugio Murakami, interview, 18 August 1979.

planners assumed . . . Hawaii would be placed under military rule: Murakami, "Hawaii no sugata," p. 208. Ike, *Japan's Decision for War*, pp. 249–253. Jones, *Japan's New Order in East Asia*, p. 331. Japan, Rikugun, Sanbō honbu, *Sugiyama memo*, 1:525–528.

Southern Regions Affairs Department: Japan, Bōei-chō, *Daihon'ei, kaigunbu*, 2:216.

150   "Land Disposal Plan": International Military Tribunal of the Far East,

Exhibit 1334, *Transcript*, pp. 11969–11973. Storry, *The Double Patriots*, pp. 317–319.

Malaya . . . served as a model: Murakami, "Hawaii no sugata," p. 210.

Koiso plan for *dōhō* Fifth Columns: Yano, *"Nanshin" no keifu*, p. 154.

Japanese forces in Philippines received tempestuous welcome: Kitamura, "Miyo, Davao-shi no dōhō o," pp. 162, 171.

151   Macassar Japanese assisted Imperial Navy: Japan, Bōei-chō, *Daihon'ei, kaigunbu*, 2:217.

using *dōhō* in occupation of Fiji: Japan, Army General Staff, "Dai riku shi," no. 1170 (3 June 1942).

Fiji's Japanese . . . sent to New Zealand: "Historical Narrative of the Fiji Islands," prepared by the U.S. Naval Liaison Officer, Fiji, to Lieutenant James A. Michener, Forces Historical Officer, 6 November 1945. Naval Archives, Washington, citing Army Board, *Pacific Story* (Wellington, 1945), p. 20.

Less than 1 percent of Hawaii Japanese was interned: Allen, *Hawaii's War Years*, p. 134.

152   National Policy Research Society: Storry, *The Double Patriots*, pp. 276–277. *Dai Nan'yō nenkan 1942*, p. 846.

Kazuo Yatsugi: Yatsugi, *Shōwa jinbutsu hiroku*. Asahi shinbunsha, *Gendai jinbutsu jiten*, p. 1438.

Greater East Asia Task Force *(Dai Tōa mondai chōsakai):* Kokusaku kenkyūkai, *Dai Tōa kyōeiken seiji keizai taiseiron*, pp. 367–369.

153   South Seas Economic Research Center: *Jiji nenkan 1939* (Tokyo 1939), p. 511. *Dai Nan'yō nenkan 1942*, p. 837.

Admiral Kasuya: *Jinji kōshin roku 1943* (Tokyo 1943), K–27.

South Seas Economic Research Center relationship with Navy Ministry: Admiral Akira Yamaki, interview, 19 January 1980.

"What Should be Done with Hawaii?" Kurokawa, "Hawaii o ika ni subeki ya."

153–   Kurokawa background: Kurokawa Papers, Honolulu, Hawaii. *Honolulu Star-Bulletin*, 19 July 1978.
154

154   "The day after the Pearl Harbor Incident . . .": Kurokawa, "Doshisha Hawaii ryō: The Friend Peace House," address delivered on the thirtieth anniversary of Friend Peace House at Doshisha University, 27 May 1966. Kurokawa Papers, Honolulu.

Yoshida Research Center: Tsugio Murakami, interview, 18 August 1979.

Japan Geopolitics Society: Horiuchi, *"Chiseigaku":* pp. 26–27.

Columbus was correct: Menefee, "Japan's Global Concept," pp. 330–332.

155   "a scientific weapon for constructing a new world order": Komaki, *Chiseigakujō yori mitaru Dai Tōa*, p. 100.

Murakami . . . developed a keen interest in the geopolitics of the Pacific: Tsugio Murakami, interview, 17 August 1979.

Murakami background: Ibid. *Jinji kōshin roku,* 2 (Tokyo 1978), MU–34–35.

[Nakamura's] principles to guide postwar occupation policies: Nakamura, "Post Bellum Management," p. 3.

156 70 percent of Hawaii Japanese would . . . collaborate: Murakami, "Hawaii no sugata," p. 208.

". . . believing in Japanese religions . . .": Ibid.

"If one speaks of a liberation . . .": Yamashita, *Hawaii shotō,* p. 7.

"For the sake of 150,000 compatriots . . .": Kanda, *Dai Tōa jōshiki tokuhon,* p. 266.

157 "Is not Imperial Japan's great mission . . .": Kurokawa, "Hawaii o ika ni subeki ya," pp. 13–14. In the original document, Kurokawa uses the expression "a temple of *ho'omaremare* in a new Pacific age." *Ho'omaremare* (written in katakana, a Japanese phonetic syllabary) could be either of two Hawaiian words: (1) *ho'omalimali,* to flatter, to mollify with soft words, to soothe, to quiet, or (2) *ho'omalemale,* to perform a marriage ceremony, (*Hawaiian Dictionary,* compiled by Mary Kawena Pukui and Samuel H. Elbert [Honolulu: University of Hawaii Press, 1971], pp. 214–215). Given the inherent ambiguity, the selection of *harmony* as an English equivalent is necessarily imperfect and tentative. Nevertheless, judging from the immediate context and from the general import of Kurokawa's recommendations, *harmony* does not seem to be far from the author's intent.

For Imperial Japan's use of puppet regimes in East and Southeast Asia during 1937–1945, see Jones, *Japan's New Order in East Asia.*

"Re-establishment of the Hawaiian Kingdom . . .": Kurokawa, "Hawaii o ika ni subeki ya," p. 13.

Kurokawa on qualifications of Hawaiians: Ibid., pp. 6–7.

dissatisfaction . . . among Hawaiian intellectuals: Kurokawa, "Hawaii o ika ni subeki ya," p. 6.

157n Princess Kawananakoa: Ibid., p. 7. *Women of Hawaii* (Honolulu 1929), pp. 155–156. *Honolulu Star-Bulletin,* 13, 18 April 1945.

Samuel Mahuka Spencer: Kurokawa, "Hawaii o ika ni subeki ya," p. 7. *Men of Hawaii,* vol. 5 (Honolulu 1935), p. 403–404. *Honolulu Star-Bulletin,* 29 February 1960. *Honolulu Advertiser,* 1 March 1960.

158 Territorial Government employees: Ibid., p. 7. Kurokawa identified the two as "the Hakuole brothers." I am grateful to Earl K. Nishimura for identifying the precise names. Interview, 8 April 1983.

Hawaii's economy . . . based upon American capital: Kurokawa, "Hawaii o ika ni subeki ya," p. 9.

Two characteristics of Hawaii's prewar economy: Murakami, "Hawaii no sugata," pp. 200–201. Kurokawa called them the "Hawaii *zaibatsu*" ("Hawaii o ika ni subeki ya," p. 2).

159–160 proposals to remodel the islands' agriculture: Nakase, "Dai Tōa kyōeiken to tōgyō seisaku," p. 7. Nakase, "Dai Tōa kyōeiken ni okeru tōgyō ni tsuite," p. 87. Murakami, "Hawaii no sugata," pp. 208–210.

160 pineapple and coffee . . . attractive potential exports to Japan: Kunimatsu, *Shin Nan'yō chishi*, p. 237.

  fishing industry . . . livestock-raising: Murakami, "Hawaii no sugata," p. 210. Kurokawa, "Hawaii o ika ni subeki ya," p. 12. Morohashi, "Hawaii to sono tai-Nichi kankei," p. 71.

  "The mainstay of Hawaii's economy today . . .": Kunitomo, *Hawaii shi*, p. 5.

  Japanese more productive in rice cultivation than were Chinese: Murakami, "Hawaii no sugata," p. 209.

  "white skinned people would have difficulty . . .": Kurokawa, "Hawaii o ika ni subeki ya," p. 12.

161 Japanese "overwhelm other ethnic groups by their numbers and activities . . .": *Nanpōken yōran 1942*, p. 358.

  "Switzerland of the Pacific": Kurokawa, "Hawaii o ika ni subeki ya," p. 13.

  referred to non-Japanese in Hawaii as *gaijin:* Yamashita, *Nipponjin no Hawaii*, p. 333.

  "a bad habit of Japanese colonists . . .": Hirano, *Taiheiyō no minzoku seijigaku*, p. 222.

  "With a background of some sixty years . . .": Yamashita, *Nippon-Hawaii kōryūshi*, p. 357.

  "In any case, given the fundamental renovation . . .": Yamashita, *Nipponjin no Hawaii*, pp. 4–5.

  "Our compatriots in Hawaii must be made to understand . . .": Ibid., p. 35.

  "When America loses . . .": Kanda, *Dai Tōa jōshiki tokuhon*, p. 266.

162 "behind us stands . . .": Haga, *Hawaii*, p. 193.

  "Wise *nisei* have probably recognized . . .": Tomomatsu, "Kaisen to zai-Bei dōhō," p. 234.

  "Nisei are prepared to sweep away . . .": Murayama, "Dai nisei to Nichi-Bei sensō," p. 10.

163 "Henceforth, we *nisei* will live up to the spirit . . .": Murayama, "We Nisei," *Japanese Abroad*, vol. 8 (September, 1942), p. 8.

  Americans might use *nisei* as sacrificial front-line troops: Kanda, *Dai Tōa jōshiki tokuhon*, p. 263.

  "They may be loyal to the United States but . . .": Ibid., p. 263.

  "What person of any color skin . . .": Miike, *Watakushi no umareta Hawaii*, p. 154.

  nisei . . . would commit suicide rather than serve the U.S. as soldiers: Yoshimori, *Hawaii o meguru Nichi-Bei kankeishi*, p. 259. Kawamura, *Amerika no shimeisen*, p. 102.

163– Home Ministry tendency to dismiss reports of formation of *nisei* units:
164 Japan, Naimushō, Keihōkyuku, Gaijika, *Gaiji geppō* (October 1943), pp. 43–44.

164 "ready to carry on the pioneer spirit . . .": Murayama, "Dai nisei no shinkyō," p. 7.

"Japanese-Americans have become accustomed to American life-styles": Nakase, "Dai Tōa kyōeiken," p. 7.

lamented the weakening of pro-Japanese sentiment: Yamashita, *Hōshu-ku kigen*, p. 218.

"sweep away the temptations . . .": Yamashita, *Nihonjin no Hawaii*, p. 408.

"Consequently, the necessity . . .": Ibid., pp. 16–17.

"As a whole, the Japanese problem . . .": Murakami, "Hawaii no suga-ta," p. 208.

165   "May I ask why has Japan been so unkind . . .": Murayama, "We Nisei," *Japanese Abroad*, vol. 16, no. 7 (August 1942), p. 10.

"But our real battle has just begun . . .": Ibid., vol. 16, no. 9 (October 1942), p. 8.

166   discrepancy between *nisei* academic achievements and job opportuni-ties: Miike, *Watakushi no umareta Hawaii*, p. 201. Haga, *Hawaii*, p. 193. Murakami, "Hawaii no sugata," p. 208.

Heishikan: Hajime Miyamoto to Tomi Knaefler, "House Divided," *Honolulu Star-Bulletin*, 9 December 1966.

"Fortunately, Japanese youth . . .": Murakami, "Hawaii no sugata," p. 208.

CONCLUSION: The Persistence of Illusion

168   For a detailed reconstruction of the Niihau incident see Ushijima, *Futari dake no sensō*, and Beekman, *The Niihau Incident*.

Niihau incident fantasy: Yamaoka, "Hawaii ni ikite ita umiwashi," pp. 12–33.

"Bombing of Washington": Ōmori, "Washington dai bakugeki," pp. 22–30.

169   "Yamaoka Parachute Brigade": Ikuhiko Hata, interview, 2 June 1980.

Ugaki fate: Ugaki, *Sensōroku*, introduction and photograph.

Tanaka hospitalization: Nihon kindai shiryō kenkyūkai, *Nihon riku-kaigun no seidō*, p. 43.

170   Komaki postwar career: *Jinji kōshin roku* (Tokyo, 1981), KO–101. Tsu-gio Murakami, interview, 17 August 1979.

Kunitomo postwar career: Kunitomo, *Chi no shio*, pp. 268–269.

Kurokawa postwar career: *Honolulu Star-Bulletin*, 19 July 1978.

Murobuse at Hibiya rally: *Gendai jinbutsu jiten* (Tokyo: Asahi shinbun-sha, 1977), p. 1396.

170–   Hirano obituary: *Asahi shinbun*, 9 February 1980 as translated and
171   published in the *Japan Foundation Newsletter*, vol. 8, no. 1 (April–May 1980), p. 17.

171   Yatsugi on wartime nationalists/postwar liberals: Yatsugi, *Shōwa jin-butsu hiroku*, pp. 290–291.

"War hath no fury . . .": Evan Esar, ed., *The Dictionary of Humorous Quotations* (New York: Horizon Press, 1953), p. 147.

in their innermost hearts most *issei* remained loyal to Japan: Ushijima, *Hawaii no nikkeijin*, p. 29. Adachi, *Hawaii nikkeijin shi*, p. 155.

[*issei*] believed in and hoped for Japanese victory: Adachi, *Hawaii nikkeijin shi*, p. 151.

"Great Japan" and the "invincible" Imperial Navy: Ushijima, *Hawaii no nikkeijin*, p. 32.

Pearl Harbor operation as . . . rescue mission: Ibid., p. 29.

issei had access to short wave sets: Yukiko Kimura, interview, 9 October 1979.

172   *kachigumi:* Ibid. Ushijima, *Hawaii no nikkeijin*, p. 29.

women wept, men . . . in stony silence: Adachi, *Hawaii nikkeijin shi*, p. 153.

issei stayed indoors: Ibid.

Rumors gave delusions sustenance: Kimura, "Rumor Among the Japanese."

apologize to emperor for bombing of Hiroshima: Adachi, *Hawaii nikkeijin shi*, p. 156.

In Hilo it was whispered: Ibid.

Rising Sun flag fluttering over Pearl City: Ibid.

appearance of interned *dōhō* gave birth to rumors: Ibid., p. 161.

172–   returnees met with more acclaim than that accorded AJA veterans: Por-
173   teus, *And Blow Not the Trumpet*, p. 230.

173   yen-dollar exchange racket: Murayama, *Hawaii nisei*, p. 150.

kattagumi: Ibid., p. 150. Ushijima, *Hawaii no nikkeijin*, p. 30. Yukiko Kimura, interview, 9 October 1979.

Hawaii Victory Society membership claim and 1949 investigation: Allen, *Hawaii's War Years*, p. 364.

doubts on 27 October Navy Day: Kimura, "Rumor Among the Japanese," p. 84.

issei flocked to Aiea Heights: Allen, *Hawaii's War Years*, p. 364.

emperor's radio broadcast on 1 January 1946: Adachi, *Hawaii nikkeijin shi*, p. 153.

collecting money for the emperor's imminent visit: Allen, *Hawaii's War Years*, p. 364.

174   disbandment of Hawaii Victory Society: *Hawaii hōchi*, 17 November 1977.

"From now on, as a resident . . .": Ibid.

Figures for Hawaii *nisei* internment: Allen, *Hawaii's War Years*, p. 134.

"This war has made me clearly realize . . .": Ibid., p. 146.

formidable hurdles [for *nisei* who chose life in Japan]: Murayama, *Hawaii nisei*, p. 150.

if Emperor Meiji had taken up King Kalakaua's 1881 proposals: Murayama, *Hawaii nisei*, p. 19.

Yomiuri poll: Tracy Dahlby, "Day Lost in Japan Generation Gap," *Honolulu Advertiser*, 7 December 1981.

175   "If it is indeed true . . .": Jim Borg, "Hawaii a 'Rome' for a New Era?" *Honolulu Advertiser*, 3 July 1980.

"cancer in the Pacific": Peattie, "Forecasting," p. 46.

Zenko Suzuki on Hawaiian society as "symbolic of Pacific solidarity": Address of 16 June attended by author. See also *Honolulu Advertiser*, 17 June 1982.

"temple of *ho'omalemale*": Kurokawa, "Hawaii o ika ni subeki ya," p. 13.

misleading to equate Pacific Community with Greater East Asia Co-Prosperity Sphere: Sōichirō Tahara, "Nihon no unmei o kimeru hito-bito" [People who decide Japan's fate], *Chūō kōron* [Central review] (May 1980), p. 271.

176   works by Ōmae, Maeda, Kuramae: Masaomi Ōmae, *Taiheiyōjin e no michi: Nihon o meguru umi no chiseigaku* [Route to Pacific man: geopolitics of Japan] (Tokyo: PHP, 1980). Tetsuo Maeda, *Taiheiyō ni nisshōki* [Rising Sun in the Pacific] (Tokyo: Century Press, 1980). Morimichi Kuramae, *Shin aku no riron: Nihon no geoporitekku wa kore da* [Theory of new evil: here is Japanese geopolitics] (Tokyo: Nihon kōgyō shinbunsha, 1980).

"Although Japan's area is narrow . . .": Kuramae, *Shin aku no riron*, p. 391.

Japan's task for the twenty-first century: Maeda, *Taiheiyō ni nisshōki*, p. 221.

collaboration in Hawaii: The postwar historian Tōru Yano writes that the Greater East Asia War energized overseas *dōhō* who enthusiastically collaborated in areas occupied by Imperial Japanese forces. Yano, *"Nanshin" no keifu*, p. 167.

177   ongoing search for an international order: Iriye, *Power and Culture*, passim.

"Pearl Harbor encore": Richard Hughes in *Far Eastern Economic Review*, 4 April 1980, p. 33.

Select Bibliography

I. *Unpublished materials in Japanese*

Japan. Army General Staff. "Dai riku shi" [Imperial operational orders]. Vol. 6, numbers 1101–1294. (7 February–30 September 1942). Deposited in War History Office, National Defense College, Tokyo.

Japan. Army General Staff. "Haruki Makoto shuki" [Handwritten notes of Captain Makoto Haruki]. 1942. Deposited in War History Office, National Defense College, Tokyo.

Japan. Army General Staff. "Iimoto nikki" [Diary of Lieutenant-Colonel Kumao Iimoto]. Vols. 18/23 (12 April–18 July 1942). Deposited in War History Office, National Defense College, Tokyo.

Japan. Foreign Ministry. "Dai Tōa sensō kankei ikken: zai tekikoku honpōjin kankei" [Matter relating to the Greater East Asia War: concerning compatriots in enemy countries]. A.7.0.0.9–11–3. Foreign Ministry Archives, Tokyo.

Japan. Imperial Navy. Combined Fleet. "Miwa nisshi" [Diary of Captain Yoshitake Miwa]. Deposited in War History Office, National Defense College, Tokyo.

Japan. Imperial Navy. Navy General Staff. "Gunreibu sakusen nisshi" [Navy General Staff operations diary]. 1941–1942. Deposited in War History Office, National Defense College, Tokyo.

Japan. Imperial Navy. Navy General Staff. "Sanagi nisshi" [Diary of Commander Tsuyoshi Sanagi]. 1942. Deposited in War History Office, National Defense College, Tokyo.

Japan. Imperial Navy. Navy General Staff. "Senji hensei ritsuan iken" [War operations proposals]. 1942. Deposited at War History Office, National Defense College, Tokyo.

Japan. Imperial Navy. Navy General Staff. Research Section. "Dai Tōa kyōeiken kensetsu taikō (shian)" [Draft outline for the construction of the Greater East Asia Co-Prosperity Sphere]. 29 November 1940. Deposited in the East Asian Library, Hoover Institution on War, Revolution, and Peace, Stanford, California.

Japan. Imperial Navy. Yokosuka Naval Air Base. "Dai Tōa sensō no senkun:

Hawaii sakusen" [Battle lessons of the Greater East Asia War: Hawaii operations]. August 1942. Deposited in the National Archives, Washington, D.C.
Kurokawa, Colbert Naoya (1890–1978). Papers. Courtesy of Tom Tomoyoshi Kurokawa. Honolulu, Hawaii.

II. *Unpublished materials in English*

Barde, Robert Elmer. "The Battle of Midway: A Study in Command." Ph.D. dissertation, University of Maryland, 1971.
Burrows, Edwin Grant. "Relations between Chinese and Japanese in Hawaii during the Sino-Japanese Conflict." First draft. Institute of Pacific Relations, Honolulu. Deposited in the Hawaii and Pacific Collection, University of Hawaii Library.
Collins, Donald Edward. "Disloyalty and Renunciation of United States Citizenship by Japanese-Americans during World War II." Ph.D. dissertation, University of Georgia, 1975.
Horiuchi, Russell Nozomi. "*Chiseigaku:* Japanese Geopolitics." Ph.D. dissertation, University of Washington, 1975.
Japan. Army Ministry. Research Section. "Land Disposal Plan in the Greater East Asia Co-Prosperity Sphere." International Military Tribunal of the Far East, Exhibit 1334. Transcript, pp. 11969–73.
Kurokawa, Colbert N. "Dōshisha Hawaii-ryō: the Friend Peace House." Address delivered at the 30th anniversary of the Friend Peace House, Dōshisha University, 27 May 1966.
Peattie, Mark. "Forecasting a Pacific War: Japanese Perspectives, 1913–1933." Paper presented at the Center for Japanese and Korean Studies, University of California, Berkeley, 15 October 1975.
United States Army. G–2 Regional Files, Hawaii. 1939–1945. Archives Division, National Archives and Records Center, Suitland, Maryland.
United States Navy. Office of Naval Intelligence. "Japanese Broadcasts: December 1941–July 1942." Operational Archives Branch, Naval Historical Center, Washington, D.C.
United States Navy. Office of Naval Intelligence. "Japanese Estimates and Comparisons of Resources as of the Beginning and End of the War." Washington Document Center Translation, no. 7 (26 June 1946).

III. *Japanese periodicals and newspapers covering Hawaii*

Asahi shinbun [Asahi news] (Tokyo). 1941–1944.
Bungei shunjū [Literary age] (Tokyo). 1941–1944.
Chirigaku [Geographical studies] (Tokyo). 1941–1944.
Chūō kōron [Central review] (Tokyo). 1941–1942.
Gaiji geppō [Monthly report on external affairs](Tokyo). 1943.
Gaikō jihō [Diplomatic bulletins] (Tokyo). 1941–1944.
Gendai [Contemporary] (Tokyo). 1941–1943.
Hawaii hōchi [Hawaii news] (Honolulu). 1937–1941, 1977.
Jikyoku jōhō [Situation reports] (Tokyo). 1942.

Jitsugyō no Hawaii [Business Hawaii] (Honolulu). 1932–1941.
Kaigai no Nippon [Japan overseas] (Tokyo). 1939–1942.
Kaigun [Navy] (Tokyo). 1944.
Kōdō sekai [Imperial world] (Tokyo). 1943–1944.
Kokusaku kenkyūkai shūhō [National Policy Society weekly reports] (Tokyo). 1941–1943.
Mainichi shinbun [Mainichi news] (Tokyo). 1941–1943.
Nippon to Amerika [Japan and America] (Tokyo). 1942.
Nippu jiji [Daily news] (Honolulu). 1932–1941.
Seikai ōrai [Political affairs] (Tokyo). 1942.
Shūkan Asahi [Weekly Asahi] (Tokyo). 1941–1942.
Taiheiyō [Pacific Ocean] (Tokyo). 1941–1943.
Tairiku [Continent] (Tokyo). 1938.

IV. *Japanese published sources*

Adachi, Nobuhiro. *Hawaii nikkeijin shi* [History of Hawaii Japanese]. Kyoto: Yanagihara shoten, 1977.

Agawa, Hiroyuki. *Yamamoto Isoroku.* Tokyo: Shinchōsha, 1966.

Akita, Kiyoshi. "Taezaru happun kentō no chikara" [Strength of an unceasing, enraged struggle]. *Kaigai no Nippon* [Japan overseas], vol. 15, no. 7 (July 1941), 7.

Amano, Keitarō, ed. *Dai Tōa shiryō sōran* [Conspectus of material on Greater East Asia]. Tokyo: Daigadō, 1944.

Asai, Jihei. "Hawaii no omoide" [Memories of Hawaii]. *Chirigaku* [Geographical studies], vol. 10, no. 2 (February 1942), 287–292; vol. 10, no. 3 (March 1942), 438–445.

Azumi, Zuimei (Hoaki). "Kokumin gaikō to dainisei no jūyōsei" [National foreign policy and the importance of *nisei*]. *Nippon to Amerika* [Japan and America], vol. 8, no. 12 (December 1938), 8–9.

_____. "Tōa kyōeiken kakuritsu to zai-Bei dōhō no kakugo" [Establishing the East Asia Co-Prosperity Sphere and the preparedness of compatriots in the United States]. *Nippon to Amerika* [Japan and America], vol. 11, no. 3 (March 1941), 12–13.

Dai Nan'yō nenkan 1942 [Great south seas yearbook]. Tokyo: Nan'yo dantai rengōkai, 1943.

Dai Tōa kōkaken kensetsu taikō [Outline for the construction of the Greater East Asia imperial sphere]. Tokyo: Dai Nippon sekisei kai, 1941.

Dai Tōa taiheiyōken no shintenbō [New view of the Greater East Asia Pacific sphere]. Tokyo: Ōbunsha, 1942.

Ebina, Kazuo. "Karifuorunia ni okeru hōjin no saikin jōsei" [Most recent condition of Japanese in California]. *Taiheiyō* [Pacific Ocean], vol. 4, no. 1 (January 1942), 64–70.

_____. *Karufuorunia to Nipponjin* [California and Japanese]. Tokyo: Taiheiyō kyōkai, 1943.

Fujita, Motoharu. *Dai Tōa nanpōken chizu chō* [Map of Greater East Asia southern sphere]. Tokyo: Nippon tōsei chizu, 1944.

Fukudome, Shigeru. *Shikan: Shinjuwan kōgeki* [The Pearl Harbor attack: a private view]. Tokyo: Jiyū Ajia sha, 1955.

Fukunaga, Kyōsuke. *Nichi-Bei sen miraiki* [Account of a future Japanese-American war]. Tokyo: Shinchōsha, 1933.

Haga, Takeshi. *Hawaii*. Tokyo: Nippon denpō tsūshinsha, 1942.

Hanme, Fumio. "Taiheiyō no shinchitsujō o ronzu" [Discussing the new order in the Pacific]. *Taiheiyō* [Pacific Ocean], vol. 5, no. 1 (January 1942), 89–95.

Hashimoto, Kingorō. *Dai Tōa kōkaken kensetsu taikō* [Outline for the construction of the Greater East Asia imperial sphere]. Tokyo: Dai Nippon sekisei kai, 1941.

Hattori, Kyōichi. *Nippon no dai shimei: sekai kaihō to kaigai dai hatten* [Japan's great mission: great overseas expansion and world liberation]. Tokyo: Nippon shokumin gakkō, 1933.

Hiraide, Hideo. "Sekai ni tatsu teikoku kaigun" [Imperial Navy bestriding the world]. In *Kaigun senki* [Navy war chronicle], edited by Kaigun jōhōbu [Navy Information Department], pp. 10–26. Tokyo: Kōa Nippon, 1942.

Hirano, Yoshitarō. *Minzoku seijigaku no riron* [Theory of ethnic politics]. Tokyo: Nippon hyōronsha, 1943.

———. *Taiheiyō no minzoku seijigaku* [Ethnic politics of the Pacific]. Tokyo: Nippon hyōronsha, 1942.

———. "Taiheiyō seikensen ni okeru Hawaii, Guamu, Hitō kogeki no igi: ko Katō Kanji taishō o omou" [Significance of attacks on Hawaii, Guam, and the Philippines in the Pacific Ocean control sphere: some thoughts about the late Kanji Katō]. *Taiheiyō* [Pacific Ocean], vol. 4, no. 1 (January 1942), 37–49.

Hirose, Hikota, ed. *Taiheiyō nisen roppyakunen shi* [2,600-year history of the Pacific Ocean]. Tokyo: Kaigun yūshū kai, 1942.

———. *Yamamoto gensui zensen yori no shokanshū* [Collection of letters from the front by Commander in chief Yamamoto]. Tokyo: Tōchō shoin, 1943.

Honma, Rakuan. *Yamamoto gensuiden* [Biography of Admiral Yamamoto]. Osaka: Kinjo shuppansha, 1943.

Ichihara, Aritsune. *Hawaii*. Tokyo: Asahi shinbunsha, 1942.

———. *Nanpōken tōchi gaisetsu* [General outline of control of southern sphere]. Tokyo: Kaiyō bunka sha, 1942.

Ienaka, Shigeru. *Hawaii no rekishi to fūdo* [Hawaii's history and natural features]. Tokyo: Seikatsusha, 1943.

Ikezaki, Chūkō. *Nichi-Bei arasowaba* [If Japan and America fight]. Tokyo: Shinchōsha, 1931.

———. *Taiheiyō senryaku ron* [Discourse on Pacific strategy]. Tokyo: Shūbunsha, 1932.

Imin mondai kenkyūkai [Research society for immigration problem], ed., *Jihenka zaigai Nihonjin no tenbō* [Prospects for overseas Japanese during the China Incident]. Tokyo: Imin mondai kenkyūkai, 1940.

Inoue, Kichijirō. "Hawaii no koto" [The matter of Hawaii]. *Jikyoku jōhō* [Situation reports], vol. 6, no. 1 (January 1942), 44–45.

Iriye, Akira. *Nichi-Bei sensō* [The Japanese-American war]. Tokyo: Chūō kōronsha, 1978.

Iriye, Toraji. *Hōjin kaigai hattenshi* [History of Japanese overseas emigration]. Tokyo: Ida shoten, 1942.

Japan. Bōei-chō. Bōei kenshūjo. Senshishitsu [Self-Defense Agency, National Defense College, War History Office]. *Chūbu Taiheiyō hōmen kaigun sakusen* [Naval operations in the central Pacific theater]. Tokyo: Asagumo shinbunsha, 1970.

_____. *Daihon'ei, kaigunbu, rengōkantai* [Imperial Headquarters, Navy General Staff, Combined Fleet]. 2 vols. Tokyo: Asagumo shinbunsha, 1975.

_____. *Daihon'ei rikugunbu* [Imperial Headquarters: Army]. Vols. 3 & 4. Tokyo: Asagumo shinbunsha, 1970, 1972.

_____. *Hawaii sakusen* [Hawaii operation]. Tokyo: Asagumo shinbunsha, 1967.

_____. *Middowe kaisen* [Battle of Midway]. Tokyo: Asagumo shinbunsha, 1972.

Japan. Gaimushō. Jōhōkyoku [Foreign Ministry, Information Section]. *Seifu kōhyō shū 1942* [Collection of government statements for 1942]. Tokyo, 1942.

Japan. Kikakuin Kenkyūkai [Cabinet Planning Board Research Society]. *Dai Tōa kensetsu no kihon kōryō* [General plan for the construction of Greater East Asia]. Tokyo: Nippon shuppan, 1942.

Japan. Naimushō. Keihōkyoku. Gaijika. [Home Ministry, Police Bureau, External Affairs Section]. *Gaiji geppō* [Monthly report on external affairs]. Tokyo, 1943.

Japan. Rikugun. Sanbō honbu. [Army General Staff]. *Sugiyama memo.* 2 vols. Tokyo: Hara shobō, 1967.

Kada, Tetsuji. *Sensō honshitsu ron* [Essential theory of war]. Tokyo: Keiō shuppansha, 1942.

_____. *Taiheiyō keizai sensō ron* [Theory of economic warfare in the Pacific]. Tokyo: Keiō shobō, 1941.

Kamei, Ken'ichirō. *Dai Tōa minzoku no michi* [The ethnic path of Greater East Asia]. Tokyo: Seiki shobō, 1941.

Kanda, Yōshi. *Dai Tōa jōshiki tokuhon* [Common sense reader on Greater East Asia]. Tokyo: Tensuisha, 1942.

Kawamura, Masahei. *Amerika no shimeisen* [America's lifeline]. Tokyo: Bunshō-dō, 1944.

Kawashima, Seijirō. "Kaigun yori mitaru Nichi-Bei mondai" [The Japanese-American problem from a naval perspective]. In *Tai Bei kokusaku ronshū* [Collection of essays on national policy toward America], edited by Kokumin tai Bei kyōkai [National Society for Policy toward America], pp. 187–224. Tokyo: Yomiuri shinbunsha, 1924. pp. 187–224.

Kidō, Itsuko. *Hawaii shi monogatari* [Story of Hawaiian history]. Introduction by Foreign Minister Masayuki Tani. Tokyo: Tōto shoseki, 1943.

Kigen nisenroppyakunen hōshuku kaigai dōhō Tokyo taikai honbu [Headquarters for the Tokyo Congress of Overseas Dōhō in Celebration of the 2,600th Anniversary of the Empire]. *Kigen nisenroppyakunen hōshuku kaigai dōhō Tokyo taikai* [Tokyo Congress of Overseas Dōhō in Celebration of the 2,600th Anniversary of the Empire]. Tokyo, 1940.

Kimura, Tatsurō. "Dai Tōa sensō no chiseigakuteki seikaku" [The geopolitical character of the Greater East Asia War]. *Chiseigaku* [Geopolitics], vol. 10, no. 6 (June 1942), 94–99.

Kitamura, Komatsu. "Miyo, Davao-shi no dōhō o" [Look at the dōhō of Davao]. *Chūō kōron* [Central review], April 1942, pp. 162–171.

Kiyosawa, Kiyoshi. *Amerika wa Nihon to arasowazu* [America will not fight Japan]. Tokyo: Chigura shobō, 1932.

Kobayashi, Tomoji. *Tairiku sakusenron* [Theory of continental operations]. Tokyo: Takayama shoin, 1937.

Kokumin gunji kyōkai [National Military Affairs Association]. *Nichi-Bei kaisen yume monogatari* [Fantasy on the outbreak of a Japanese-American war]. Tokyo: Hakushindō, 1913.

Kokusaku kenkyūkai [National Policy Research Society]. *Dai Tōa kyōeiken seiji keizai taiseiron* [Theory of the political and economic system of the Greater East Asia Co-Prosperity Sphere]. Tokyo: Nippon hyōronsha, 1943.

Komaki, Saneshige. *Chiseigakujō yori mitaru Dai Tōa* [Greater East Asia from a geopolitical perspective]. Tokyo: Nippon hōsō shuppan kyōkai, 1942.

————. *Dai Tōa chiseigaku shinron* [New theory of geopolitics in Greater East Asia]. Tokyo: Hoshino shoten, 1943.

————. "Dai Tōa kensetsu no chiseiteki kōsatsu" [Geopolitical consideration of the construction of Greater East Asia]. *Gendai* [Contemporary], vol. 23, no. 10 (October 1942), 54–63.

————. "Dai Tōa no chiseigaku" [Geopolitics of Greater East Asia]. *Seikai ōrai* [Political affairs], vol. 12 (March 1942), 24–28.

————. "Dai Tōa no chiseigakuteki gaikan" [General geopolitical view of Greater East Asia]. *Chirigaku* [Geographical studies], vol. 10, no. 4 (April 1942), 473–480.

————. *Nippon chiseigaku* [Japanese geopolitics]. Tokyo: Kōdansha, 1942.

————. "Taiheiyō no chiseigaku" [Geopolitics of the Pacific Ocean]. *Gendai* [Contemporary], vol. 23, no. 1 (January 1942), 98–105.

Kunimatsu, Hisaya. *Shin Nan'yō chishi* [Geographical description of the new South Seas]. Tokyo: Kōkin shoin, 1941.

Kunitomo, Tadao. *Chi no shio* [Salt of the earth]. Tokyo: Chūō kōron jigyō shuppan, 1970.

————. Preface to H. Gregory [*sic.*], *Hawaii shi* [History of Hawaii]. Tokyo: Sanseido, 1943.

Kurokawa, Naoya. "Hawaii o ika ni subeki ya" [What should be done with Hawaii?]. Nan'yō keizai kenkyūjo [South Seas Economic Research Institute]. *Nan'yō shiryō* [South Seas materials], no. 236 (April 1943).

Maebara, Mitsuo, et. al. *Dai Tōa kyōeiken no minzoku* [Peoples of the Greater East Asia Co-Prosperity Sphere]. Tokyo: Rokumeikan, 1942.

Maeda, Tetsuo. *Taiheiyō ni nisshōki* [Rising Sun flag in the Pacific]. Tokyo: Century Press, 1980.

Matsukawa, Jirō. *Dai Tōa chiseijigaku* [Geopolitics of Greater East Asia]. Tokyo: Kasumigaseki shobō, 1942.

Matsumoto, Gorō. *Ajia minzoku to Taiheiyō* [Asian peoples and the Pacific]. Tokyo: Seibi shokaku, 1942.

Matsuo, Kinoaki. *Sangoku dōmei to Nichi-Bei sen* [Tripartite alliance and a Japanese-American war]. Tokyo: Kasumigaseki shobō, 1940.

Mehnert, Klaus and Yoshirō Suetsune. "Hawaii: Taiheiyō no Jiburarutaru" [Hawaii: Gibralter of the Pacific]. *Kokusai bunka kyōkai kaihō* [Bulletin of the International Cultural Association], no. 173 (April 1942), 113–134.

Miike, Noboru and Shirō Takahara. *Watakushi no umareta Hawaii* [My native Hawaii]. Tokyo: Seitoku shoin, 1942.

Miyashiro, Sō. *Hawaii*. Tokyo: Kaizōsha, 1942.

———. "Hawaii no gunbi" [Hawaii's armaments]. *Manshū keizai* [Manchukuo economics], vol. 3, no. 8 (August 1942), 90–94.

Mizuno, Hironori. *Dakai ka, hametsu ka: kōbō no kono issen* [A way out? Ruin? Rise and fall of this war]. Tokyo: Tōkai shoin, 1932.

Mochizuki, Hajime. *Amerika dō deru ka* [How will America come out?]. Tokyo: Hasegawa shobō, 1942.

Moriyasu, Shinjirō. *Dai Nan'yō no genjitsu* [Reality of the Greater South Seas]. Tokyo: Endō shoten, 1942.

Morohashi, Hiroshi. "Hawaii to sono tai-Nichi kankei no kyūtenkan" [Hawaii's sudden change of relations with Japan]. *Bōeki tōseikai kaihō* [Bulletin of the Trade Regulation Society], vol. 1, no. 4 (August 1942).

Motogawa, Fusazō. "Hawaii no chiseigakuteki kōsatsu" [A consideration of Hawaii's geopolitics]. *Chiseigaku* [Geopolitics], vol. 1, no. 4 (April 1942), 58–71.

Murakami, Tsugio. "Hawaii no sugata" [The shape of Hawaii]. In *Dai Tōa chiseigaku shinron*, edited by Saneshige Komaki, pp. 186–211. Tokyo: Hoshino shoten, 1943.

Murayama, Tamotsu. "Dai nisei no seikatsu" [The *nisei*'s life]. *Kaigai no Nippon* [Overseas Japan], vol. 16, no. 10 (December 1942), 15–17.

———. "Dai nisei no shinkyō" [The *nisei*'s state of mind]. *Kaigai no Nippon*, vol. 16, no. 6 (July 1942), 6–8.

———. "Dai nisei to kyōiku" [The *nisei* and education]. *Kaigai no Nippon*, vol. 16, no. 8 (September 1942), 12–15.

———. "Dai nisei to Nichi-Bei sensō" [The *nisei* and the Japanese-American war]. *Kaigai no Nippon*, vol. 16, no. 7 (August 1942), 7–10.

———. *Hawaii nisei*. Tokyo: Jiji tsūshinsha, 1966.

Murobuse, Kōshin. *Nihon no risō* [The ideals of Japan]. Tokyo: Gengen shobō, 1942.

Nakamura, Kaju. "Hoku-Bei zendo saido no yūkōki" [A second tour of all North America]. *Kaigai no Nippon*, vol. 16, no. 4 (May 1942), 26–33.

Nakamura, Ryōzō. "Dai Tōa sen no tenbō" [A view of the Greater East Asia War]. *Taiheiyō* [Pacific Ocean], vol. 5, no. 1 (January 1942), 12–24.

———. "Seikaiken waga te ni kisu" [Control of the sea belongs to us]. In *Dai Tōa shinron* [New theory of Greater East Asia], edited by Yomiuri shinbunsha. Tokyo: Kenshinsha, 1942.

Nakase, Setsuo. "Dai Tōa kyōeiken ni okeru tōgyō ni tsuite" [On the sugar industry in the Greater East Asia Co-Prosperity Sphere]. *Taiheiyō* [Pacific Ocean], vol. 5, no. 3 (March 1942), 81–89.

———. "Dai Tōa kyōeiken to tōgyō seisaku" [Greater East Asia Co-Prosperity

Sphere and sugar policy]. *Kokusaku kenkyūkai shūhō* [National Policy Society weekly reports], vol. 4, no. 6 (7 February 1942), 1–19.

Nanpō nenkan 1943 [South Seas yearbook]. Tokyo: Nanpō nenkan kankōkai, 1943.

Nanpōken yōran [Handbook for southern areas]. Osaka: Asahi shinbunsha, 1942.

Nan'yō nenkan, 1943 [South Seas yearbook]. Edited by Taiwan sōtokufu gaijibu [Taiwan Governor-general's Office, External Affairs Department]. Taihoku (Taipei): Nanpō shiryōkan, 1943.

Nihon gaikō nenkan [Japan foreign affairs annual]. Tokyo: Nihon gaikō nenkan sha, 1943.

Nihon kindai shiryō kenkyūkai [Japan Modern Sources Research Society]. *Nihon rikukaigun no seidō, soshiki, jinji* [The system, organization, and personnel of the Japanese Army and Navy]. Tokyo: Tokyo daigaku shuppankai, 1971.

Nihon yūsen kabushiki kaisha [Japan Mail Lines]. *Hawaii annai* [Guide to Hawaii]. Tokyo, 1934.

Niina, Masuo, ed. *Kaigun sensō kentō kaigi kiroku* [Records of conferences on naval battle operations]. Tokyo: Mainichi shinbunsha, 1976.

Noyori, Hideichi. *Bei-Ei gekimetsu* [Destroy America and England]. Tokyo: Shūbunkaku, 1942.

Nozaki, Keisuke. *Hawaii to Hiripin* [Hawaii and the Philippines]. Tokyo: Nimatsudō, 1932.

Nukada, Hiroshi. *Rikugunshō jinjikyokuchō no kaisō* [Memoirs of chief of the Army Ministry's Personnel Section]. Tokyo: Fuyō shobō, 1977.

Ōkubo, Gen'ichi. *Hawaii Nihonjin hatten meikan* [Directory of Hawaii Japanese]. Hilo: Hawaii shōgyōsha, 1940.

Ōmori, Kiyoshi. "Washinton dai bakugeki" [Great bombardment of Washington]. *Kaigun* [Navy], vol. 1, no. 1 (May 1944), 22–30.

Ōtake, Rokurō. "Bakugekika no Hawaii" [Hawaii under bombardment]. *Shūkan Asahi* [Weekly Asahi]. 21 December 1941. pp. 12–14.

Ōto, Yoshikatsu. *Nichi-Bei moshi kaisen seba* [If Japan and America fight]. Tokyo: Shoseidō, 1914.

Rōyama, Masamichi. "Dai Tōa kōikikenron" [Theory of a broad area Greater East Asia]. In *Taiheiyō mondai no saikentō* [Re-examining the problem of the Pacific Ocean], edited by Taiheiyō kyōkai [Institute of Pacific Relations], pp. 1–58. Tokyo: Asahi shinbunsha, 1941.

Saitō, Chū. *Taiheiyō senryaku joron* [Prologue to Pacific strategy]. Tokyo: Shunyōdō, 1941.

Sakurai, Heigorō et. al. "Ajia no saiken o kataru" [Discussing the reconstruction of Asia]. *Kokusaku kenkyūkai shūhō* [National Policy Research Society weekly reports], vol. 4, no. 1 (3 January 1942), 1–2.

Satō, Kenryō. *Dai Tōa sensō kaisōroku* [Memoirs of the Greater East Asia War]. Tokyo: Tokuma shoten, 1966.

Satō, Kōjirō. *Nichi-Bei sensō yume monogatari* [Japanese-American war fantasy]. Tokyo: Nippon Hyōronsha, 1921.

Satō, Seitarō. *Kaigai shinshutsu to Nipponjin* [Overseas advance and Japanese]. Tokyo: Endō shoten, 1942.

Sawada, Ken. *Kaigai hatten to seinen* [Overseas expansion and youth]. Tokyo: Chōbunkaku, 1943.

Shibuya, Shōji. *Minami Taiheiyō shotō: chiseijiteki kenkyū* [Islands of the South Pacific: geopolitical research]. Tokyo: Senjō shoten, 1943.

Shishimoto, Hachirō. *Nikkei shimin o kataru* [Speaking of citizens of Japanese ancestry]. Tokyo: Shokasha, 1934.

Sōga, Yasutarō, *Gojūnen no Hawaii kaikō* [Fifty years of Hawaii recollections]. Osaka: n.p., 1953.

Sorimachi, Eiichi. *Ningen Yamamoto Isoroku* [The human Isoroku Yamamoto]. 2 vols. Tokyo: Kōwa-dō, 1956–1957.

Stephan, John. "Nippongun Hawaii senryō keikaku no zenbō" [Full account of Japanese military's Hawaii occupation plans]. *Rekishi to jinbutsu* [History and people] *zōkan* [special issue] no. 142 (January 1983), 264–272.

Tahara, Harutsugu. "Kaigai dōhō wa Shina jihen o dō mita ka" [How do overseas dōhō view the China Incident]. *Tairiku* [Continent], November 1938, pp. 104–119.

Takagi, Kinnosuke. "Beikoku no tai-Nichi dai issen" [America's first war against Japan]. *Jikyoku jōhō* [Situation reports], vol. 6, no. 12 (December 1942), 146–147.

Takagi, Shinsuke. "Dai Nippon ni chiiki kōzō" [Great Japan's area structure]. *Takushoku ronsō* [Colonization debates], vol. 5, no. 1 (September 1943), 39–62.

Takagi, Sōkichi. *Taiheiyō kaisenshi* [History of the opening of the Pacific War]. Tokyo: Iwanami shoten, 1959.

————. *Taiheiyō sensō to rikukaigun no kōsō* [Pacific War and the Army-Navy struggle]. Tokyo: Keizai ōraisha, 1967.

————. *Yamamoto Isoroku to Yonai Mitsumasa.* Tokyo: Bungei shunjū shinsha, 1950.

Takei, Atsushi, [Nekketsu]. *Hawaii ōchō shi* [History of the Hawaiian monarchy]. Honolulu, 1918.

Tamaru, Tadao. *Hawaii ni hōdō no jiyū wa nakatta* [There was no freedom of the press in Hawaii]. Tokyo: Mainichi shinbunsha, 1978.

Tanaka, Shin'ichi. *Tanaka sakusen buchō no shōgen* [The testimony of chief of Operations Department Tanaka]. Tokyo: Fuyō shobō, 1978.

Tanemura, Sakō. *Daihon'ei kimitsu nisshi* [Secret Diary of Imperial Headquarters]. Tokyo: Daiyamondo-sha, 1952.

Taniguchi, Kichihiko. *Dai Tōa keizai no riron* [Economic theory of Greater East Asia]. Tokyo: Chigura shobō, 1942.

Tominaga Kengo, ed. *Taiheiyō sensō* [Pacific War]. Vol. 39 of *Gendaishi shiryō* [Sources for contemporary history]. Tokyo: Misuzu shobō, 1975.

Tomomatsu, Toshio. "Kaisen to zai-Bei dōhō" [Outbreak of the war and dōhō in America]. In *Teikoku Amerika* [The enemy America], edited by Masuo Katō, pp. 215–234. Tokyo: Dōmei tsūshinsha, 1942.

Toyama, Tetsuo. *Haran chōjō hachijūnen no kaikō* [Turbulent accumulated eighty years of memoirs]. Tokyo: Toyama Sadako, 1971.

Tsuneya, Moriyuki. *Kaigai shokuminron* [Theory of overseas colonization]. Tokyo: Hakubunsha, 1891.

Tsurumi, Yūsuke. "Shin Taiheiyō mondai" [Problem of the new Pacific]. *Gaikō jihō* [Diplomatic bulletins], 1 February 1942, pp. 47–54.

Ueda, Yutaka. "Hawaii no jitsujō" [Actual conditions in Hawaii]. *Gendai* [Contemporary], vol. 23, no. 1 (January 1942), 160–167.

Uehara, Keiji. *Nichi-Bei no setten Hawaii* [Hawaii: Where Japan and America meet]. Tokyo: Senshinsha, 1932.

Ugaki, Matome. *Sensōroku* [War records]. Tokyo: Hara shobō, 1968.

Ushijima, Hidehiko. *Futari dake no sensō* [A war of only two]. Tokyo: Mainichi shinbunsha, 1980.

————. *Hawaii no nikkeijin* [People of Japanese ancestry in Hawaii]. Tokyo: Sanseidō, 1969.

————. *Shinjuwan: dokiyumentari* [Pearl Harbor: documentary]. Tokyo: Jiji tsushinsha, 1976.

Watanabe, Akira. "Hawaii no shutō Oahu-to no chikei" [The topography of Hawaii's main island: Oahu]. *Taiheiyō* [Pacific Ocean], vol. 4, no. 1 (January 1942), 96–104.

Watanabe, Ikujirō. *Shiden Yamamoto gensui* [Biography of Fleet Admiral Yamamoto]. Tokyo: Chikura shobō, 1944.

Watanabe, Shūjirō. *Sekai ni okeru Nihonjin* [Japanese in the world]. Tokyo: Kei shobō, 1893. Reissued in 1942.

Yamamoto, Yoshimasa. *Chichi Yamamoto Isoroku* [My father Isoroku Yamamoto]. Tokyo: Kōbunsha, 1969.

Yamaoka, Sōhachi. *Gensui Yamamoto Isoroku* [Fleet Admiral Isoroku Yamamoto]. Tokyo: Dai Nihon yūbenkai kōdansha, 1945.

————. "Hawaii ni ikite ita umiwashi" [The sea eagle that lived in Hawaii]. *Kaigun* [Navy], vol. 1, no. 4 (August 1944), 12–33.

Yamashita, Sōen. *Hawaii shotō* [Hawaii Islands]. Tokyo: Tokyo kōenkai shuppanbu, 1942.

————. *Hōshuku kigen nisen roppyakunen to kaigai dōhō* [Celebrating the 2,600th anniversary of the empire and overseas *dōhō*]. Tokyo, 1941.

————. *Nihonjin no Hawaii* [The Hawaii of Japanese]. Tokyo: Sekaidō shoten, 1942.

————. *Nikkei shimin no Nihon ryūgaku jijō* [Conditions of people of Japanese ancestry studying in Japan]. Tokyo: Bunseisha, 1935.

————. *Nippon-Hawaii kōryūshi* [History of Japan-Hawaii intercourse]. Tokyo: Daitō shuppan, 1943.

————. "Tai-Bei senden kōsaku to zai-Bei Nihonjin no tachiba" [Propaganda strategy toward the United States and the position of Japanese in the United States]. *Nippon to Amerika* [Japan and America], vol. 8, no. 1 (January 1938), 20–29.

————. "Zai-Nichi dainisei no shōrai" [Future of nisei in Japan]. *Nippon to Amerika*, vol. 8, no. 10 (November 1938), 24–26.

Yano, Tōru. *"Nanshin" no keifu* [The pedigree of "southern advance" thought]. Tokyo: Chūō kōronsha, 1975.

Yatsugi, Kazuo. *Shōwa jinbutsu hiroku* [Private records of Shōwa people]. Tokyo: Shinkigensha, 1954.

Yoshimori, Saneyuki. *Hawaii o meguru Nichi-Bei kankeishi* [Japanese-American relations with respect to Hawaii]. Tokyo: Bungei shunjūsha, 1943.

Published sources in western languages

Agawa, Hiroyuki. *The Reluctant Admiral.* Tokyo: Kōdansha, 1979.

Allen, Gwenfread. *Hawaii's War Years, 1941–1945.* Honolulu: University of Hawaii Press, 1950.

Asada, Sadao. "The Japanese Navy and the United States." In *Pearl Harbor As History: Japanese-American Relations, 1931–1941,* edited by Dorothy Borg and Shumpei Okamoto, pp. 225–259. New York: Columbia University Press, 1973.

Bailey, Thomas A. "Japan's Protest Against the Annexation of Hawaii." *Journal of Modern History,* 3 (March 1931), 46–61.

Barber, Joseph Jr. *Hawaii: Restless Rampart.* New York: Bobbs-Merrill, 1941.

Beekman, Allan. *The Niihau Incident.* Honolulu: Heritage Press of the Pacific, 1982.

Berger, Gordon M. *Parties Out of Power in Japan, 1931–1941.* Princeton: Princeton University Press, 1977.

Blakeslee, George. "Hawaii: Racial Problem and Naval Base." *Foreign Affairs,* vol. 17, no. 1 (1938), 90–99.

Burroughs, Edgar Rice. "Our Japanese Problem." *Hawaii,* vol. 5, no. 11 (30 June 1944), 7, 13.

Burrows, Edwin Grant. *Chinese and Japanese in Hawaii during the Sino-Japanese Conflict.* Honolulu: Institute of Pacific Relations, 1939.

Butow, Robert J. C. *Tojo and the Coming of the War.* Stanford: Stanford University Press, 1961.

Bywater, Hector C. *The Great Pacific War: A History of the American-Japanese Campaign of 1931–33.* London: Constable, 1925.

Clark, Blake. "Some Japanese in Hawaii." *Asia* (December 1942), 723–725.

Conn, Stetson, Rose C. Engelman, and Byron Fairchild. *Guarding the United States and Its Outposts.* Washington: Office of the Chief of Military History, Department of the Army, 1964.

Conroy, Hilary. *The Japanese Frontier in Hawaii, 1868–1898.* Berkeley: University of California Press, 1953.

Coox, Alvin D. and Saburō Hayashi. *Kōgun: the Japanese Army in the Pacific War.* Quantico: United States Marine Corps Association, 1959.

Crowley, James B. "Japan's Military Foreign Policies." In *Japan's Foreign Policy, 1868–1941,* edited by James W. Morley, pp. 3–117. New York: Columbia University Press, 1974.

Daws, Gavan. *Shoal of Time: A History of the Hawaiian Islands.* New York: Macmillan, 1968.

de Mendelssohn, Peter. *Japan's Political Warfare.* London: Allen & Unwin, 1944.

Dingman, Roger. *Power in the Pacific: The Origins of Naval Arms Limitation.* Chicago: University of Chicago Press, 1976.

Donaldson, Richard. "They Want to be American Citizens." *Paradise of the Pacific,* vol. 52 (April 1940), 9–10.

Dull, Paul S. *A Battle History of the Imperial Japanese Navy (1941–1945).* Annapolis: Naval Institute Press, 1978.

Embree, John. *Acculturation Among the Japanese of Kona, Hawaii.* Supplement to *American Anthropologist,* no. 43, part 2 (1941).

Fitzpatrick, Ernest Hugh. *The Coming Conflict of Nations, or the Japanese-American War.* Springfield, Illinois: H. W. Bokker, 1909.

Havens, Thomas R. H. *Valley of Darkness: the Japanese People and World War Two.* New York: W. W. Norton, 1978.

Holmes, W. J. *Double-edged Secrets: U.S. Naval Intelligence Operations in the Pacific during World War II.* Annapolis: Naval Institute Press, 1979.

Honolulu Japanese Chamber of Commerce. *The Rainbow: A History of the Honolulu Japanese Chamber of Commerce.* Honolulu, 1970.

Ike, Nobutaka, trans. and ed. *Japan's Decision for War: Records of the 1941 Policy Conferences.* Stanford: Stanford University Press, 1967.

Iriye, Akira. *Pacific Estrangement: Japanese and American Expansion, 1897–1911.* Cambridge: Harvard University Press, 1972.

————. *Power and Culture: The Japanese-American War, 1941–1945.* Cambridge: Harvard University Press, 1981.

————. "Wartime Japanese Planning for Post-War Asia." In *Anglo-Japanese Alienation, 1919–1952,* edited by Ian Nish, pp. 177–197. Cambridge: Cambridge University Press, 1982.

Jones, F. C. *Japan's New Order in East Asia: Its Rise and Fall, 1937–1945.* London: Oxford University Press, 1954.

Jones, Stephen B. and Klaus Mehnert. "Hawaii and the Pacific: A Survey of Political Geography." *Geographical Review,* vol. 30, no. 3 (July 1940), 358–375.

Kimura, Yukiko. "Rumor Among the Japanese." *Social Process in Hawaii,* 11 (May 1947), 84–92.

Knaefler, Tomi. "House Divided." *Honolulu Star Bulletin,* December 5–10, 1966.

Layton, Captain Edwin T. "Rendezvous in Reverse." United States Naval Institute, *Proceedings,* vol. 79, no. 5 (May 1953), 478–485.

Lea, Homer. *The Valor of Ignorance.* New York: Harper & Brothers, 1909. Reprint 1942.

Lebra, Joyce C., ed. *Japan's Greater East Asia Co-Prosperity Sphere in World War II.* London: Oxford University Press, 1975.

Lind, Andrew W. *The Japanese in Hawaii Under War Conditions.* Honolulu: Institute of Pacific Relations, 1943.

Magistretti, William. "Japan's New Order in the Pacific." *Pacific Affairs,* vol. 14, no. 2 (June 1941), 198–206.

Mahan, Alfred Thayer. *The Interest of America in Sea Power.* Boston: Little, Brown, 1898.

Maki, John M. *Japanese Militarism: Its Cause and Cure.* New York: Alfred A. Knopf, 1945.

Marder, Arthur J. *Old Friends, New Enemies: The Royal Navy and the Imperial Japanese Navy, Strategic Illusions, 1936–1941.* Oxford: The Clarendon Press, Oxford University Press, 1981.

Marumoto, Masaji. "Vignette of Early Hawaii-Japan Relations." *The Hawaiian Journal of History,* vol. 10 (1976), 52–63.

Mehnert, Klaus. "Die Japaner auf Hawaii." *Zeitschrift für Geopolitik,* vol. 16 (August–September 1939), 596–603.

————. *Ein Deutscher in der Welt.* Stuttgart: Deutsche Verlags-Anstalt, 1981.

————. "Problem XIX: U.S.-Flottenmanöver im Pazifik 1938." *Zeitschrift für Geopolitik,* vol. 15 (July 1938), 559–569.

Menefee, Selden C. "Japan's Global Concept." *Asia* (June 1943), 330–332.

Michel, Henri. *The Second World War.* Translated by Douglas Parmee. 2 vols. New York: Praeger, 1975.

Miyamoto, K. *A Nisei Discovers Japan.* Tokyo: Japan Times Press, 1957.

Morison, Samuel Eliot. *Coral Sea, Midway, and Submarine Actions, May 1942–August 1942.* Boston: Little, Brown, & Co., 1949.

_____. *The Rising Sun in the Pacific: 1931–April 1942.* Boston: Little, Brown, & Co., 1960.

Morley, James W., ed. *The Fateful Choice: Japan's Advance into Southeast Asia, 1939–1941.* New York: Columbia University Press, 1980.

_____. *Japan's Foreign Policy, 1868–1941: A Research Guide.* New York: Columbia University Press, 1974.

Murayama, Tamotsu. "We Nisei." *Japanese Abroad*, vol. 16, no. 7 (August 1942), 8–10; no. 8 (September 1942), 7–8; no. 9 (October 1942), 7–8.

Murphy, Thomas D. *Ambassadors in Arms.* Honolulu: University of Hawaii Press, 1954.

Nakamura, Kaju. "Building Greater East Asia, i.e. Ultimate Stable Peace in the World." *Japanese Abroad*, vol. 16, no. 2 (February 1942), 2–6.

_____. "First American-Detained Japanese Exchange Vessel Arrives at Japan." *Japanese Abroad*, vol. 16, no. 8 (September 1942), 2–5.

_____. "A Grandiose Policy Needed: Do Not Be Content with a Mere Leader of East Asiatic Races." *Japanese Abroad*, vol. 16, no. 3 (April 1942), 2–5.

_____. "Post Bellum Management of Southern Provinces." *Japanese Abroad*, vol. 16, no. 5 (June 1942), 2–5.

Nisei Survey Committee. *The Nisei: A Study of Their Life in Japan.* Tokyo: Keisen Girls' School, 1939.

Ogawa, Dennis M. *From Japs to Japanese: The Evolution of Japanese-American Stereotypes.* Berkeley: McCutchan, 1971.

_____. *Kodomo no tame ni—For the Sake of the Children: The Japanese-American Experience in Hawaii.* Honolulu: The University Press of Hawaii, 1978.

Peattie, Mark B. *Ishiwara Kanji and Japan's Confrontation with the West.* Princeton: Princeton University Press, 1975.

Pelz, Stephen E. *Race to Pearl Harbor.* Cambridge: Harvard University Press, 1974.

Porteus, Stanley D. *And Blow Not the Trumpet: A Prelude to Peril.* Palo Alto: Pacific Books, 1947.

Potter, John Deane. *Yamamoto: The Man Who Menaced America.* New York: Viking, 1965.

Prange, Gordon W. *At Dawn We Slept.* New York: McGraw-Hill, 1981.

Rademaker, John A. *These Are Americans: The Japanese-Americans in Hawaii in World War II.* Palo Alto: Pacific Books, 1951.

Robinson, Eric. *The Japanese File.* Singapore: Heinemann Asia, 1979.

Schmitt, Robert C. *Historical Statistics of Hawaii.* Honolulu: The University Press of Hawaii, 1977.

Schwantes, Robert S. "Japan's Cultural Foreign Policies." In *Japan's Foreign Policy, 1868–1941: A Research Guide*, edited by James W. Morley, pp. 153–183. New York: Columbia University Press, 1974.

Shibutani, Tamotsu. *The Derelicts of Company K.* Berkeley: University of California Press, 1978.

Shillony, Ben-Ami. *Politics and Culture in Wartime Japan.* London: Oxford University Press, 1981.

Shirota, Jon. *Lucky Come Hawaii.* New York: Bantam, 1965.

Storry, Richard. *The Double Patriots: A Study of Japanese Nationalism.* New York: Houghton, Mifflin, 1957.

Tahara, Harutsugu. "For Sake of Fatherland: Japanese Abroad Voluntarily Offer Many Material Help to Nation." In *The Pulse of Japan,* pp. 110–115. Tokyo: Tokyo Information Bureau, 1938.

Tasaki, Hanama. *Long the Imperial Way.* New York: Houghton, Mifflin, 1950.

Thomas, David A. *Japan's War at Sea: Pearl Harbor to the Coral Sea.* London: Andre Deutsch, 1978.

Toland, John. *The Rising Sun.* New York: Random House, 1970.

United States. Congress. Commission on Wartime Relocation and Internment of Civilians. *Personal Justice Denied.* Washington: U.S. Government Printing Office, 1982.

United States. Department of Defense. *The "Magic" Background of Pearl Harbor.* 8 vols. Washington: U.S. Government Printing Office, 1977.

United States. Strategic Bombing Survey. Naval Analysis Division. *The Campaigns in the Pacific War.* Washington: U.S. Government Printing Office, 1946.

_____. *Interrogations of Japanese Officials.* 2 vols. Washington: U.S. Government Printing Office, 1946.

United States. War Office. *Final Report: Japanese Evacuation from the West Coast.* Washington: U.S. Government Printing Office, 1943.

Wakukawa, Ernest K. *A History of the Japanese People in Hawaii.* Honolulu: Tōyō shoin, 1938.

Watson, Mark Skinner. *The War Department: Chief of Staff: Prewar Plans and Preparations.* Washington: Department of the Army, 1950.

Yoshida, Jim. *The Two Worlds of Jim Yoshida.* New York: William Morrow, 1972.

Zacharias, Ellis M. *Secret Missions.* New York: G. P. Putnam, 1946.

Index

Adachi, Nobuhiro, 171
Akamatsu, Sukeyuki, 166n
Akita, Kiyoshi, 44, 50, 53, 129n
Alaska, 1, 4, 11, 130, 142; proposed annexation of, 130; proposed cession to Japan, 187
Aleutian Islands, 111, 112, 115, 118, 133, 134, 166
Alexander & Baldwin, 3
Allen, Gwenfread E., xiii, 3–4
Allison, John, 29, 29n
Aloha Society, 44
American Factors, 3
Aoyama Gakuin, 45, 170
Arita, Hachirō, 46, 53, 79, 147n
Ariyoshi, George, 19
Arizona, USS, 19, 22
Army General Staff (Japanese), xi, 5, 73, 96, 98, 103, 118–119; decision to seize Hawaii, 115–116; on Midway operation, 112–113, 115; opposition to Hawaii invasion, 98, 101, 105; plans to use *dōhō* in Fiji, 151; position on war strategy, 96
Asahi shinbun, 170
Asahikawa, 117
Asai, Jihei, 132
Ashida, Hitoshi, 30, 147n
Attu Island (Atsuta-jima), 115, 120, 134
Australia, 1, 4, 17, 57, 92, 94, 96, 97, 100, 104, 106, 107, 128, 137, 144
Austria, 27
Azumi, Zuimei, 38

Bataan, 119
Batavia, 96, 105
Big Five (Hawaii corporations), 3, 25, 143, 158, 159, 160

Big Island. *See* Hawaii, island of
Bismarck Islands, 96
Bolivia, 144
Bougainville, 169
Brazil, 24, 144
Burma, 100, 102, 138, 153, 157
Butow, Robert J. C., x
Bywater, Hector C., 57–59

C. Brewer, 3
California, 1, 2, 5, 11, 13, 36, 59, 60, 69, 75, 105, 125, 126, 129, 132, 133, 137, 168, 169; anti-Japanese agitation in, 13; planned suicide raid against, 169; scenarios for conquest, 56, 57, 60, 105, 129–130; shelling of, 106, 125
Camp McCoy, 163n
Campbell, James, 157n
Canada, 144
Caroline Islands, 15, 64
Castle & Cooke, 3
Celebes Islands, 151
Ceylon, 92, 94, 100, 102, 103, 104, 106, 107, 110, 113
Chiang Kai-shek, 78, 87, 122, 135
China, 11, 24, 28, 29, 35–39, 56, 69, 78, 79, 87, 88, 106, 113, 117, 118, 123, 128, 137, 157, 158
Chinese in Hawaii, 12, 15, 26, 28, 36, 158, 160
Chirigaku, 128
Chiseigaku, 130
Columbia, 144
Columbus, Christopher, 140, 154
Combined Fleet (Japanese), 1, 5, 30n, 61, 64, 67, 68, 71, 76, 77, 80, 82, 83, 90, 96–98, 100, 101, 105, 109, 110, 113, 119, 120, 168, 169, 172; disagreements

with Navy General Staff, 82, 96, 101–
102, 109; postwar rumors about, 172;
war strategy, 96
Cook, James, 11, 140, 141, 143
Corregidor, 119
Czechoslovakia, 27

Dai nisei rengōkai [League of *nisei* organi-
zations], 46
Davao, 150
Democratic Party in Hawaii, 21
Diamond Head Crater, 61, 132
Dickinson College, 45
Dillingham Corporation, 159
Dōhō: definition of, 2n
Dōmei news agency, 29, 30, 134
Doolittle, James, 113
Doolittle raid, 113–114
Dōshisha University, 41, 46, 154
Dutch East Indies, 78, 81, 85, 96, 137, 157

East-West Center, Honolulu, 175
Eastern Brotherhood Society, 173
Ebina, Kazuo, 145
Ebizaka, Seikō, 38
Embree, John, 29, 31–32, 33
Emigrant's Office (in Japanese Foreign Min-
istry), 144–145, 146
Emmons, Delos C., 134
Emperor of Japan. *See* Hirohito, Meiji
England, 11, 27, 38, 57, 71, 73, 130, 144
Equador, 144
Erimo (training ship), 32
Etō, Jun, 9
Exclusion Act (1924), 13, 37, 62, 123

Federal Bureau of Investigation, 145
Fiedler, Kendall J., 198
Fiji, 96, 97, 100, 101, 104, 106, 109, 111,
113, 151; Army guidelines for *dōhō* in,
151
Filipinos in Hawaii, 11, 12, 26, 40, 158
Fitzpatrick, Ernest Hugh, 56, 57
Fort Armstrong, 58
Fort De Russy, 22, 58
Fort Shafter, 58, 145
Fortune magazine poll on Hawaii (1940),
93–94
France, 27, 38, 59, 163
Fujii, Shigeru, 77, 91, 101
Fukudome, Shigeru, 81, 84, 97, 98, 103,
106, 112
Fukunaga, Kyōsuke, 60–61, 168
Fukuoka, 13

Gakushūin University, 158
Garvey, Marcus, 60
Germany, 11, 27, 30, 38, 39, 48, 51, 56–

57, 71, 73, 78, 87, 102, 115; joint operations with Japan on U.S. mainland,
129–130
Gilbert Islands, 96
Grand Congress of Overseas Compatriots
(1940), 48–54, 150
Greater East Asia Co-Prosperity Sphere, ix,
3, 4, 18, 38, 41, 48, 50n, 51, 52n, 54,
65, 78, 79, 121, 134, 135–147, 148,
153, 155, 158, 161, 162, 163, 164, 165,
175; origins of, 78–79, 136; scope of,
51, 79, 136–138
Greater East Asia Deliberation Council,
138
Greater East Asia Ministry, 148
Greater East Asia Task Force, 152
Greater East Asia War, 135, 163, 167, 169,
171, 174, 175, 176
Guadalcanal, 119, 166, 167
Guam, 1, 63, 65, 75, 95, 123, 137, 174

Haga, Shichirō, 52
Haga, Takeshi, 138, 140, 152, 162, 165
Hakuole, James, 158
Haleiwa, 45
Hamada, Yoshijirō, 49, 51
Hanme, Fumio, 137
Hara, Kei, 139
Harada, Tasuku, 37
Harbottle, Isaac, 158
Harvard University, 74
Hashimoto, Kingorō, 136
Hashirajima, 77, 89, 97, 101, 107
Hata, Ikuhiko, xiii, 118, 169
Hattori, Takushirō, xi
Haushofer, Karl, 76
Hawaii: in Admiral Yamamoto's calcula-
tions, 2, 73–75, 81, 88, 92–94; *dōhō*
population, 5, 11, 21, 23; Japanese im-
migration to, 12–13; Japanese invest-
ment in, 19–20; Japanese nationals in,
20; position in Pacific Basin, 10–11;
projected Japanese administration of,
155–158; proposed economic reforms
in, 158–160; proposed Japanese annexation of, 130; proposed social reforms in,
161–166; potential wartime collaboration in, 7–9; U.S.-Japanese cooperation
in, 19
Hawaii hōchi, xiii, 26, 27, 28, 34, 36, 39,
174
Hawaii, island of, 10, 13, 16, 31, 32, 44,
49, 53, 67, 81, 110, 157, 160, 172;
scenarios of landings on, 81, 104–105,
110, 111
Hawaii, Kingdom of, 16, 17, 139, 141–
142; possible revival of, 157

Hawaii, Republic of, 12, 15, 16, 18
Hawaii Victory Society, 173, 174
Hawaiian monarchy, 12, 15, 17, 141–142, 155; possible revival of, 155, 157
Hawaiians and part-Hawaiians, 11, 12, 141, 157, 161, 168; projected role under Japanese rule, 156–158
Hayashi, Senjūrō, 129n
Heishikan, 166
Higashikuni, Prince, 50
Hilo, 13, 16, 29, 32, 40, 44, 59, 67, 157, 172; as base for Oahu campaign, 67; shelling of, 133
Hiraide, Hideo, 127, 128
Hirano, Yoshitarō, 131, 142, 161, 170–171
Hirohito, Emperor of Japan, x, 20, 40, 107, 111, 113, 126n, 169, 170, 172, 173
Hiroshima, 13, 35, 46, 77, 89, 118, 172
Hitler, Adolf, 27, 57, 87
Hong Kong, 5, 95, 123, 137
Honolulu, 13, 19, 20, 22, 30, 31, 32, 33, 44, 45, 46, 52, 53, 57, 66, 84, 92, 97, 124, 131, 132, 134, 139, 140, 142, 153, 163, 166n, 168, 175; bombing of (March 4, 1942), 106; scenario of uprising in, 58
Honolulu Advertiser, 29
Honolulu Star-Bulletin, 29, 153, 170
Honouliuli, 145n
Hoshi, Tōru, 18–19

Ienaka, Shigeru, 141
Iida, Kōichi, 49
Iimoto, Kumao, 103, 117
Ikezaki, Chūkō, 64–65, 124
Imonbukuro (comfort bags), 33, 34
Imperial Japanese Army, xi, 3, 6, 7, 8, 15, 23, 24, 25, 27, 28, 29, 30, 36, 39, 51, 55, 58, 67, 101, 123–124, 131, 157, 168, 173, 177; divisions designated for Hawaii invasion, 116–117; lack of interest in Hawaii, 69–70, 98; and postwar administration of Hawaii, 150; rivalry with Imperial Navy, 95, 101–102, 149. *See also* Army General Staff
Imperial Japanese Navy, x, 6, 8, 15, 24, 29–32, 39, 51, 52, 55, 58, 62, 82, 104, 125, 132, 133, 171, 177; internal factions, 70–71, 82, 149; noncooperation with Army, 102, 149; visit to Hawaii, 15–16, 30–33, 69, 88; war strategy evolution, 72–87; wartime destruction of documents, x. *See also* Navy General Staff
Imperial Rule Assistance Association, 48
India, 128, 137, 144
Indochina, 39, 78, 87, 88, 137
Inoue, Kaoru, 18

Inoue, Keishirō, 18
Inoue, Kichijirō, 132
Inoue, Shigeyoshi, 76, 86
Institute of Pacific Relations, 46, 137
International Military Tribunal for the Far East, x
Internment of Japanese-Americans, 5, 126, 145, 146, 172–173; reparations claims discussed in wartime Japan, 146
Iolani School, Honolulu, 46
Iriye, Akira, x, 177
Ishiwara, Kanji, 98n
Isobe, Takashi, 52
Issei (first generation Japanese-Americans), 6, 7, 14, 21, 23, 24, 26–29, 32, 36, 38, 39, 41, 118, 161, 164, 170, 176; in California, 36; contributions to war effort in China, 33–35; in Hawaii, 6, 15, 16; and Imperial Japanese Navy visits, 31, 32; in Japan, 7, 41–42; projected role under Japanese rule, 162; postwar victory illusions of some, 171–174
Italy, 27, 30, 38, 39, 48, 51, 130, 163
Itō, Masanori, 30
Itō, Seiichi, 82
Iwo Jima, 8

Japan-America Hawaii Society, 44
Japan Geopolitics Society, 154
Japanese Chamber of Commerce (Hawaii), 14, 19, 33, 34
Japanese Consulate in Honolulu, 15, 24, 25, 33, 34, 46
Japanese language schools in Hawaii, 14, 15, 25
Japanese vernacular press in Hawaii, 14, 15, 20, 26–29, 31–34, 38, 39, 40
Java, 118
Java Sea: Battle of, 105
Jitsugyō no Hawaii, xiii, 26, 27, 28, 29, 30, 31, 32, 34, 38, 39–40, 129n
Johnston Island, 91, 100, 104, 110, 111, 113, 118, 133

Kachigumi [victory groups], 172, 173
Kada, Tetsuji, 127, 137–138, 197
Kahoolawe, 10
Kahului, 44, 49, 133; shelling of, 133; thirteenth-century Japanese landing at, 141
Kaigai dōhō [overseas compatriot], 53
Kaigai dōhō chūō kai [Central society for overseas compatriots], 53
Kaigai no Nippon [Japan overseas], 44, 124, 126, 128, 131, 165
Kalakaua, David (Hawaiian monarch), 17, 18, 141–142, 157n, 158, 174

Kaleo (Kauai), 145n
Kalihi (district of Honolulu), 37
Kalihi Eight Corners Society, 173
Kamchatka, 114
Kami, Shigenori, 99, 107
Kanda, Yōshi, 131, 152, 156, 161, 163, 177
Kanna, Kenwa, 30, 47, 147n
Kapiolani, Queen, 157n
Kasumigaura Air Base, 74, 81
Kasuga, Muneichi, 153
Katō, Kanji (Hiroharu), 18, 61, 65, 71, 72, 142, 175
Katō, Tomosaburō, 70
Kattagumi [victory groups]. *See kachigumi*
Kauai, 10, 12, 13, 109, 110, 157n, 168
Kaumualii (king of Kauai), 157n
Kawakami, Shōzō, 49, 51
Kawamura, Masahei, 142, 163
Kawananakoa, Princess Abigail, 157
Kawasaki, Matsuhei, 31
Kawashima, Seijirō, 60, 62, 63, 65
Kaya, Okinori, 106
Keio University, 127, 137
Kibei [*nisei* educated in Japan and return-ing to the U.S.], 25–26, 25n, 36, 41, 43, 84
Kidō, Itsuko, 138–139, 142, 144, 152
Kiska Island (Narukami-jima), 115, 120, 134
Kobe, 113
Koiso, Kuniaki, 47, 53, 150
Kokusai gakuyūkai [International student friendship society], 45
Kokusaku kenkyūkai. See Policy Society
Komaki, Saneshige, xii, 127–128, 131, 132, 137, 141–142, 149, 154–155, 170, 171, 175, 177
Kona, 13, 29, 31–32, 33, 36, 53, 160
Konoe, Fumimaro, 39, 50, 53, 79, 80
Konpira Shrine (Honolulu), 32
Korea, 11, 15, 35, 79, 137, 140
Kress, 159
Kumamoto, 13, 35, 118
Kunimatsu, Hisaya, 160
Kunitomo, George Tadao, 44–45, 46, 47, 136, 138, 139, 140, 141, 147, 152, 160, 170, 171
Kuramae, Morimochi, 176
Kure, 10, 35
Kurile Islands, 85, 96, 117, 118, 131
Kurokawa, Colbert Naoya, 45–46, 47, 142, 147, 153–154, 156–158, 160, 161, 170, 171, 175, 177
Kuroshima, Kameto, 77, 81, 82, 90, 91, 93, 97, 105
Kusaka, Ryūnosuke, 81
Kuwashima, Kazuo, 147n

Kuykendall, Ralph S., 138
Kyoto, 117, 154, 160, 165
Kyoto Imperial University, xi, 127, 132, 137, 141, 145, 149, 154, 155, 170

Lahaina, 84–85
Lanai, island of, 10, 12
Lea, Homer, 56–57
Lebra, Joyce, x, xiii
Lenin, Vladimir, 55, 139
Liaison conferences, 78, 79, 83, 86, 87, 102, 106, 107, 138
Lind, Andrew W., xiii, 43
Lions Club of Honolulu, 45–46, 153, 170
Lodge, Henry Cabot, 56
London Naval Treaty (1930), 70–71
Long Beach (California), 8
Los Angeles, 56, 169
Luce, Clare Boothe, 57

MacArthur, Douglas, 170, 172
Macassar, 151
Maeda, Tetsuo, 176
Mahan, Alfred Thayer, 55–56
Mainichi shinbun, 30, 37, 132
Makapuu Point (Oahu), 141
Makaweli (Maui), 145n
Malaya, 78, 81, 85, 96, 150; possible model for Hawaiian occupation, 150
Manchuria (Manchukuo), 15, 25, 35, 37, 41, 42, 51, 69, 78, 79, 86, 98, 115, 117, 118, 131, 136, 140, 155, 157, 158; pos-sible model for Hawaii, 157
Manila, 5, 75, 95, 105, 123
Mao Tse-tung, 170
Marcus Island, 114
Mariana Islands, 15, 80, 153, 169
Marquesas Islands, 11
Marshall Islands, 15, 64, 80, 96, 101, 103, 114
Massie case, 143
Masuda, Seiichi, 174
Matsumoto, Gorō, 142
Matsumura, Hideitsu, 51
Matsumura, Kan, 37
Matsuo, Kinoaki, 65–66
Matsuoka, Yōsuke, 34, 48, 50, 53, 78, 83, 136
Maui, 10, 12, 31, 36, 44, 49, 76, 81, 84, 85, 141; possibility of assault against, 81; thirteenth-century Japanese landings on, 141
McKinley High School (Honolulu), 45
McKinley, William, 18
Mehnert, Klaus, xii, 76
Meiji, Emperor of Japan, 12, 14, 18, 27n, 141, 174

Meiji Restoration, 27, 49
Meiji University, 41
Mexico, 144
Micronesia, 15, 64, 75, 78, 79, 136, 137; as springboard for Hawaii invasion, 64
Michener, James A., 201
Mid-Pacific Institute (Honolulu), 45
Midway Island, 60, 66, 75, 91, 93, 100, 104, 108, 109, 110, 111, 133
Midway Operation, ix, x, 108, 109, 119–120, 163, 166, 167, 169, 172, 176; called a Japanese victory, 134; genesis of, 110–111
Miho, Fumiye, 42
Miho, Katsuichi, 49
Miike, Fred Noboru, 143–144, 145, 152, 163, 165
Mikami, Kaiun, 49
Mindanao Island, 80, 137, 145, 150
Mitchell, William ("Billy"), 74
Miwa, Yoshitake, 77, 91, 98–99, 107, 111
Miyake, Setsurei, 129n
Miyashiro, Sō, 130, 131, 132, 144
Miyazaki, Shūichi, 179
Miyo, Tatsukichi, 111, 112
Mizuno, Hironori, 63–64, 65
Mochizuki, Hajime, 128–129, 131, 171
Molokai, 10
Montague, Charles Edward, 171
Monterey (California), 8
Mōri, Iga, 49
Morimura, Tadashi. *See* Yoshikawa, Takeo
Morishige, Torao, 37
Moriyasu, Shinjirō, 134
Motogawa, Fusazō, 130
Murakami, Masayoshi, 125
Murakami, Tsugio, xii, 131, 132–133, 145, 149, 155, 156, 159, 160, 164–166, 170, 177
Murayama, Tamotsu, 11, 162–163, 164, 165, 174
Murobuse, Kōshin, 126, 170, 171
Mutō, Akira, 106

Nagano, Osami, 86, 95, 100, 107, 112, 133
Nagaoka, 74
Nagasawa, Setsu, 17
Nagoya, 113, 134n
Nagoya, Setsu, 17
Nagumo, Chūichi, 89, 90, 91, 102, 103, 107, 109, 119
Nakajima, Chikubei, 129n
Nakajima, Kesago, 129n
Nakamura, Kaju, 44, 124, 126, 128, 131, 144, 145, 155, 156
Nakamura, Ryōzō, 46, 133
Nakano, Seigō, 30, 129n
Nakase, Setsuo, 159–160, 164

Naniwa: in Hawaii, 15–16, 19
Nanking, 29, 30n, 31, 34
Nan'yō [South seas], 136, 137
Nan'yō keizai kenkyūjo. See South Seas Economic Research Center
National Memorial Cemetery of the Pacific (Honolulu), 7, 22
National Policy Research Society. *See* Policy Society
Navy General Staff (Japanese), 5, 33, 70, 72, 73, 76, 77, 79, 81, 82, 83, 84, 87, 91, 100, 101, 103, 105, 107, 108, 110, 153, 156, 169; disagreements with Combined Fleet, 82, 101–102, 109; plan for Greater East Asia Co-Prosperity Sphere, 79; position on war strategy, 96; rivalry with Imperial Army, 95, 101–102
Navy Torpedo School, 74
New Caledonia, 104
New Order in East Asia, 28, 37, 38, 42, 48, 51, 53, 78
New York: Japanese invasion scenario, 60, 128; triumphal entry of Imperial Japanese Navy into, 129
New Zealand, 1, 4, 57, 104, 137, 144, 153
Nihoa, 10
Nihon bunka shinkōkai [Society for promotion of Japanese culture], 29
Niigata, 74
Niihau, 10, 168
Nippon rengō kyōkai [United Japanese society], 32
Nippu jiji, 26, 27, 30, 31, 32, 33, 34, 36, 37, 39, 46, 52, 127, 139, 164
Nisei (second generation Japanese-Americans), 3, 6, 11, 21, 24–29, 31, 38, 39, 161, 162–166, 174, 177; in California, 5; combat units in Europe, 6, 7–8; in Hawaii, 3, 5, 6–7, 21; and Imperial Japanese Army, 24–25, 35–37, 44; and Imperial Japanese Navy, 31, 32, 41; in Japan, 6, 7–8, 25–26, 36, 41–45, 46; Japanese expectations of, 37–38, 43, 47; projected role under Japanese rule in Hawaii, 162–166; prewar citizenship status, 23–25, 26, 32
Nishimura, Shinji, 137
Nogi, Marshal Maresuke, 57
Nomura, Kichisaburō, 46, 53, 147n
Nōnin, Kuwaichi, 35, 49
Nosaka, Sanzō, 126, 170
Noyori, Hideichi, 129–130, 171
Nuuanu YMCA, 45, 142, 153

Oahu, 10, 12, 31, 32, 45, 49, 59, 60, 75, 76, 85, 89, 90, 94, 104, 105, 109, 110,

118, 133, 141, 172; Army General Staff invasion study of, 119; Combined Fleet invasion timetable of, 111; north shore landing scenarios, 60, 62, 65, 66, 67, 81–82, 133
Oberlin College, 45
Ogasawara, Naganori, 129n
Ōhashi, Hachirō, 152
Ōhira, Masayoshi, 175
Oikawa, Koshirō, 50, 53, 81
Oka, Takazumi, 106–107, 149, 153
Okada, Keisuke, 84
Okawara, Yoshio, 175
Okinawa, 8, 176
Ōkōchi, Denshichi, 31
Ōkuma, Shigenobu, 18
Ōkuma, Yuzuru, 51
Ōkura, Kimmochi, 152
Ōkura, Kishichirō, 30
Ōmae, Masaomi, 176
Ōmori, Kiyoshi, 168
Ondo (training ship), 32
Oregon, 1, 57, 125, 129–130; scenario of conquest of, 129–130
Ōto, Yoshikatsu, 60, 61, 62, 168

Pacific and Asian Affairs Council, 45
Pacific Community, 175, 177
Palama Rebirth Society, 173
Palmyra Island, 91, 97, 98, 100, 104, 111, 113, 118, 133
Pan American Airways, 75
Pan Pacific Union, 45, 153
Panama Canal, 1, 57, 59, 65, 105
Panay Incident (1937), 30, 30n
Pearl City, 172
Pearl Harbor, 1, 2, 3, 4, 10, 19, 20, 22, 40, 54, 58, 59, 62, 65, 66, 67, 69, 73, 75, 81, 82, 83, 84, 87, 88, 91, 109, 110, 111, 122, 123, 124–126, 130, 132, 133, 136, 137, 139, 142, 144, 154, 168, 171, 172, 173, 174, 175; assessment of operation results, 89–90; as future Japanese naval base, 105; in Japanese media (1942), 124–126; in 1936 Navy War College Plan, 75; Yamamoto planning for, 81–83, 88
Peattie, Mark R., xiii, 61
Perry, Matthew, 123
Peru, 144
Philippines, 1, 8, 11, 21, 40, 58, 59, 60, 63, 65, 69, 79, 80, 81, 95, 129, 137, 138, 142, 145, 150, 157, 174
Phnom Penh, 169
Piikoi, Prince David Kawananakoa, 157n
Policy Society, xii, 152, 159, 164, 171
Port Darwin raid, 106
Porteus, Stanley D., 4

Portugal, 11, 94
Portuguese in Hawaii, 12, 158
Potsdam Declaration (1945), x
Prange, Gordon, xiii, 193
Princeton University, 103

Rabaul, 105, 114
Radio Tokyo, 125, 126, 133, 134, 141, 154
Rangoon, 105
Relocation of Japanese-Americans. *See* internment of Japanese-Americans
Reparations: planned claims against U.S. in wartime Japan, 146
Republican Party in Hawaii, 21, 157
Roosevelt, Franklin D., 2, 7, 39, 86, 88, 93, 123, 125, 157
Roosevelt, Theodore, 58, 123
Rōyama, Masamichi, 46, 79
Russia, 11, 15, 69, 139
Russo-Japanese War (1904–1905), 15, 16, 45, 56, 69, 74, 117, 123
Ryukyu Islands, 75

Saigō, Takamori, 27, 27n
Saipan, 8, 176
Saitō, Chū, 67
Sakhalin, 15, 78, 117, 118, 140, 155
Sakurai, Heigorō, 139
Samoa, 11, 96, 97, 100, 101, 104, 106, 109, 111, 113
San Diego, 75, 81n, 105
San Francisco, 60, 75, 109, 131, 145, 162
Sand Island Internment Center, 145n, 146
Sansei (third generation Japanese-Americans), 21, 24, 37, 162, 168
Santa Barbara, 106, 125, 169
Santa Monica, 169
Sasaki, Akira, 100
Satō, Kenryō, 98n
Satō, Kōjirō, 60, 61, 168
Scandinavia, 11
Schofield Barracks, 19, 58
Scotland, 11
Sears Roebuck, 159
Seattle, 162
Seikai ōrai, 128
Sendai, 117
Shanghai, 28, 31, 75, 95
Sherman, John, 18
Shiga, Shigetaka, 140
Shiga University, 170
Shiina, Noriyoshi, 179
Shimada, Shigetarō, 138
Shinmura, Yuzuru, 130
Shiozawa, Kōichi, 51
Shiratori, Toshio, 53
Shiriya (training vessel), 32
Shūkan Asahi, 125

Siberia, 11, 17, 69, 128
Singapore, 5, 39, 67, 95, 118, 123, 139, 150
Sino-Japanese War (1894–1895), 15, 69
Sino-Japanese War (1937–1945), 28–39, 51, 122, 135
Soejima, Taneomi, 18
Sōga, Yasutarō, 31
Sogabe, Shirō, 29
South Manchuria Railroad Company, 130
South Seas Economic Research Center, xii, 152, 153, 176
Southern Regions Affairs Department [*Nanpō seimubu*], 149–150, 153
Soviet Union, 27, 38, 69, 78, 86, 98, 113, 115, 117
Spain, 11, 37, 94, 145
Spencer, Samuel Mahuka, 157, 157n
Stanford University, 56
Stoddard, Lothrop, 60, 60n
Storry, G. R., vi, xiii, 152
Suetsugu, Nobumasa, 30n, 61, 71, 72, 73, 74
Sugamura, Yoshihiro, 53
Sugiyama, Gen, 34, 100, 107, 111, 113, 169
Sun Yat-sen, 56
Sunosaki (warship), 32
Suzuki, Eijirō (naval aviation officer), xii, 193
Suzuki, Kantarō (naval officer, prime minister), 84
Suzuki, Kyūman (diplomat), 144, 146
Suzuki, Suguru (naval officer), xii, 32–33, 84–85, 92, 94
Suzuki, Takao (army officer), 84n
Suzuki, Teiichi (army officer and bureaucrat), 138
Suzuki, Yoshiyuki (army officer), 49, 52, 53
Suzuki, Zenkō (prime minister), 19, 175
Sweden, 94, 146

Tachikawa Army Air Base, 51
Tago, Ichimin, 129n
Tahara, Harutsugu, 35, 47, 49, 50, 147n
Tahiti, 11
Taiheiyō, 133
Taiwan, 15, 78, 79, 131
Takaishi, Shingorō, 30
Takamatsu, Prince, 172
Takeda, Isamu, 32
Tamaru, Tadao, 27
Tanabe, Moritake, 106
Tanaka, Shin'ichi, 98, 99, 101, 105, 106, 111, 112, 114, 119, 169, 177; reaction to Doolittle raid, 114–115
Tani, Masayuki, 138, 146
Taniguchi, Kichihiko, 125

Tantalus, Mount, 172
Tasaki, Hanama Harold, xii, 35–36
Teitō nichinichi, 129
Terasaki, Takaji, xii, 31, 34, 182, 183
Texas: as scene of Japanese invasion, 57
Thailand, 137, 138
Theo. H. Davies, Co., 3
Tōfukuji, Koshirō, 49
Tōgō, Heihachirō, 16, 40, 72, 74
Tōjō, Hideki, 50, 53, 95, 102, 124
Tokugawa shogunate, 12n, 14, 16n, 27n, 142, 168n
Tokyo Hawaii Society, 44
Tokyo Imperial University, 45, 46, 79, 163
Tokyo shinbun, 128, 131
Tomioka, Sadatoshi, 82, 97, 98, 99, 100, 101, 103, 111, 112, 114, 115
Tomomatsu, Toshio, 162
Tomoyuki, Seo, 182
Tōyama, Mitsuru, 53, 129n
Tōyama, Tetsuo, 26, 31
Tōyō bunka kaki daigaku [Oriental Culture Summer University], 44, 124
Toyotomi, Hideyoshi, 63n
Truman, Harry, 172
Tsuda, Shingo, 129n
Tsurumi, Yūsuke, 46, 53, 140
Tsushima, Battle of, 16, 72, 74
Twain, Mark, 142

Ugaki, Matome, 76, 77, 85, 91, 92, 94, 97, 100, 101, 103, 105, 107, 109, 110, 114, 118, 120, 169, 177; comparing Hawaii to Ceylon as targets, 103; reaction to Doolittle raid, 114; work on Hawaii invasion plan, 94
United States Army, xi, 4, 7, 19, 40, 57, 163, 174
United States Asiatic Fleet, 95
United States Department of State, 8
United States Navy, x, 19, 40, 86
United States Pacific Fleet, 1, 59, 60, 62n, 65, 66, 69, 72, 75, 81, 82, 85, 87, 88, 90, 92, 93, 96, 100, 104, 107, 110, 113, 119; Japanese accounts of its destruction, 125
University of Hawaii, xii, xiii, 4, 6, 20, 26, 29, 36, 37, 41, 42, 45, 76, 136, 138, 143, 166
University of Oregon, 51
Ushijima, Hidehiko, 171

Venezuela, 144
Vietnam, 11, 171

Waikiki, 20, 22, 58, 61, 76
Wailuku, 141
Wakatsuki, Reijirō, 47

Wake (Ōtorijima), 75, 91, 96, 98, 109, 114,
    119, 123
War planning in Japan, 85–88, 95–96,
    106–107, 148–149
Waseda University, 41, 45, 137
Washington, D.C.: Japanese bombing sce-
    narios of, 128, 168
Washington, George, 125
Washington Naval Conference (1921–
    1922), 61, 70, 73, 123
Washington, state of, 1, 57, 125, 129–130;
    scenario of conquest of, 129–130
Watanabe, Shūjirō, 140
Watanabe, Yasuji, 77, 81, 82, 91, 110–111,
    120
Wells, H. G., 55
White Russians, 158
Wilhelm II (German kaiser), 56, 59

Yamaguchi (city and prefecture), 13, 155
Yamaguchi, Tamon, 103–104, 118, 119–
    120, 169
Yamamoto, Eisuke, 129n
Yamamoto, Isoroku, x, 1, 2, 60, 73–75, 76–
    78, 80, 81, 82–83, 88, 90–95, 97, 99,
    100, 101, 102, 103, 107, 120, 124, 169,
    177; and Midway operation, 109, 110,
    111, 112; reaction to Doolittle raid,
    114; reaction to Pearl Harbor operation,
    90–91, 92; view of Ceylon operation,
    102; views on Hawaii invasion, 2, 73–
    74, 81, 92–94
Yamamoto, Yūji, 101
Yamaoka, Mannosuke, 49–50
Yamaoka, Daiji, 169
Yamaoka, Sōhachi, 168
Yamashita, Sōen, 45, 46, 47, 49, 50, 127,
    139, 141, 142, 144, 147, 152, 156, 161,
    164
Yamashita, Tomoyuki, 150
Yano, Tōru, 150
Yasukuni Shrine, 7, 84n
Yatsugi, Kazuo, 152, 171
Yōgeki sakusen [interceptive operations],
    72–73, 74
Yokohama, 109, 113
Yokosuka Naval Base, 51
Yomiuri poll on Pearl Harbor, 174–175
Yonai, Mitsumasa, 34, 71, 73
Yonsei (fourth generation Japanese-Ameri-
    cans), 21
Yoshida Research Center, 152, 154–155,
    164
Yoshida, Shigeru, 177
Yoshikawa, Takeo (alias Tadashi Morimura),
    83, 84
Yoshimori, Saneyuki, 163